ID0983175

THE RED PENCIL

A SPECIAL STUDY OF THE
KENNAN INSTITUTE
FOR
ADVANCED RUSSIAN STUDIES

WOODROW WILSON INTERNATIONAL CENTER FOR SCHOLARS

THE RED PENCIL
Artists, Scholars, and Censors in the USSR

Edited by

Marianna Tax Choldin and **Maurice Friedberg**

Russian portions translated by

Maurice Friedberg and **Barbara Dash**

Boston
UNWIN HYMAN
London   Sydney   Wellington

© 1989 by Unwin Hyman, Inc.

Unwin Hyman, Inc.
8 Winchester Place, Winchester, MA 01890, USA

Published by the Academic Division of
Unwin Hyman, Ltd,
15/17 Broadwick Street, London W1V 1FP, UK

Allen & Unwin Australia Pty Ltd,
8 Napier Street, North Sydney, NSW 2060, Australia

Allen & Unwin (New Zealand) Ltd, in association with the Port
Nicholson Press Ltd, 60 Cambridge Terrace, Wellington, New Zealand

Library of Congress Cataloging in Publication Data

The red pencil : artists, scholars, and censors in the USSR / edited
by Marianna Tax Choldin and Maurice Friedberg : Russian
portions translated by Maurice Friedberg and Barbara Dash.
    p.   cm.
  Bibliography : p.
  Includes index.
  ISBN 0–04–445203–9
    1. Censorship—Soviet Union—History—20th century. 2. Arts–
–Censorship—Soviet Union—History—20th Century. 3. Mass media–
–Censorship—Soviet Union—History—20th century. 4. Soviet Union–
–Intellectual life—20th century.   I. Choldin, Marianna T.
(Marianna Tax)   II. Friedberg, Maurice, 1929–   . III. Dash,
Barbara.
Z658.S65R43   1989
363.3'1'0947—dc19   88–17126
                                                          CIP

British Library Cataloguing in Publication Data

The Red pencil : artists, scholars and
censors in the U.S.S.R.
1. Russia. Censorship
I. Title   II. Friedberg, Maurice
363.3'1'0947
ISBN 0–04–445203–9

Set in 10 on 12 point Garamond.
Printed in Great Britain at the
University Press, Cambridge

Contents

Acknowledgments   ix

Contributors   xi

Introduction   xiv

1   Soviet Culture of the Mid-1980s: A New Thaw?
    Alexander Gershkovich   1

Part I   *Soviet Censorship*

2   Soviet Censorship: A View from the Inside
    Leonid Vladimirov   15
3   Soviet Censorship: A View from the Outside
    Maurice Friedberg   21
4   Censorship Via Translation: Soviet Treatment
    of Western Political Writing
    Marianna Tax Choldin   29

    Soviet Censorship: Discussion   53

Part II   *The Scientist's Laboratory*

5   Coping with the Censor: A Soviet Scientist Remembers
    Yuri Yarim-Agaev   71

    The Scientist's Laboratory: Discussion   75

Part III   *Literature and Intellectual Life*

6   Censoring Artistic Imagination
    Maurice Friedberg
    Vassily Aksyonov
    Vladimir Voinovich
    Andrei Siniavsky   81

Literature and Intellectual Life: Discussion   101

Part IV *The Mass Media*

7   Film Censorship in the USSR
    Valery Golovskoy   117
8   Censoring the Journalist
    Ilya Suslov   145
9   Censorship at the Editorial Desk
    Boris Zaks   155
10 Censorship in the Theater
    Alexander Gershkovich   163

    The Mass Media: Discussion   191

Annotated Bibliography   215

Appendix: Conference Participants   231

Index   234

Acknowledgments

Many people helped us prepare this book for publication. The editors would like to express their special thanks to Evan Raynes, formerly of the Kennan Institute, for editorial assistance; Raya Veil (Jersey City, New Jersey) foir her expert transcribing from our conference tapes of Russian-language material; Marita Romine, formerly secretary in the Department of Slavic Languages and Literatures, for transcribing the English-language discussion from those tapes; John Glad (University of Maryland) and Vladmir Padunov (Wheaton College) for their extremely helpful comments; and last but far from least, Victoria Miller, secretary at the Russian and East European Center, University of Illinois, for her painstaking preparation of the manuscript.

Contributors

Vasily Aksyonov: Russian novelist, one of the leading authors of the period of post-Stalin thaws, best known for his *Half-way to the Moon*. Among his recent works available in English are *The Burn*, *The Island of Crimea*, and *In Search of Melancholy Baby*. Now living in Washington, D.C.

Marianna Tax Choldin: professor, head of Slavic and East European Library, and director of Russian and East European Center, University of Illinois at Urbana-Champaign; author of, among other works, *A Fence around the Empire: Russian Censorship of Western Ideas under the Tsars*.

Leonid Finkelstein (Vladimirov): former member of the editorial board of the Soviet popular science journal *Znanie-Sila*. In the West he has published a book, *The Soviet Cosmic Bluff*. Now lives in Great Britain.

Maurice Friedberg: professor and head of the Department of Slavic Languages and Literatures, University of Illinois at Urbana-Champaign; author of, among other works, *Russian Classics in Soviet Jackets*, *A Decade of Euphoria: Western Literature in Post-Stalin Russia, 1954–64*, and *Russian Culture in the 1980s*; co-editor, most recently, of *Soviet Society under Gorbachev*.

Alexander Gershkovich: specialist in Soviet and East European, particularly Hungarian, theater; author of, among other works, *Teatr na Taganke (1964–1984)* (Taganka: The Rebellious Soviet Theater). Now lives in Boston.

Valery Golovskoy: specialist in Soviet and East European, particularly Polish, television and film. Author of, among other works, *Behind the Soviet Screen: The Motion-Picture Industry in the USSR 1972–1982*. Now lives near Washington, D.C.

Andrei Siniavsky: novelist, critic, and literary scholar. A co-defendant in a 1966 Soviet trial for the crime of publishing abroad under a pseudonym, which is described in his recent novel *Spokoinoi nochi (Good Night)*. Now lives near Paris.

Ilya Suslov: journalist and satirist; former editor of the humor column called The Twelve Chairs Club in the Moscow newspaper *Literaturnaia gazeta*. Author of three collections of comic short stories in Russian, as well as of a comic novel in English, *Here Is To Your Health, Comrade Shifrin*. Now lives in Washington, D.C.

Vladimir Voinovich: Russian novelist, best known for a series of satirical novels, of which *Private Chonkin* is the first volume, and the recently published *Moscow 2042*. Now lives in the Federal Republic of Germany.

Yuri Yarim-Agaev: A physicist and human rights activist, member of the Moscow Helsinki Watch Group; since emigrating to the U.S. he has been active as a physicist at Stanford, MIT, and Bell Communications Research; founder in 1986 of the New York-based Center for Democracy, which monitors human rights violations in the Soviet Union.

Boris Zaks: Former member of the editorial board of *Novyi mir*, the Moscow literary monthly that was the flagship of the liberal cause during the Khrushchev thaws of 1956 and 1962. Now lives in New Jersey.

Introduction

Governments, Trotsky is alleged to have said, come and go, but the police remain. So it is also with Soviet censorship. Established by Lenin within days of the Communist takeover in November 1917 as a temporary measure to be rescinded as soon as normalcy was restored, it shows every sign of surviving, in Solzhenitsyn's words, Methuselah-like, into the 21st century. There were rumors of its demise in the heady days of Gorbachev's reforms, but these appear to have been laid to rest, at least for the time being. Compared with the Brezhnev years, to say nothing of the Stalin era, since 1985 Soviet censorship has been relatively lax and at times downright generous and permissive. Nevertheless, censorship's initials continue to appear on Soviet books and periodicals, and the reversal, in late 1987, of an earlier promise to allow some cooperative publishing was an ominous sign. Coming at a time when cooperative ventures manufacturing a wide variety of consumer goods and providing an array of services received official blessing and assistance, the ban on cooperative publishing of fiction and poetry, including the closing of the three or four such enterprises already in existence, was most likely the result of one serious consideration. Publishing under nongovernment auspices would inevitably contribute to an erosion of the efficacy of Soviet censorship and also advance the cause of ideological pluralism. And that, apparently, exceeded the limits of liberalism of the Gorbachev administration. Soviet censorship, then, not only continues to exist; its functions and structure, fragmentary evidence indicates, are not very different from those of the preceding decades, even if its stringency is, as of this writing, much relaxed.

On May 2–3, 1983, a conference on "Soviet Direction of Creative and Intellectual Activity" was held at the Kennan Institute for Advanced Russian Studies of the Woodrow Wilson International Center for Scholars in Washington, D.C. The conference was cosponsored and partially funded by the U.S. Department of State's Office of External Research, now the Office of Long-Range Assessments and Research, which is part of the department's Bureau of Intelligence and Research. Intended to build on and update the 1969 symposium on Soviet censorship held in London, the proceedings of which were edited by Martin Dewhirst and Robert Farrell and published as a book in 1973 (*The Soviet Censorship*; Metuchen, NJ: Scarecrow Press), the 1983 conference brought together a dozen Western and Soviet émigré writers and scholars to report on results and first-hand experiences with the Soviet system. A lively and large audience (scores of people were denied admission because we ran out of space), which included both Western specialists and recent arrivals from the USSR, added many valuable observations and raised interesting and provocative questions.

Émigré participants had been asked to share with us in the West their knowledge of recent Soviet conditions in their own areas of intellectual life, which spanned a wide variety of fields, and to give their assessment of the impact of censorship restrictions on the activities of Soviet intellectuals and artists. They discussed the definition of censorship (including self-censorship) in their areas and addressed the question of how censorship (again, including self-censorship) affects artistic and intellectual creativity. In their papers they told us, on the basis of personal experience, how they and their colleagues who are still in the Soviet Union coped with censorship intervention and still remained functioning authors, artists, and intellectuals. The émigrés' personal experience was relevant, of course, but they generalized their observations and attempted to give us a sense of how the system affects people in their fields.

Following are contributions from the conference and summaries of the discussion during each session. Participants and audience ranged over many areas of intellectual and artistic endeavor, including science, scholarship, publishing, creative writing, literary criticism, journalism, radio and television, cinema, and theater.

In gatherings of this kind there tend to be as many perspectives as there are people present, but in this particular conference the variety of views took on special significance. The formal papers and discussion established beyond any doubt that in the absence of clear-cut legal and administrative definitions of the role of Soviet censorship in various fields of endeavor, there is much inconsistency, improvisation, and even contradiction. Those entrusted with the task of censorship, as well as those subjected to it, often seemed guided by intuition and by personal and highly subjective extrapolations of current Communist Party policies. They differed in their appraisal of the implications of these policies to what may appear to an outside and non-Soviet observer [may appear] as totally irrelevant problems. All too often both the censors and those censored were equally convinced that their mutually exclusive interpretations of current political desiderata and taboos represented "correct" readings of the leadership's political moods. It goes without saying that these served to confuse even further the already chaotic picture of censorship activity conducted in the absence of official guidelines and legal restrictions. What emerged, then, was a picture of great bureaucratic complexity further aggravated by a diversity of local conditions and even personalities.

The reason, of course, is that unlike its prerevolutionary, imperial Russian antecedent, Soviet censorship is not institutionalized (its existence, though universally known, is not even openly acknowledged) and thus it takes on a very different character from traditional censorship. Moreover, Soviet censorship (normally referred to as Glavlit, originally meaning Chief Board for Literary and Publishing Affairs, now the Chief Board for the Preservation of State Secrets in the Press) is not merely "negative," with its function restricted to prevention of the appearance of undesirable materials. It also serves a "positive" function, seeing to it that desired information or attitudes are incorporated into a work to be released to the public. This new censorship, at once preventative and constructive, permeates every aspect of artistic and intellectual life and functions with infinite variety, from the innermost workings of an artist's or scholar's mind to the public reporting of actions of the Central Committee and even of the country's undisputed leader.

As suggested, then, the presentations that follow contain many contradictions, disparate views, and conflicting interpretations. The two organizers of the conference, respectively long-time students of pre-Soviet and Soviet censorship, are convinced that these are by no means mutually exclusive. On the contrary, they may *all* be correct, each supplementing the other. Taken together they constitute a kind of outline map of the Soviet system of censorship. The 1969 London symposium presented some basic sketches and measurements and an approximate scale of the enterprise of Soviet censorship. The Washington conference of May 1983 refines and hones some of the earlier meeting's concepts and operational guidelines and, above all, supplements it with many reports by more recent Soviet eyewitnesses and participants. The Washington conference thus imparts to the sketch an enhanced sense of perspective, immediacy, detail, color, texture, and some new points of reference. Finally, Alexander Gershkovich's essay maps out the general trends in Soviet culture up to the first years of Gorbachev's rule, i.e, beginning of 1987.

The existence and workings of Soviet censorship bear some resemblance to another taboo "nonsubject," that of the Soviet concentration camps. Full and official data may never become available, but that does not absolve students of the Soviet system from the task of collecting as much of the fragmentary evidence as possible in an attempt to establish an approximate but necessary picture of the structure and workings of this important Soviet institution. In some respects the findings of the 1983 censorship conference in Washington bear the same relationship to the 1969 London symposium on censorship as do recent studies of the Soviet labor camps, such as Solzhenitsyn's *Gulag Archipelago*, to those written in the West before Stalin's death. The former supplement the latter and will, in turn, it is hoped, be supplemented and updated again when new information becomes available.

More than five years have elapsed since the holding of the Kennan Institute conference, of which the last three, those of Mikhail Gorbachev's administration, have been marked by a number of spectacular developments in the country's cultural and intellectual life. We have been following closely the impact of the new policies of *glasnost, perestroika* and *uskorenie* — roughly "openness," "restructuring," and "acceleration" — on the workings of Soviet institutions most affected by the system of direct and indirect censorship controls. One of us, Maurice Friedberg, was cochair of the conference convened late in 1986 by the Department of State. Several of the papers from that conference appear in Maurice Friedberg and Heyward Isham (eds.), *Soviet Society under Gorbachev* (Armonk, NY: M. E. Sharpe, 1987). Friedberg was also codirector of the Summer Seminar on Soviet Literature and Cinema of the 1980s held in 1987 at Yale University under the sponsorship of the Social Science Research Council. As of the spring of 1988, the situation appears as follows.

Soviet censorship is now unquestionably more permissive and less stringent than it was before Gorbachev's assumption of power. A number of previously proscribed subjects, ranging from prostitution to drug addiction, are now discussed in the press and dealt with in literature. An open letter to Gorbachev from a group of émigré artists and writers expressing deep skepticism about his reforms was actually printed in *Moscow News*, a weekly read primarily by foreigners residing in the USSR but a *Soviet* journal nevertheless. Novels, such as Anatolii Rybakov's *Children of Arbat* and Vladimir Dudintsev's *White Robes*, described the horrors of Stalin's terror with greater candor than ever before, while Chingiz Aitmatov's *The Executioner's Block* portrayed with much sympathy a young Soviet man's religious quest, attributes quite unthinkable in Soviet writing only a few years earlier. Still, on the whole the situation in Soviet literature and journalism is, as of this writing, hardly encouraging. At the Sixth Congress of the USSR Union of Journalists held in March 1987, Viktor Afanas'ev, editor-in-chief of *Pravda*, warned his colleagues against blandishments of investigative reporting, while in literature a seemingly successful counteroffensive against liberal tendencies was mounted in spring 1987 by the Russian Federation's Union of Writers, long a stronghold of Stalinist orthodoxy.

By contrast, censorship's grip is being loosened in Soviet theater and the cinema. In the summer of 1986, the Union of Cinema Workers succeeded in establishing a commission charged with investigating the reasons for banning individual motion pictures. It was the first time that a procedure had been set up to appeal capricious censorship interference in the arts. Some 50 films have been examined. Most, though not all, have since been released. While not questioning the *principle* of censorship (indeed, the term itself was bashfully never used), the reform nevertheless represented an attempt to curb Soviet censorship's unlimited and totally arbitrary powers.

Soviet filmmakers' success inspired a similar revolt among actors and directors of the legitimate theaters, who succeeded in replacing the docile All-Russian Theater Society with an activist Union of Theater Workers. One of the new organization's foremost purposes is the protection of its members from arbitrary treatment by the numerous groups and individuals wielding censorship powers. Specifically, the union is empowered to prevent the implementation of "unqualified administrative decisions" — a euphemism for censorship tyranny by nontheatrical authorities.

What is at issue then, in this age of *glasnost*, is whether the oppressive status quo will remain in place, whether all cultural and intellectual life in the USSR will continue to be controlled by a faceless censor endowed with unlimited powers, or whether some degree, however modest, of procedural legality is to be introduced. If the latter tendency prevails, then the Soviet Union may be cautiously edging from its current practices toward those of the far more benign and enlightened censorship of imperial Russia. That the situation is fluid is attested by the fact that while the identity of the chief of Glavlit, the central Soviet censorship authority, remains an official secret, some rumors in Moscow identify him as Vladimir Alekseevich Boldyrev.

Marianna Tax Choldin
Maurice Friedberg
University of Illinois at Urbana-Champaign

1
Soviet Culture of the Mid-1980s: A New Thaw?

Alexander Gershkovich

In the 70 years of its existence, Soviet culture has experienced a variety of seasons. There was the intoxicating spring of the 1920s, then the long Stalinist winter with its subzero temperatures, and the brief and fickle Khrushchev thaw, which, by the late 1960s, turned into more permanent-looking Brezhnev frosts. Here we are, in the mid-1980s, and the weather is changing again.

Voices were heard proclaiming that a new thaw has arrived. The highly respected Italian Slavist, Vittorio Strada, even formulated a law about "regular changes from frosts to thaws and the other way around in Russia's literary world."[1] It is quite true that the high and low tides of Soviet culture indeed, in their changes of ideological weather, manifest certain patterns that are characteristic of a society of victorious socialism. The most important of them, one might say, is the fact that the evolution of culture does not bring about any changes in the subsoil of culture; that is, the process is confined to the parameters of the existing political system.

It is true that events in Soviet culture since Mikhail Gorbachev's accession to power, and particularly after his launching at the 27th Party Congress of the new policy of "openness" and "revolutionary restructuring," indeed point to a continuation, after a long interval, of the process of liberalization of culture that was begun and also brought to a halt in Khrushchev's time. A series of telltale signs attest that the period of the thaw is with us again. The most important symbol of cultural life — censorship — while not abolished altogether, has assumed a low profile and pretends not to notice what is happening around it. Censorship has assumed new forms of camouflage.

There is an avalanche of books, films, and theatrical performances, independent-minded and critical, that never would have seen the light of day only two or three years ago. Pasternak's *Doctor Zhivago*, anathematized in Khrushchev's day, has been published and the author, expelled from the Writers Union in his lifetime and humiliated in every way, is posthumously readmitted to the same Writers Union. Some of the writings of Nabokov, Khodasevich, and other Russian émigrés are being printed. A "happening" was organized in Manege and hitherto forbidden rock'n'roll youth ensembles took part in it. The former minister of culture, the "dogmatist" Demichev, was kicked upstairs. A democratic coup d'état took place in the union of film workers, currently the most militant organization of the artistic intelligentsia, bringing into the leadership real artists rather than bureaucrats.

The editorial boards of such journals as *Novyi mir*, *Znamia*, *Oktiabr*, and even *Ogonek*, once the preserve of the ultra-Stalinist Sofronov, have changed their composition. They now include such men of the Khrushchev era as Sergei Zalygin, Georgi Baklanov, and Vladimir Lakshin. The editorial boards have become more independent from the Writers Union, where, alas, almost nothing has changed and Brezhnev's favorite, the hack Georgii Markov, continues as honorary chairman.

Newspapers are filled with exposés, debates, heated discussions, diametrically opposed evaluations of works of art and literature and of moral problems, all of which hardly attest to a unanimity of views in a society of "real socialism." People want renewal, but it turns out that the farther they march along the path mapped out by the Party, the more they become lost in the labyrinth of an obsolete political system, insoluble contradictions, and chronic ailments of social consciousness in the state mechanism of a culture they are powerless either to replace or to change.

Yet people speak of a new thaw. However strange, those shouting the loudest about it are men and women who lived through the thaw of the 1960s, who rose on its crest and then witnessed what became of it, how it came to an end. The most vocal champions of the movement may have grown old, they may have lost their youthful enthusiasm, they may have grown wiser and richer, but they are still leftovers from the Khrushchev era. These are the poets Voznesenskii and Evtushenko, the playwrights Victor Rozov and Mikhail Shatrov, and theatrical directors Mark Zakharov and the late Anatolii Efros.

Nevertheless, the present stage in the evolution of Soviet culture, if measured by the depth of change and the atmosphere, differs significantly from that of 20 years ago. If the metaphor is to be continued, then, the thaw should be described as Gorbachev's "Indian summer."

The old Russian dictionary of Dal' defines Indian summer as the wondrous time in autumn when "the cobwebs fly over fields and forests. The abundance of cobwebs is a harbinger of a dry autumn."[2] Yes, a dry autumn.

A belated, languid little wave of nature still alive, its resistance to death, and some kind of nostalgic sadness that fills everything. Perhaps it is nostalgia for the spring that was or for the spring that will be. The cobweb may fall off various nooks and crannies, but the nooks and crannies endure. It may not be accidental that Viktor Astaf'ev's *A Sad Thriller* bears the mark of late autumn, as do the naked trees of a weeping park in R. Bykov's film *The Scarecrow*. Late autumn pervades the Kirghiz steppe of Chingiz Aitmatov's God-seeking novel, *The Executioner's Block*; late autumn is felt in Valentin Rasputin's *Fire*, in the midst of a taiga devastated by mindless destruction of the forest. Nevertheless, with all that we must not forget that not a few movements and events that shaped the destinies of Russia began in quiet autumn and winter.

An anonymous author of a samizdat document, whom we have no reason to suspect of great partiality to the regime, now writes from Moscow as follows:

> Upon assumption of power in the spring of 1985 by Mikhail S. Gorbachev, the Soviet Union has entered a new era. Everybody shares this view, from government bureaucrats to intelligentsia that is critical of the regime. What is less clear is the historic essence of this period, the outlook of the country's evolution.[3]

The testimony is particularly valuable because it emanates from inside the country.

Hopes that had been abandoned for some time that changes might be effected within the confines of the present political system have come to life again among the democratic intelligentsia and young people. The well-known dissident historian Roy Medvedev discusses in his latest writings changes in social psychology. During the period of Brezhnev's stagnation he thought that confrontation with the authorities was both necessary and unavoidable. By contrast, Gorbachev, in his view, needs critical support, especially as his policies encounter increasing resistance from conservative and orthodox elements.[4] Medvedev's opinion is seconded by Ludmila Alekseeva[5] and Yurii Orlov, democratic dissidents now in the West. In one of his interviews (in the Paris *Russkaia mysl'*, October 31, 1986), Orlov said that Gorbachev "may himself only inch the country forward but others will take his place. Of course, they are all tied to dogma and to the social structure that confines them. But if they are true patriots, they will strive to effect reforms."[6]

A different point of view is expressed by a number of Western experts on the USSR and, however strange this may seem, by the majority of Russian émigré authors. They are almost unanimous in viewing recent developments in Soviet culture with much skepticism. In their view it is the usual Soviet Potemkin village. Insofar, they say, as the system remains unchanged, nothing will work out anyway and there is no reason to get your hopes up.

I am in no position to comment on other aspects of Soviet life, but as far as Soviet culture of the 1980s is concerned, in literature, theater, and especially cinema some very real changes are taking place and I hope that these are irreversible. Perhaps it is premature to speak of a new *era*, but there is every justification for speaking of a new historical interval.

Nevertheless, one must enter an important caveat. The new stage in Soviet culture began some time before Gorbachev's arrival on the scene. His new cultural policy followed a process that had begun earlier. It merely recognized — or, more precisely, retroactively recognizes — that process, or, to use a new Soviet buzzword, imparts to it *uskorenie*, speed-up; it turns it into parameters that are acceptable for the new policies. It is only a slight exaggeration to say that Gorbachev follows the little that is still viable in Soviet art, after the slaughters of the past. He tries to enlist support for his reforms from that part of the Soviet artistic intelligentsia that is still respected by the masses, which are suspicious of state-sponsored art. There is not much of an alternative, however. The emasculated, faceless bureaucratic official art of Gribachev, Markov, Chakovskii, Kuniaev, and Isaev leaves the Soviet public cold, particularly the young.

Like all Soviet leaders who preceded him, Gorbachev loves art for good utilitarian reasons; his love of art is the result of cold calculation. In that respect, as in so many others, he models himself after Lenin. As is known, the founder of the Soviet state, upon his arrival in Moscow in 1918, began his contacts with culture with a visit to the Moscow Art Theater. Eyewitnesses attest that he was very pleased with A. N. Ostrovskii's comedy *Enough Simplicity in Every Wise Man*. Lenin roared with laughter at the tsarist general, Krutitskii (played by Konstantin Stanislavskii), to the point that his wife, Nadezhda Konstantinovna Krupskaia, found his behavior unbecoming.

It was surely a coincidence that upon his assumption of office, Mikhail Sergeevich Gorbachev chose for his first visit to the theater the same theater Lenin visited, where the same play was then being performed (this revival of the play was directed by Oleg Efremov). In the third act of the play General Krutitskii, while glancing over projected reforms, says, quite literally, the following: "What is a reform? Reform contains two activities: first, abolition of the old; and second, its replacement with something new. Which of these two acts is more harmful? Both are harmful to the same degree." Gorbachev, we can assume, roared with laughter at this scene, just as his predecessor did.

The new secretary-general was also taken with another play that Lenin saw in his time at the Moscow Art Theater, Chekhov's *Uncle Vanya*. In that play the central character, who lost all of his life's goals, finds solace in selfless labor devoid of any ideals or lofty dreams. Theater critics panned the performance. On the other hand, in his conversation with Oleg Efremov, Gorbachev underscored that he personally found the performance useful and quite consonant with the spirit of the times and with classic traditions of the Russian theater. "I am not a specialist in this field," he said modestly, "but I think that you are on the right track."

Both plays were staged by the Moscow Art Theater prior to Gorbachev's ascension to power and before the new policy of openness (*glasnost*) was announced. This is additional confirmation of the fact that the process of change in the theater and in other areas of art began before the new policies were enunciated. The process, it must be emphasized, began quite independently of either Gorbachev or his predecessors — indeed, at times notwithstanding their desires. Mikhail Shatrov's play *Thus Shall We Conquer*, which is set during Lenin's last days, was often banned both under Brezhnev and under Chernenko. Revived again under Gorbachev, the play was now awarded the highest state prize. The process of emancipation of art from the dogmas of socialist realism began spontaneously, not from above but from below. It was the most courageous and honest among the playwrights and editors who were willing to take risks. This was their answer to the bureaucratic tutelage over art, to the spiritual famine in the country, to the dishonesty, indifference, and decline of morals in the society of "real socialism." At the same time, it served to affirm their faith in the nation's vitality that survived despite all odds, in the sense of justice, truth, and beauty, which needed ideas other than those promulgated by the bureaucrats. In short, what was needed was real art, not art for show.

It is my belief that Soviet propaganda is to blame for the notion that absolutely everything that happens in Soviet culture is planned and programmed by the Party and the government. Since Stalin's time, Soviet propaganda views this notion as a way to paralyze the author's will, his creative initiative, as a way to subjugate art to utilitarian politics. The myths of the monolithic character of Soviet culture that allegedly owes all of its successes to the wise policies of the ruling party was hardly true of literature and the arts in earlier times, including the Stalin era. It is even less justified today.

Even earlier, side by side with such orthodox prose writers as Fadeev and Fedin, there were also Platonov and Zoshchenko. Conformists Surkov and Bezymenskii wrote their kind of verse at the same time that Pasternak and Akhmatova wrote their poetry. The official composer Khrennikov was a contemporary of Shostakovich. The Stalinist playwright Pogodin wrote at the same time that Bulgakov did. Official Soviet criticism of our day considers them all part and parcel of Soviet culture, even though in their time many of these artists were declared inimical to that culture.

Even at that time, strictly speaking, Soviet culture was not one — either in its essence or in its form. A careful reading of the minutes of the founding Congress of Soviet Writers of 1934 reveals that side by side with the official hosannas in the auditorium there were also muted voices that expressed their concerns. These voices called for a sober recognition of the danger to Russian literature of the doctrine of socialist realism that would impose on it obligatory uniformity. Suffice to mention the speeches of Iurii Olesha, Lidiia Seifullina, and Mikhail Koltsov. Suffice to recall Nikolai Bukharin's report on poetry or the five-minute melancholy speech by Boris Pasternak. As the Congress was about to close, Pasternak uttered prophetic words about the writer's conscience. He appealed to writers "not to sacrifice their identity for the sake of their well being"; he warned them not to change from writers into literary functionaries.

At that time Soviet literature failed to heed the advice of one of its true, if unofficial leaders. Pasternak's words were forgotten for 50 years, for eternity — forgotten until need forced their recollection. Only when all the other ideological norms that were artificially imposed on Soviet culture lost their significance, in the eyes of not only the artists themselves but also of their audience, were the words remembered. At the 27th Party Congress, General Secretary Gorbachev seized on the notion of "conscience" as if this were his salvation. He called for "openness" and "revolutionary restructuring" (*perestroika*) of the people's consciousness. The artistic intelligentsia was assigned by him the foremost role in that task. It goes without saying that Gorbachev resorted to this extreme measure because things were getting desperate.

By the mid-1980s, it seems, the Brezhnev-Chernenko policy of thwarting the artistic potential of Soviet art was obviously exhausted. Chernenko (who succeeded the *éminence grise*, Mikhail Suslov), then the chief ideologist of the country, was a run-of-the-mill Party functionary. At a plenary session of the Central Committee in June 1983, Chernenko heaped fire and brimstone upon nonconformist artists. First he expelled from the country a number of troublesome writers, artists, and cinema and theater directors who dared violate commandments of socialist realism. Following that he proclaimed a Soviet ideological slogan: "There are truths that brook no revision. They are problems that were solved long ago once and for all."[7] In translation from Sovietese to Russian, this meant "You won't get away with it!"

Then another high-placed expert on Soviet culture made his appearance. He was a former KGB boss, a specialist in combatting corruption, and now the first deputy prime minister — Gaidar Aliev. Speaking at a plenary session of Soviet filmmakers, he appealed to them to model themselves on the best films of the 1930s. When he mentioned, among others, the motion picture "Chapaev" (a primitive propagandistic western), laughter broke out in the auditorium. After that experience the "expert" on Soviet culture never again spoke in public on artistic matters. USSR Minister of Culture P. Demichev (who learned to be cautious in Khrushchev's days, when he irresponsibly proposed at the 22nd Party Congress that Stalin's body be removed from the Lenin Mausoleum) kept quiet, obviously waiting for the situation to become clearer.

That was a troubling and ominous time. Kremlin sentries frequently changed the guard to the sounds of funeral marches commemorating a series of leaders who were dying one after another. There was general confusion, skepticism, cynicism, lack of faith, and, at times, despair. Old ideological slogans, appeals, and promises were no longer believed. Ideological control over art no longer worked.

The Party ideologists were particularly concerned about the young, who seemed quite demoralized. Anarchists and extreme nihilists appeared among the country's young men and women. They rejected not only the Party role in providing leadership for art but even questioned collectivistic principles of Soviet society. Iurii Kuznetsov, a poet, composed a quatrain that hailed individualism as one way to survive in a world filled with cynicism and lies. Critics pounced on him for the following:

> Let them live to ripe old age.
> Still, they will be tossed aside by the hands of the clock.
> My name is Kuznetsov and there is only one of me.
> All the rest are forgeries and deception.

In Soviet art the years 1981 to 1985 were a period of awakening and preparing to effect a change of aesthetic principles. The old fairy tale about a happy land of socialism, where everything is clear and where the struggle is not between Good and Evil but between the Good and the Better, was a thing of the past. Those artists who, in the period of the Brezhnev stagnation, were preparing the ground for the following stage in the development of Soviet art, with its appeals to conscience and for openness, played a great role in that process. Put crudely, the reorientation of Soviet art meant exchanging Gorkii for Dostoevsky. Suddenly people became aware that all criteria are confused, that the world, in the words of the central protagonist of Iurii Trifonov's *The Old Man*, is divided not into "black and white, not into obscurantists and angels, but are something inbetween." The old Bolshevik Pavel Efgrafovich concluded his sermon as follows: "Every human being has in him something from the darkness and from the devils as well as from the angels . . . one may kill a million people" — he reasoned, as if arguing with Dostoevsky's Raskolnikov — "one may dethrone a tsar, explode half of the globe with dynamite, but *one cannot save a single human*" (italics in the original). So thought the hero of Trifonov's novel, a man who helped make the revolution and who then experienced its fruits, as did his children in the 1970s. He had seen the light, but it was too late — his life was over.

But all life was not over. The transition from Gorky to Dostoevsky, from illusions to serious probing of the human condition, was reflected in the 1980s in all branches of Soviet arts and letters. It was reflected in Igor Volgin's literary study, *Dostoevsky's Last Year*, even though the illusion of Russian society was directly and at times tastelessly linked to Gorbachev's appeals to begin reconstruction by tackling the "human factor." It was reflected in Viktor Astaf'ev's *The Sad Thriller*, a novel that created quite a stir, in which the author quoted Dostoevsky's loud declaration that he "will not accept any revolution if it entails the suffering of a single child."

The beginning of this turnabout antedates Gorbachev: it may be found in rehearsals of Trifonov's *House on the Embankment* at the Taganka Theater. I personally saw the play's author and the director, Liubimov, who were sitting next to each other in the auditorium, trying to influence Alexander Sabinin, the actor playing Professor Ganchuk, to show the audience how a one-time believer in Gorky's illusions sees the light, even if belatedly. Professor Ganchuk, who in his old age was suddenly accused of kowtowing to the West, is shown alone and ill, on his way to a store carrying a mesh bag filled with empty milk bottles. He is shuffling along and figuring out that Gorky turned out to be wrong, and that it was Dostoevsky who turned out to be right: that same Dostoevsky with whom he, old fool that he is, spent a lifetime polemicizing in his lectures. Ganchuk mutters to himself, "All is permitted if there is nothing except for a dark room with spiders."

This brief episode in the play was rehearsed for several days. All it showed was a lonely old man with a cane and a mesh bag crossing the stage for a single minute in front of the curtain. Liubimov would not leave the actor alone; he would make him do it again and again.

Sasha, it is all superficial. Very superficial . . . Please keep in mind that this is the old man's swan song. He is a lonely old man. It happens just before his death. Try to see that: you are on your way to the store with empty milk bottles. Empty ones. Do you get it? Empty! And you are saying that Gorky, it turns out, was wrong about something and you concede that Dostoevsky, for whom you had no use in the past, turns out to be right. For you, this is the tragedy of seeing the light. Had it been the other way around, you wouldn't be going to the store with empty bottles. You would always have yogurt at home. But because, at the end of your life, you prefer Dostoevsky, then, naturally, God himself ordered that you have no yogurt.

I also saw Trifonov trying to help the actor to find the necessary psychological state. "Ganchuk," he said, "arrived at the criminal idea that Dostoevsky was right. He arrived at it only recently, overcoming with great difficulty his previous convictions. What is happening is that he is saying aloud for the first time what has been on his mind for awhile. He is groping for words. He can't find them yet, but we are witnesses to the moment when he does find them. You must show that you are groping for words."[8]

The situation in the arts in the years 1980 to 1985 was quite paradoxical. On the other hand, there was a flood of opportunistic writing of which Andrei Voznesenskii's verses on the struggle against alcoholism are typical. The one-time rebel wrote:

Truth is growing stronger.
Truth is filled with hopes
For a sobered-up Russia.
Sober and bright-eyed.

There was also Voznesenskii's article and then a volume of articles entitled *Supervisors of the Spirit*, in which the poet calls on artists to seek patrons among the high and mighty. He cites the example of bygone days. It was the high and mighty, according to Voznesenskii, who were the true "movers of culture," the "true supervisors of the spirit."

There were the phony, insincere war novels by Ivan Stadniuk, written according to Stalinist criteria. There was the primitivism of the much-decorated poet Egor Isaiev. It was he who described Pushkin from the vantage point of the poet's nurse Arina Rodionovna; who held forth about some mysterious "genes of ordinary people" that, he claimed, made Pushkin what he was. There was the combination of false patriotism and cheap lyricism of Evgenii Evtushenko's *The Kindergarten*. This was a film that related the story of his difficult wartime childhood, and that included shockingly tasteless scenes showing Red Square, in which we see either fat cows being evacuated to the East or else soldiers singing diligently, "Do the Russians Want War?" — a song that sounds unintentionally ironic at a time when the Soviet Union is bogged down in a war in Afghanistan.

Another example is A. Misharin's *Four Times as Much as France*, advertised by official propaganda as the best play of the season. Its plot was almost a joke. A Communist Party provincial committee somewhere in the Far East is trying to solve the problem (solving it takes up the entire play!) of whether a Soviet trawler disabled in the stormy Pacific should be allowed to signal SOS; would this not hurt Soviet prestige in the eyes of foreigners and result in having to spend precious dollars for the saving of the crew? At the end of the play the Solomonic judgment was to ask Moscow for instructions.

The decline in the quality of art brought about a precipitous drop in theater and cinema attendance. It also brought about the appearance of mountains of scrap paper in bookstores. Such venerable theatrical directors as G. Tovstonogov, M. Zakharov, and V. Monastyrskii wrote that it is difficult to perform to half-empty houses and that a far-reaching reform of theater is overdue. Some anecdotal excesses were recorded. Thus in the Volkov Theater in the city of Iaroslavl, the management ordered the hat-check girls not to return overcoats to spectators who wished to leave after the first act. A fist fight ensued in the theater and the police were called out.

At the very same time, however, quite different works appeared in Soviet art, works impressive for their courage, depth, and color. Let us name a few of them. There was Vasil' Bykov's *A Sign of Distress*, a tragic canvas about a peasant family in wartime Belorussia under German occupation. The work unfolds, with astonishing acumen, the psychology of the peasantry, whose faith in the Soviet government had been undermined long before the war by Stalin's collectivization of agriculture. The reminiscences of the protagonist of Bykov's short novel about those times of injustice were the first "signal of distress." A misfortune that touched the entire nation: that was the author's subject.

Roland Bykov's film *The Scarecrow* (1984) shows a schoolgirl in an old Russian town who did not wish, and did not know how, to lie, for which sin she was burned on a bonfire by her classmates, members of the Young Pioneer Communist Youth Organization. To be sure, she was not burned in person. What was burned was her effigy, a scarecrow with a sign on its chest. She was burned, so to speak, symbolically, but that made the truth of the film and its artistic power even more merciless. A storm of viewers' reactions was unleashed. Soviet newspapers were filled with letters from readers. The film had its defenders, but it also had embittered foes from among "ordinary" people who demanded that the film's director be put behind bars. It was not because he had lied — everybody conceded that Soviet schools educate cruel children who lie — but because the film's creator dared to tell the truth and washed dirty linen in public.

The journal *Nash sovremennik* (*Our Contemporary*, No. 5, 1985) featured a new novella by Valentin Rasputin entitled *The Fire*. It was a hastily written work smacking of journalism, but it succeeded in tying into a single knot indifference toward destruction of nature and the degradation of the human soul. The author's pain was caused by outrages perpetrated in Russia that sounded like a prophetic warning about the nuclear accident in Chernobyl. Another Siberian writer, Viktor Astaf'ev, brought out in 1986 his novella *The Sad Thriller*. The narrator, Leonid Soshnin, is a policeman from a small Siberian town several times wounded in the course of duty. He is trying to guess a riddle of the Russian soul: why is it, Astaf'ev asks, that Russians are always compassionate to criminals but indifferent to their neighbors and to themselves? The author's criticism of his own nation, his sense of despair for its despoiled environment, for the good that turned into weakness and for the evil that gathered so much strength, is really a saga of Russia. It is not the Russian state, however, that Astaf'ev describes but the Russians as a cultural and ethnic community that was degraded under the Soviet regime to the point of moral decline, to the point where the primary cell of society — the family — begins to fall apart.

One cannot readily evaluate present conditions in Soviet culture. Things are in flux. Conditions change; they are filled with contradictions; complexities abound. The Soviet journalistic apparatus that administers culture, though possessing little initiative, may nevertheless paralyze any initiative without particular risks to itself. Naturally one must not expect too much from literature and the arts. And yet one recalls that when Lev Tolstoi was once asked, "What can art accomplish?" he replied, "Art cannot accomplish much, but were it not for art, God knows where we would be today!"

The "Indian summer of Soviet culture" is approaching its end. As indicated, however, by events of 1986–87, the struggle inside the various artistic guilds is only beginning. Whatever the outcome, one thing is already certain: there is no single literature and art in the USSR. Artists representing various views and tendencies coexist there and compete with one another. That in itself is no small thing.

By the end of 1987, defenders of the status quo, after initial defeats from reformers who appear to have taken them by surprise, mounted a counterattack. Thus at the Plenary Session of the Writers Union of the Russian Federation in the spring of 1987, Iurii Bondarev threatened to lure the reformers into a "Stalingrad" while Alexander Prokhanov, the author of "colonial" Soviet novels glorifying the exploits of Soviet arms in Afghanistan and elsewhere, proclaimed an all-out war against proponents of reforms.[9]

The situation, then, remains unclear. One may have sympathized with the late Viktor Nekrasov, a prominent Soviet novelist then still living and writing in exile in Paris. In the fall of 1986, Nekrasov was elated by the news from the recent Seventh Congress of the Union of Soviet Writers. "At long last!" he shouted in jubilation. Within days, however, he read in a Moscow paper that nonconformist painters were anathematized as in the past, and he decided, sadly, that his jubilation was premature, that little has changed. Still, such extremes and contradictions are normal and attest that not one but two cultures exist now in the Soviet Union.

Notes

[1] Vittorio Strada, "Il Romanzierre Russo e il Suo Popolo," *Corriere della Sera*, August 25, 1986.

[2] Vladimir Dal', *Tolkovyi slovar' zhivogo velikorusskogo iazyka*, vol. I (Moscow, 1978), p. 34.

[3] Anonymous, "Ot 'stabilizatsii' k 'uskoreniiu," *Problemy Vostochnoi Evropy* (New York), nos. 15–16, (1986), p. 60.

[4] Anonymous, "Ot 'stabilizatsii' K 'uskoreniiu," p. 63.

[5] L. Alekseeva, "Pis'mo o nadezhde," *SSSR: Vnutrennie protivorechiia*, No. 15 (Benson, VT: Chalidze Publications), pp. 10–15.

[6] Iurii Orlov, "Est' tsel' kotoroi khochetsia dostich' – eto demokratizatsiia," *Russkaia mysl'* (Paris), October 31, 1986, pp. 4–5.

[7] Cited from *Izvestiia* (Moscow), June 15, 1983, p. 2.

[8] For a detailed discussion, see Aleksandr Gershkovich, *Teatr na Taganke* (1964–1984) (Benson, VT: Chalidze Publications, 1986), p. 25.

[9] See the stenographic report of the Plenary Session of the Board of the Writers Union in *Literaturnaia gazeta*, May 6, 1987, p. 4.

PART I

Soviet Censorship

2

Soviet Censorship: A View from the Inside

Leonid Vladimirov

As long as censorship exists, all civil liberties remain illusory.

— *Karl Marx*

The Soviet Government was the first in history to establish a total state monopoly not only over the production and distribution of worldly goods, but also over the production and distribution of ideas, opinions and feelings.

— *Arthur Koestler*

It is unlikely that the introduction of censorship in Russia was carefully planned by Lenin before he came to power in November 1917. He knew, after all, the words of Karl Marx quoted above. More than once he thundered in articles and speeches against censorship — especially in prerevolutionary Russia. Yet the Decree of the Press that, in effect, reintroduced censorship (lifted by the Provisional Government in March 1917) was signed by Lenin almost immediately (in two days) after the Bolsheviks seized power. Since then Soviet censorship has grown stricter all the time, with only minor fluctuations in its severity over certain periods. Even the death of Stalin and the so-called de-Stalinization did not seriously affect the well-oiled censorship machine, today one of the most efficient (if nonproductive) in the Soviet totalitarian system.

Why, then, did Lenin establish censorship so quickly? In my opinion, he was forced to muzzle the free press in Russia by the very logic of events. Indeed, Russia of 1917 was very much a free country. It would probably be fair to assert that neither before nor after the period between March 1 and November 7, 1917, did Russia enjoy such civil liberties as within that period.

Many people were looking forward to taking part in the election of the Constitutional Assembly and to the subsequent transformation of the country into a democratic republic. The war was still raging; there were enormous internal problems; in many ways, chaos reigned supreme. Yet there was hope, and the general direction of political developments seemed to be clearly chosen.

The Bolsheviks, however, had their own ideas about the country's future. Taking advantage of the existing liberties, of antiwar feelings among the military and the peasants, and of the general weakness of the government, they managed to seize power in a rather easy coup d'état. But the very next morning they had to deal with a much more difficult problem: how to justify their seizure of power. Civil liberties and the free press still in place, the new rulers were exposed and severely criticized from all quarters. They were not able to answer this criticism as they could not explain their actions without lying — and lies do not stick in the environment of a free press. The Bolsheviks, for example, kept saying that their aim was still to convene the Constitutional Assembly, but the remaining papers of other political parties asked ironically whether it was necessary to overthrow the government by force in order to proceed with democratic elections.

Thus exposed, Lenin most probably faced a stark choice: either to gag all critics or to lose power. And, logically, he "temporarily" banned all nonsocialist publications.

The events that followed — the defeat at the general elections (25 percent of the votes were cast for the Bolshevik candidates), the dispersal of the Constitutional Assembly by force, the civil war — had polarized the society as deeply as before. The return to civil liberties looked, to Lenin, utterly suicidal. He said as much in his angry rebuff of Miasnikov, who in 1920 reminded people that the press restrictions of 1917 and 1918 were "temporary." But even if Lenin had been inclined to lift censorship after the civil war, he would have found it very difficult to accomplish. For the totalitarian "growth" had already permeated the tissue of society. There was the Cheka with its arbitrary executions, there were military tribunals sentencing people summarily to death or long prison terms, and there were commissars at all levels who had already tasted the heady wine of unrestricted power and would not tolerate any criticism.

In a way, all this was the *effect* of the suppression of free press and of general freedom of speech — but this kind of reasoning was not for Lenin. For him, of course, there was only "the resistance of defeated classes," and strengthening that resistance by lifting censorship looked extremely dangerous.

In 1921 such danger became, if anything, more real. The disturbances in Petrograd, the Kronstadt uprising, and associated events led — again, logically — to the introduction of "internal censorship" inside the Bolshevik Party itself.

The 10th Party Congress (held, by coincidence, simultaneously with the Kronstadt uprising) decided to ban all factions within the Party. It would be unthinkable after the 10th Congress even to raise the matter of censorship: to many communists it had become by then a necessary element of the system, a weapon in their "class struggle."

A more or less similar logic would probably guide any group that comes to rule a country by unlawful means, not as a result of a democratic process. Such groups feel vulnerable to exposure and tend to muzzle all independent voices as quickly as possible.

Today the logic of Soviet censorship remains the same: there is still no legitimate ground for Communist Party rule in the Soviet Union, and this dangerous information must be strictly and continuously suppressed. However, the functioning of censorship, as a result of long experience, has become rather sophisticated and sometimes even subtle. Not one word appearing in print can be disseminated on USSR territory, not one radio or TV broadcast can go on the air, the curtain cannot rise on one play, no motion picture can be screened, not a single exhibition – admission charged or open to the public – can be opened, if the censor's special permission has not been obtained. The censor's stamp, a large rectangular rubber stamp bearing his personal number with permission to print and date of issue — is placed on each number of *Pravda*, on the "master" copy of any bottle label, and on the "permission" copy of the script of every TV transmission — in other words, on absolutely everything. The very existence of censorship is, however, secret, and any direct reference to it is strictly forbidden.

All these rules are enforced by means of the clause of the Penal Code dealing with state secrets. If the manager of a printing works puts any uncensored material through the presses, he is likely to be charged with "divulging of a state secret" and sentenced — *in camera* — to eight years of imprisonment. I am not aware of any such court case in the post-Stalin period, but the threat is there and works perfectly. To ensure observance of the rules, there is a censor at every printing establishment in the country, and if the printing shop has several presses or works in shifts, the number of censors grows proportionately.

Sometimes the printers produce only certain periodicals or books that are censored elsewhere and do not take any other jobs. Their local censors have virtually no work to do: they simply look at other censors' permission stamps and pass the material without even reading it. However, these "printing censors" are sitting there nevertheless: their task is to see that nothing *else* is published. The only exception is the arrangement at the print shops of big-circulation newspapers, if those shops are housed within editorial buildings, but in such buildings there are, of course, censors' offices "responsible" for the papers themselves, and the censors of the paper are watching the print shop as well.

Strictly speaking, the censor's task is simple: to ensure that no state secret is published. Each censor has the full list of items that are not for publication. It is an impressive volume entitled *List of Information Not to Be Published in the Open Press* [*Perechen' svedenii, ne podlezhashchikh opublikovaniyu v otkrytoi pechati*]. When I last saw a *Perechen'*, in 1966, it had more than 400 pages of rather small type. On its green cover, above the title, the words "Secret. Copy No.____" were embossed in gold.

To check a text against the list is, however, not a simple or straight-forward task. The censor reads the text through with maximum attention, putting question marks against any "doubtful" word, line, or passage. Then he (or she; there are a great many female censors) checks each suspected item against the list — called by all censors the "Talmud" — to eliminate as many question marks as possible. The remaining marks must be "clarified" with the editor of the censored publication. For example, the description of all scientific projects in a certain field may be permitted only conditionally, if it can be shown that there was a previous and recent open publication on a given project. The editor must bring whatever "open sources" he can gather to satisfy the censor. Sometimes foreign publications are enough; sometimes only recent Soviet publications are required, especially in cases in which a piece of Soviet research is described in the text.

There are also "direct restrictions" in the list, such as naming certain factories or persons. For example, only the chairman of the Committee for Cultural Relations with Foreign Countries could be mentioned by name, but not other members of the committee; the same restriction applies to the KGB. A great many items could be published only with special dispensation from various authorities such as the Central Committee of the CPSU, the KGB, the Military Censorship, or the Space Censorship. To this category belongs, for instance, all information on air crashes, floods, earthquakes, forest fires, and epidemics in the USSR or other "socialist countries." Absolutely forbidden are numerical crime statistics (unless published officially, which almost never happens), any information on price increases, and even absolute figures of individual incomes. The list of such forbidden items is very long indeed.

Checking against the list, however time-consuming, is only part of the censoring process. The other part, more subtle and difficult, is an ideological assessment. The subtlety here lies in the formal position of Glavlit, or Chief Directorate for the Protection of State Secrets in the Press [Glavnoe Upravlenie po Okhrane Gosudarstvennykh Tain v Pechati], as censorship is known in the USSR. Technically this organization is not supposed to concern itself with anything other than protection of state secrets. In fact, however, this is not the case. Every censor is clearly instructed to be an ideological watchdog also. To this end, each censor attends frequent political "seminars," regularly organized not only in Moscow, Leningrad, or union republics capitals but also in all provincial centers.

Having noticed in a text something incompatible with the current ideological directives, the censor makes a "recommendation" to the editor who submitted the text. Officially he cannot cross out anything or alter a single word: this may be done by editors only. Usually a censor's "recommendation" is quite enough for an editor to introduce the required amendment, but not always. If an editor does not want to change the text as "recommended," the censor passes it as it is and warns the editor that he or she will report the case. The report goes to the Press Department of the Central Committee of the Communist Party of the Soviet Union; in republics, to the Central Committee of the republican party; and in the provinces, to the Provincial Party Committee.

Such situations are extremely rare. I know of only one case, the appearance in *Literaturnaia gazeta* of *Babii Yar*, a poem by E. Yevtushenko. The editor-in-chief of *Literaturnaia gazeta*, the late Valery A. Kosolapov, resisted the censor's "advice" not to publish the poem. It did appear, and Kosolapov survived: he received only a severe dressing-down at the Central Committee. However, this happened during a relatively "mild" period of Khrushchev's rule; at any other time Kosolapov's "revolt" could have cost him his job and maybe even his Party card.

The ideological "vigilance" of censorship sometimes hits the editors quite unexpectedly. In January 1960, the magazine *Znanie-Sila* (*Knowledge Is Power*), where I used to work, published an article that argued that science fiction was important not only as entertainment but also as a stimulator of scientific innovations. The article was passed by the magazine's censor but subsequently, at some higher level of censorship, was found to be ideologically wrong. This happened too late: the magazine had already been printed. The editor-in-chief of *Znanie-Sila* received a Party reprimand from the Ideological Committee [Ideologicheskaia Komissiia] of the Central Committee and soon lost his job!

The ideological "side" of censorship is well known to all editors, although there is nothing about it in "The Talmud." This awareness leads to careful editing of everything *before* the material reaches the censor. In other words, censorship begins much earlier than at the Glavlit stage. Mr. Ilya Suslov, one of the participants in our conference, worked for many years as a department editor of *Literaturnaia gazeta*; he has counted at least seven stages of censorship. I fully subscribe to his findings, as they coincide with my own experience.

The most complex are the relations existing between Glavlit and various publishers of fiction in the USSR; that is, literary magazines and publishing houses. The very appearance of unorthodox literary works (one may think of the late Abramov, of Mozhaev, Rasputin, and others) shows that the process of editing and censoring of fiction has become very sophisticated indeed. We know from Solzhenitsyn of the way his *One Day in the Life of Ivan Denisovich* saw the light of day: Aleksandr Tvardovskii, the celebrated editor of *Novyi mir*, managed to make Khrushchev read the manuscript, and so the work was passed by the very top censor, the ruler himself. No doubt there are also editors in Russia today anxious to publish worthy literary works, and sometimes they manage to overcome the resistance of censorship.

But the resistance *is* there, and this fact explains such phenomena as samizdat and tamizdat. More deeply, censorship in the USSR is fully responsible for severe deformation — one could even say mutilation — of Russian literature and also for poisoning the literary tastes of readers. Trash is published everywhere in the world; it is, if you like, the inevitable "filler," the "ore," while good books are as rare as precious metals. Yet the literary process, the very complex "sieves" of criticism and readers' judgment, serve as sensitive filters, separating out those precious metals and rejecting the trash. In the Soviet Union, however, both literary criticism and readers' reactions are inadequate and in many cases hypocritical; gradually it became more and more difficult to tell the trash from genuine literature. It is in such an environment that the "works" of Yuri Pilar, Yulian Semionov, Chingiz Aitmatov, and other surrogates grow enormously popular in the country; that the plays of Arbuzov or Arro are performed in hundreds of theaters, playing to full houses; that people queue for hours to see films like the recent *Private Life* or *The Station for Two*. This kind of stuff is passed by the censorship without hindrance, despite the fact that in such material there may be episodes depicting some negative aspects of Soviet life. Thus the very borderline between genuine literature and cunning fakes is blurred. Censorship at all levels continues to conduct, quite methodically, this "unnatural selection," giving a green light to "useful" works and raising barriers before anything arising from the creative human spirit. "I cannot stop feeling astounded by the keenness of our literary critics," wrote Vladimir Lakshin in *Novyi mir* in 1964. "They immediately pick out everything fresh and talented in our literature in order to profane and disgrace it."

This is not, however, the "keenness" of some vile critics. This is the logic of censorship — the same logic that made Lenin sign his Press Decree two days after the Bolshevik Revolution.

3
Soviet Censorship: A View from the Outside

Maurice Friedberg

That censorship in the USSR affects every form of public expression in matters of culture, politics, and so forth will no doubt be attested by all the speakers at this conference. This all-pervasiveness of Soviet censorship has already been described in general terms by Mr. Finkelstein. Fewer people are aware of the fact that similar, if not more stringent censorship in the USSR affects the writing of foreign authors as well. In a way this is a departure from the way censorship operated under the tsars. You may recall that a number of Pushkin's poems bear the subtitle *Podrazhanie Parni*, imitation of Evariste Parny, a minor eighteenth-century French poet. If you go through the poetry of Parny, you will see there nothing of the sort. What Pushkin did was merely a ruse to mislead the censor into believing that his original verse was just an imitation of a foreign poet. He did it because foreign poets were treated with considerable leniency at a time when Russian poets were subject to rather rigid limitations.

Those limitations, of course, pale into insignificance when you view them against the censorship restrictions in the 20th century. You will not find an entry for the words *tsenzura v sovetskii period* ("censorship in the Soviet period") in any Soviet reference work. In *Literaturnaia entsiklopediia* the article stops with the abolition of censorship in 1917 — incidentally in a censored manner, because the implication is that censorship was abolished *under the Soviets*. The reverse is, of course, the case. Censorship was established, or reestablished, by Lenin, literally within two days of the coup d'état of November 1917, but censorship had been abolished the previous February by the Provisional Government that was established in the wake of the abdication of the tsar.

Evidence of Soviet censorship of all Western writing, as well as of the spoken word, is both abundant and readily proven, but it is readily proven and visible only to those of us who have access to the originals of these literary works, which means those of us who live abroad. To those Soviet citizens who read translations of Western European, American, Latin American, Australian, or any other type of writing produced outside the confines of the Soviet Union, the proof is not readily available at all. They cannot check the published Soviet translation against the original text, and often even the published Soviet version of the text in the *original* language against the same text published abroad in that same original language. The Soviet Union must be the only country in the world in which they carry coals to Newcastle (I guess the Russian equivalent is samovars to Tula). Books are published *in English* in the Soviet Union (even something as innocent as Mark Twain) instead of being imported from the United States. The alleged excuse is that some of these books are provided with introductions, annotations, and so forth. Occasionally, however, the texts themselves are affected, as I have had the opportunity to demonstrate on other occasions.

Censorship of the spoken and of the printed word originating abroad is attested, above all, as every Soviet citizen knows, by the regular jamming of many Western broadcasts, a fact that can be ascertained by virtually anyone in the USSR who owns a radio or a television set. Systematic interference with radio broadcasts to the point where they become totally inaudible is the most blatant type of censorship of the spoken word that tries to penetrate the USSR from abroad. There are more innocent ways of trying to ascertain that fact. Try to give somebody in the USSR the traditional Christmas present — namely a gift subscription to a European or American journal, no matter how innocent — and see what happens. The official Soviet excuse for the inability of Soviet citizens to subscribe to Western periodicals is that they are saving currency. But try and pay the hard currency right here, and send somebody a journal, an ordinary one, neither anti-Soviet nor pornographic. The journal is not likely to reach the subscriber.

There is another way to see how censorship works in the USSR, and any Washingtonian can check this very readily. Ask any Soviet visitor to these shores, after taking him to the bookstore of Victor Kamkin, what is the opposite number of Kamkin's bookstore in the Soviet Union. Where in the Soviet Union will you find a store stocked with every conceivable type of publication manufactured in the United States and countries of Western Europe? The answer, of course, will be silence. Here and there you may find a Soviet bookstore that may stock a classic, something like Racine or Corneille or Molière in Librairie Hachette editions. You may also occasionally find purely technical books, but a magazine that has anything other than pure technology, as you will see from the paper by my colleague Marianna Choldin, is quite another matter.

A third way to see Soviet censorship in action is to pay attention the moment you enter the Soviet Union. Your luggage is going to be searched, and you will see that what they are looking for is not a bottle of whisky for which no customs duty is being paid, nor is it an extra pair of silk stockings. They will be looking for journals and books, and they will search for them with the thoroughness that is normally reserved in the West for people suspected of trying to smuggle cocaine.

In fact, hardly any Soviet libraries have significant collections of foreign books. The Library of Foreign Literature in Moscow, one of the country's major repositories, does not even have the kind of collection that my own university and Marianna's has, in the state of Illinois, where the number of books from the Soviet Union and Eastern Europe approaches something like the half-million mark. When you arrive at the Library of Foreign Literature, you will discover that Arkadii Raikin, the Soviet comedian, was right when he said, *"U nas est' vsë, no ne dlia vsekh."* We have everything, but not for everybody. There is rationing of access to foreign books. You will see that there are certain books that one is allowed to read on the premises, and fewer books that one is allowed to take home. Furthermore, when it comes to photocopying a work of foreign literature, one must actually produce a contract from a Soviet publisher attesting that the bearer, a translator, is herewith issued a contract for the translation of a book by such and such an author. It is only when one is armed with this kind of evidence that one is allowed to order a copy of the book. Otherwise even a professional translator cannot get a photocopy. You can *read* it, so that you can then propose a translation, but to obtain a copy you must have an actual contract.

I emphasize all these barriers because it is only after running this formidable obstacle course that the printed word originating abroad may be approved for eventual translation in the USSR, and it is only then that the normal process of censorship begins. Very few books, of course, survive this rigorous test, but there is, to be fair, no watertight method of ascertaining which books were turned down for normal commercial reasons, or literary or artistic ones, and which were vetoed by the censors. In one of his beautiful stories, *The Graphomaniacs*, Andrei Siniavsky says that in the USSR graphomania — compulsive writing — will exist as long as censorship exists, because nobody will ever concede that his manuscript was turned down by the editors for legitimate literary reasons. Authors will always believe that they have been discriminated against on political grounds.

Be that as it may, it is only after its formal acceptance that the manuscript is turned over to people armed with various-colored pencils.

Marianna Choldin will speak about the procedures that affect Soviet trans-lations of Western scholarship and nonfiction generally. One would expect Marianna's material to be censored more thoroughly because, after all, this is politics, hard social science, serious economics, whereas fiction deals with fictitious characters and fictitious situations. In reality, however, the intensity of censorship interference is more or less equal. I have been following the process of censorship in the USSR rather closely ever since I published my first article on the subject three decades ago, and shall attempt to identify a number of continuities.

What is the most fundamental type of censorship? It is, of course, the nonpublication of any writings by authors whose works may be innocent enough but whose personae are considered odious by the Soviet publishing authorities. For instance, there are at this time no fewer than three living American Nobel Prize winners falling into this category: Czeslaw Milosz, Isaac Bashevis Singer, and Saul Bellow. (Not a single book by Bellow has ever been published in Russian.) The case of Milosz is simple enough. Milosz is an émigré and that is bad enough, because in Soviet publishing the only good émigré is a dead émigré. The Russian émigré Ivan Bunin — also a Nobel Prize-winning author — began to be published only after his death. Isaac Bashevis Singer is also an émigré, but he is even more objectionable because he happens to be writing in Yiddish.

Saul Bellow's crimes are more clear-cut. Bellow is a traditional realist and not addicted to smut, an excuse that is very often used by Soviet publishers to explain the unavailability in the USSR of certain types of books that are really banned for political reasons. In the case of Bellow, it is obviously his anticommunist politics that are the barrier to his publication in Russian, including his support for anti-Soviet recent Russian émigrés. (He has, curiously, been published in Estonian and other Baltic languages that "restrict" their accessibility to about two percent of the Soviet population.) It is Bellow's politics, rather than the contents of his books, that Soviet publishers find objectionable. I am not speaking of *Dean's December*, which is, in fact, quite political, but of such books as *Herzog* or *Mr. Sammler's Planet* or *Humboldt's Gift*. All could otherwise be translated into Russian, but because of their author's persona they are not.

Examples can, of course, be multiplied. To retain a sharper focus, let me restrict my examples to Americans. Take, for instance, Jerzy Kosinski, who was until recently president of the American PEN. A refugee from Communist Poland, Kosinski was attacked not long ago by the *Village Voice* in New York and simultaneously by General Jaruzelski's newspapers in Warsaw. This is what I find fascinating. When his *Painted Bird* appeared some years ago, he was subject to a campaign of vilification for having written a vicious book. The latest campaign of vilification uses as an excuse the claim that he did *not* write those vicious books, that somebody else wrote those vicious books. You see, it is a no-win situation. You write a book, and that is bad. You *don't* write a book, and that is bad too. You just can't win. Take the example of another writer whose books, with minor cosmetic changes by the censors, would probably do well in the Soviet Union. I am strongly convinced that Herman Wouk's best sellers *The Winds of War* and *War and Remembrance* would be successful in the USSR, especially if a few negative references to the Soviet Union were to be removed. The trouble is that Wouk is a political conservative and, to add insult to injury, a devout Orthodox Jew.

Then there are, of course, the writers whose defections from pro-Soviet and communist causes make them hateful as turncoats. The foremost living American example is Howard Fast, during the years 1945–56 far and away the Soviet Union's most widely printed contemporary American author. However, he became an unperson literally overnight after his break with communism in 1956 over Hungary. Fast's old books were withdrawn from circulation and destroyed. For years his name was retroactively expunged even from cumulative Soviet bibliographies. The most painful, however, was the fate of a poor, perfectly innocent lady who was stripped of her *kandidat nauk* (candidate of science) degree because she wrote a dissertation on Howard Fast; I think it was called *Govard Fast, amerikanskii pisatel' i borets za mir* (Howard Fast, American writer and fighter for peace). They took away the degree on the grounds that *nikakoi on ne pisatel', i nikakoi on ne borets za mir* — he is neither a writer nor a fighter for peace. In Nikolai Gogol's *Inspector General*, someone decides toward the end of the play that the impostor Khlestakov is neither important nor a person. That was written a century before George Orwell. Hence the "unperson" is really a concept invented in the 1820s and 1830s in Mother Russia. It goes without saying that Fast's recent books describing generations of emigrants in San Francisco, strongly reminiscent of traditional Russian realism in the 19th century and remarkably free of obscenity (perhaps because Fast does not want to compete with his daughter-in-law, Erica Jong) as well as of anti-Soviet politics, are not to be found anywhere in the USSR.

Some bans of this sort are observed for decades at a stretch. Upton Sinclair and John Dos Passos are cases in point. On rare occasions these bans may be lifted. For instance, Richard Wright, the black American novelist, had once broken with the Communist Party and related his experiences in the famous collective volume of the late 1940s, *The God that Failed*. Wright's *Native Son*, however, was reprinted in the USSR after Wright's death.

What are the routine manifestations of censorship intervention? A resolution of the Central Committee of June 4, 1959, decreed that in the translation of Western books, "passages of no scholarly or practical interest are to be deleted." The directive was aimed at translations of works in the social sciences, but practices during the quarter-century that followed amply demonstrate that this type of censorship is very much the standard operating procedure in Soviet translations of literary works as well. Affected are occasional disrespectful remarks about the USSR or communism in foreign books, whether in authorial speech or voiced by literary personages. Incidentally, Soviet legal authorities obviously never had any training in literature because they do not distinguish in this respect between what a character says, what the narrator says, and what the author may think. So in Hemingway's *For Whom the Bell Tolls* all derogatory quips about communists during the Spanish Civil War are gone.

Speaking of Hemingway, about a year and a half ago, in this very room at the Wilson Center, Raisa Orlova, who was active in the USSR in the 1960s as a critic and translator of American literature, spoke, and I wanted to know how they dared, in the USSR, to rewrite Hemingway. Orlova looked at me with some compassion; obviously I was a child who did not understand the facts of life. She said that they had to censor Hemingway because there was no other way to publish him. That may well be so, but nevertheless I did not relent, and I asked her whether she and her colleagues had tried to obtain Hemingway's permission to censor his books, because at that time he was still very much alive and one would think that the author should have some say in the matter. What if Hemingway preferred not to appear in Russian at all, rather than to appear in Russian in censored form? Since I was a child asking naive questions, I was not favored with an answer.

In more recent works, Soviet editors or censors have done a very thorough job of removing all disrespectful observations about communism and the USSR from Gore Vidal's *Washington DC*, even though *Washington DC* is above all an attack on McCarthyism in America; and from Kurt Vonnegut's antimilitaristic novel *Slaughterhouse Five*. In John Steinbeck's *Travels with Charlie*, they got rid of a funny scene describing Khrushchev pounding the table with his shoe at the UN, even though at that time Khrushchev had already been deposed.

All of these instances are examples of removal of passages that are overtly critical of the USSR, of Soviet policies, of communism. But Soviet censors are not always content with that. Occasionally they also do the reverse — they suppress material that is in their view overly favorable to the Soviet Union's capitalist adversaries. In Truman Capote's *In Cold Blood*, most of the information suggesting that American farmers are reasonably prosperous people was removed because, I suspect, it would invite invidious comparisons with Soviet collective farms. The Soviets suppressed the entire narrator's part in Arthur

Miller's play *The Crucible* — the part attacking intolerance and witch hunts and extolling freedom of speech – again, I suspect, because this would suggest undesirable parallels with Soviet conditions. It is worth emphasizing that none of these changes was authorized by the American writers concerned, or at least by those among them who are still alive, because I wrote to every one of them, and every one of them wrote back and assured me that permission to censor their books was not sought and was certainly not granted.

While politically motivated censorship of American literary texts as well as of Western European ones is often unacknowledged, Soviet writers and editors readily concede that overly blunt language and excessively frank portrayals of sex are, in fact, toned down in Soviet translations of foreign literary texts. They are indeed, and the following offenders recently had their mouths washed out with soap: James Baldwin (*If Beal Street Could Talk*), John Updike (*Marry Me*), and Kurt Vonnegut (this time for *Breakfast of Champions*). Vonnegut's book was also cleansed of its dirty drawings, the kind associated in America with *Mad* magazine. Occasionally the Soviet censors do ridiculous things simply out of ignorance. In 1978, *Teatr* magazine published a translation of Neil Simon's comedy *The Prisoner of Second Avenue*. The Russian text omitted references to the mythical pilot named the Red Baron and also to Red Label Whiskey, because these sounded like slurs on the communist movement. Just to be on the safe side, they also got rid of the Zionist name of New York's Beth Israel Hospital.

More sinister was an excision in 1977 from the Soviet translation of the classic scholarly work *The Literary History of the United States*, which was published to look like not just a complete translation but a *literal* one. The English title page faced the Russian title page, leading one to believe that the Russian version faithfully reproduced the complete and unabridged text of the original. In fact, however, the translation contained the usual cosmetic changes — odious people were unmentioned, lines omitted. One chapter, however, was practically cut out; only a quarter of it remained. This was a chapter on foreign-language culture in the United States. Soviet editors and censors retained those parts of it that dealt with Swedish theaters in Minnesota, with Slavic enclaves, and with the French colonies in Maine and Louisiana. They got rid, however, of material dealing with Jewish literary life in Yiddish, again because this would invite invidious comparisons with the USSR. There were also some mistranslations, perhaps intentional. Thus "a fervent Jewish religious faith" became *"evreiskim religioznym fanatizmom,"* Jewish religious fanaticism.

That there is literary censorship in the USSR is hardly news to Soviet citizens, even though in contrast to the situation that prevailed under the tsars, it is not admitted. Moreover, I suspect that Soviet citizens are quite aware that there is serious censorship of literature written by Soviet authors. Censorship of works by non-Soviet authors is particularly dishonest for two reasons: it suggests to Soviet readers that even writers who live in the West are strongly critical of the capitalist way of life (but never of the USSR), and, conversely, that they have nothing positive to say about their homeland. It also suggests to unsuspecting Soviet readers that the Western authors who are critical of capitalism find the Soviet way of life if not attractive, then at least tacitly acceptable and definitely superior to the life and values of the bourgeois democratic society that they criticize.

4

Censorship via Translation: Soviet Treatment of Western Political Writing

Marianna Tax Choldin

Introduction: Soviet Censorship and Its Imperial Roots

Since the end of the 17th century, when Peter the Great promulgated his great reforms, Russian rulers have displayed a consistently ambivalent attitude toward things foreign. They covet Western technology and know-how but are uneasy with Western values and ideas. However, because the latter always seem to infiltrate along with the former, the government is constantly confronted with the problems of dealing with these potentially dangerous influences. Ideas of any kind are elusive, but the government has always taken the position that control of at least their written expression must nonetheless be attempted. Consequently, printed works from abroad have always been controlled at the borders and domestic works closely examined for unwelcome foreign concepts and values.

The essential continuity of the Russian attitude is especially striking in the case of foreign publications. There are numerous accounts by 19th-century travelers of foreign publications confiscated from their luggage upon entering Russia. As almost any visitor to the Soviet Union can attest, at present too, foreign visitors arriving in the Soviet Union are invariably questioned as to whether or not they are bringing in foreign books or magazines. The regime has changed,

This paper was written while the author was a visiting scholar at the Center for the Book at the Library of Congress and at the Kennan Institute for Advanced Russian Studies at the Smithsonian Institution. Thanks are extended to both institutions for their support.

but the concern remains the same. It is important to recognize this continuity — that Soviet censorship is deeply rooted in prerevolutionary Russia. An examination of these roots enhances our understanding of current conditions.

I have recently completed the first phase of an envisioned comprehensive study of Russian and Soviet censorship of foreign publications. There I describe Russia's 19th-century censorship operation, particularly the ways in which the imperial government attempted to protect Russians from insidious Western influences, and examine the themes that caused official concern.[1] These themes can be grouped into four main categories: disrespect toward Russian royalty, opposition to the existing social order, the portrayal of Russians as non-European barbarians, and ideas offensive to religion and morality. Each of these themes has numerous variations.

It is generally acknowledged by Western students of Soviet history and ideology that the essential concerns underlying the institution of censorship in imperial Russia are still central to the operation today: the fear of alien values and ideas and the belief that the West is out to subvert the populace ideologically. Today such beliefs are expressed in the Soviet view of bourgeois ideas as inherently hostile toward the Soviet Union and the consequent need to protect Soviet citizens from dangerous foreign values, concepts, fashions, and fads.

In striking contrast to tsarist Russia, however, even the existence of censorship is no longer officially acknowledged in any published Soviet source. Therefore the researcher must rely less on official sources and more on material of an inferential nature. Fortunately, this may be found in abundance: oblique references to various publications, and secondary sources such as national bibliographies, subject encyclopedias, and critical and biographical works on Western writers and thinkers reveal much about the system.[2] However, perhaps the most direct way to identify the themes in foreign publications that concern the authorities and the techniques employed to bring these publications into line before allowing them to reach the readers is to examine Soviet translations because it is through translation that most Western publications now reach Soviet audiences. I made such an examination, comparing several Soviet translations with the foreign originals; the results are discussed later.

First, however, let me review the general situation with regard to foreign publications before and after the revolution, and raise some questions that I hope will be answered in the course of this conference.

In imperial Russia there were four general categories of foreign publications: those permitted by the censorship authorities to circulate freely; those banned absolutely; those under a ban "for the public," accessible only to individuals who applied at the Foreign Censorship Committee offices and were approved by the authorities; and those permitted for circulation only after the excision (by blacking or pasting over or by cutting out) of specified words, lines, or pages.

In the Soviet Union there appear to be four analogous categories.

(1) Foreign publications that circulate freely include some writings with a socialist orientation as well as some science and technology titles. (Some, but not all, of these materials circulate freely: in times of crisis in recent years, such as occurred in Hungary, Poland, and Czechoslovakia, communist newspapers from the West as well as from Eastern Europe were banned temporarily; and issues of *Science*, the prestigious journal published by the American Association for the Advancement of Science, are routinely subjected to excision techniques very much like those used in tsarist times.)

(2) It is difficult to describe the category of works banned absolutely because we do not have access to official Soviet lists, as we do for much of the tsarist period. We may assume, however, that some kind of list probably does exist; and in any case, there is no doubt that most foreign publications are not permitted to circulate in the Soviet Union. Therefore we would be justified in considering these works to be "banned absolutely."

(3) The equivalent of the ban "for the public" of tsarist times is the Soviet system of restricted "special" collections and reading rooms in libraries and institutes to which only authorized individuals — those who require access for professional reasons or who have top clearance — are admitted.

(4) The fourth category, consisting of publications permitted only with excisions, has its Soviet analogy in the group of works selected for translation. This category proved to be extremely valuable for understanding censorship in the tsarist period because it revealed very clearly and directly the themes of concern to the imperial censorship. Lists prepared by the Foreign Censorship Committee indicated precisely which passages were to be excised before the book or magazine could be released for circulation. My study of translations suggests that the analogous category is equally valuable for understanding at least some aspects of Soviet concern regarding foreign publications.

Of course, one must proceed with great caution when evaluating translations. As any experienced translator knows (and I am one myself), there is often more than one "correct" way to express the meaning of a given word or phrase, and choices may well be made for reasons other than censorship — for example, literary style. But taking such factors into account — indeed, bending over backward in order to be objective — the researcher cannot help but be struck by certain patterns that seem to characterize Soviet translations. Taken together, they reveal a system of control that goes beyond the tsarist system of censorship, so far beyond it that one hesitates even to use the term "censorship."

Webster defines "censor" in several ways, two of which seem to be relevant here: "an official empowered to examine written or printed matter (as manuscripts of books or plays) in order to forbid publication, circulation, or representation if it contains anything objectionable"; and "an officer or official charged with scrutinizing communications to intercept, suppress, or delete material harmful to his country's or organization's interests."[3] Both definitions describe fairly accurately the role of the prerevolutionary Russian censor of foreign publications — a role one might call *reactive* rather than *active*. My study suggests that his Soviet counterpart, on the other hand, has an additional, active role to play: the contemporary censor must not merely delete "harmful" material but must also translate, edit, amend, and rewrite the foreign work. This process differs significantly from the earlier form of censorship and might better be called "rewriting" or simply "control." And what should we call the practitioner? Indeed, who exactly *is* responsible for this process or set of processes? The translator? The editor? A higher official? Some combination of all of these?

In any case, the resulting "translation" may differ substantially from the original, and given that most Soviet readers do not have access to the original, they cannot know the extent and nature of the differences. It is common knowledge that Soviet readers, again like their forebears, are experts in reading and interpreting texts.[4] However, what about translated foreign works? The wary Soviet reader must certainly realize that rewriting, and not merely translation, has taken place, but how can he or she possibly guess the extent of the changes? The reader gets no help from Aesopian language here, for the book in hand has been, in effect, written by the Soviet authorities and not by the American, French, or German author whose name it bears. The reader, while realizing this, is powerless to do anything about it.

The foreign author has also been badly treated, of course. Before 1973, when the USSR joined the Universal Copyright Convention, it was common for authors to be unaware that changes had been made in their works; in some cases they were unaware even that Soviet translations had been published.[5] Although the situation has improved somewhat since 1973, there is still ample evidence that unauthorized changes continue to be made.[6]

There is also the question of self-censorship. Again, we hear a great deal about this complex phenomenon that is such an important factor in the Soviet system of control. What role, if any, does self-censorship play in the translation of foreign works? Certainly the author himself did not have the Soviet authorities in mind as he wrote, although he may have been dealing with other constraints placed on him by his own environment. But what about the Soviet translator? Does this person have the responsibility of rewriting a foreign book to make it acceptable? Does the translator take on the persona of the author and "clean up" the text, as if it were his own, before passing it on to the next level of review? Does he "clean it up" as he translates, or is the translator merely responsible for a faithful translation, leaving the rewriting to superiors?

No doubt there is variation in the handling of these matters. Maurice Friedberg has been studying the process of literary translation that precedes the publication of foreign works, and no doubt he has answers to some of these questions with regard to belles lettres. My own research, the preliminary results of which are discussed later, deals with the translation of nonfiction works on politics and international relations, works that might be called "neutral" or even "friendly" toward the Soviet Union. I hope that participants in this conference, especially those with direct Soviet experience, will be able to help me understand how the system functions with regard to this kind of material.

Four Books and Their Soviet Translations

The first work selected for comparison was *The Arrogance of Power* by Senator J. William Fulbright (1966, Soviet translation 1967). Based on a series of lectures delivered at the Johns Hopkins School of Advanced International Studies, this is a compelling book written in one of our nation's darker hours, the period of deep involvement in Vietnam. Fulbright, then chairman of the Senate Foreign Relations Committee, was very critical of U.S. foreign policy. He believed that we were wielding our great power for the wrong ends and the wrong reasons, and that by so doing we stood to lose everything. He wanted to see our government change its self-destructive course:

> It is my hope — and I emphasize it because it underlies all of the criticism and proposals to be made in these pages — that America will escape those fatal temptations of power which have ruined other great nations and will instead confine herself to doing only that good in the world which she *can* do, both by direct effort and by the force of her own example.[7]

The Arrogance of Power seemed particularly well suited to this study precisely because it was so critical of the United States. Perhaps a literal translation would be permitted because the message was one that the Soviet authorities wanted their readers to receive, especially coming from such a prominent source as Senator Fulbright.

The study was to focus on Fulbright's book, but three other works were included to broaden the picture: *The Evolution of Diplomatic Method* by Sir Harold Nicolson (1954, Soviet translation 1962);[8] *I Speak of Freedom* by Kwame Nkrumah, president of Ghana (1961, Soviet translation 1962);[9] and *India's Foreign Policy: Selected Speeches, September 1946–April 1961* by Jawaharlal Nehru, prime minister of India (1961, Soviet translation 1965).[10] Nicolson's book, the text of a lecture series delivered at Cambridge University, deals with the development of diplomacy from Greek and Roman times via Machiavelli's Italy and Richelieu's France through Woodrow Wilson's America. *I Speak of Freedom*, subtitled *A Statement of African Ideology*, is a political autobiography by the first president of Ghana. Nkrumah discusses such topics as the history of the independence movement, the development of institutions in the new state, and Africa's role in world affairs. The volume of Nehru's speeches, published by the Ministry of Information and Broadcasting of the government of India, consists of nearly 200 selections dealing with foreign policy-related subjects, including India's policy of nonalignment; its role in the United Nations; the Cold War and disarmament; and India's relations with other countries of Asia, Africa, Europe, and America. The Soviet publishers represented are the Institute of International Relations (Nicolson, Fulbright), Foreign Literature (Nkrumah), and its successor, Progress (Nehru). The Soviet version of Nicolson's book had a print run of 23,000; Fulbright's, a run of 10,000; no figures are available for Nkrumah and Nehru.[11]

Let me insert a caveat at this point: obviously it would be foolish to draw grand conclusions about translation or censorship, or differences between the Khrushchev and Brezhnev eras, based on a sample of four books. It is worth noting that the first two translations were published under Khrushchev and the last two under Brezhnev, and there are indeed some differences that may be significant.[12] But, of course, one must resist the temptation to do more than mention these points. Clearly, more material would have to be reviewed before more than tentative conclusions could be drawn. But it is at least a beginning. The explorer charting *terra incognita* starts by noting what is observed, indicating the outlines of hills and valleys in a necessarily crude way and leaving the finer work until later.

Techniques

When comparing the translations with their originals, one is struck first by certain structural differences, mainly in the form of deletions and additions. Deletions are least evident in the Nicolson and Nkrumah translations, but Nicolson in particular has substantial additions. The original has no introduction, notes, or index, but more than one-third of the translation is composed of a lengthy introductory essay and extensive notes. A brief preface and a few notes have been added to the Nkrumah translation, but the original preface and notes are also included, making this the most "faithful" of all translations. There are a few deletions, however: the dedication to the late Patrice Lumumba is not included, nor is the acknowledgment of the Ghana Information Services for the photographs used in the text. Five of these photographs are not reproduced in the translation — Nkrumah with Macmillan, Nasser, Eisenhower, Tito, and Hammarskjold—but the photograph with Khrushchev is included, not surprising in a 1962 publication. Incidentally, most of the photographs have been relocated in the translation, but if there is any significance in this, it is not immediately apparent. There is also a blank page where a photograph may have been removed at the last moment.[13]

The Fulbright translation omits acknowledgments and the preface by Francis O. Wilcox, dean of the Johns Hopkins School of Advanced International Studies, as well as all references and an end-page "About the Author." Added is an eight-page Soviet preface and a number of notes.

By far the most extensive structural changes are found in the Nehru translation. The comparison is complicated by the fact that the translation extends the period covered by the original through January 1, 1964, with additional material for the years 1961–1964 added from the official *Foreign Affairs Record*.[14] Of the 189 selections in the original volume, 39 were included in the translation; 13 selections were added from the *Foreign Affairs Record*.

One cannot make the comparison without a full-scale examination of those speeches in the two original sources included in, as well as excluded from, the translation. However, even confining oneself to the two-thirds of the translation taken from the 1961 volume, as I have done, clear differences emerge. The 612-page original reduces to a 254-page translation that is not only a shorter book but a substantially changed one. (The fact that 60 percent of the English text was cut is unacknowledged in the Soviet edition.)

Comparison of the tables of contents gives some indication of the difference. The original is divided into 12 topical sections: "India's Emergence," "An Independent Policy," "Opposition to Military Pacts," "Panchsheel and Co-Existence," "Foreign Possessions in India," "People of Indian Origin Abroad," "Commonwealth," "United Nations," "Cold War and Disarmament," "Personnel and Publicity," "Asia and Africa," "Europe," and "America." The last three are subdivided into sections on individual countries arranged alphabetically. Within sections and subsections, speeches are presented in chronological order.

The translation, on the other hand, has an entirely different format: the 52 selections (39 from the 1961 original) are simply presented in chronological order. Without going into a detailed comparison at this time, let me simply note that all three items in the section on opposition to military pacts are included in the translation; that no items on people of Indian origin, the Commonwealth, or personnel and publicity are included; that all seven of the included selections on Europe deal with countries of Eastern Europe,[15] although countries of Western Europe are well represented in the original by eleven selections; and that no speeches on America are included. (I was rather surprised at the omission of the single speech on Cuba, which is critical of U.S. intervention; however, a nearly identical speech taken from the *Foreign Affairs Record* is included.)

There is evidence of editing within selections, too; in one case three separate items from the original have been combined in a rather complicated way into a single speech in the translation.[16] It should also be noted that several of the translated titles of speeches bear little or no resemblance to the titles given them in the original; similar title changes are found in the Nkrumah and Fulbright translations.

As mentioned earlier, each of the Soviet translations examined is preceded by a Soviet introduction. Judging by the four cases under consideration, such introductions can play different roles in the staging of a translation. The Nkrumah introduction is brief and upbeat, emphasizing the good relations between Ghana and the Soviet Union. The Nicolson essay, published the same year, is lengthy — almost one-third of the entire book — and polemical, taking a hard line vis-à-vis the bourgeois world and chastising Nicolson for largely neglecting Soviet diplomacy and misunderstanding it when he does mention it. The author of the biographical essay on Nehru mentions several times the good relations existing between India and the USSR and quotes the Indian leader regarding the great accomplishments of Soviet Russia.[17] The Fulbright introduction emphasizes this important senator's criticism of his country's policies but also reminds the reader that Fulbright is still very much in the imperialist camp. Comparing the translation with the original, we see that the author of the essay has quoted Nehru's positive impressions of the Soviet experience while omitting his reservations. Here is the original, with the omitted section underlined:

> A study of Marx and Lenin produced a powerful effect on my mind and helped me to see history and current affairs in a new light. The long chain of history and of social development appeared to have some meaning, some sequence, and the future lost some of its obscurity. The practical achievements of the Soviet Union were also tremendously impressive. *Often I disliked or did not understand*

some development there and it seemed to me to be too closely concerned with
the opportunism of the moment or the power politics of the day. But despite all
these developments and possible distortions of the original passion for human
betterment, I had no doubt that the Soviet Revolution had advanced human
society by a great leap and had lit a bright flame which could not be smothered,
and that it had laid the foundations for the "new civilization" towards which the
world would advance.

Incidentally, this passage is translated in its entirety in the Soviet edition of *The Discovery of India*.[18]

After examining closely portions of the texts of these books and comparing them with the originals, what strikes me as especially interesting about the introductions is the different ways in which they relate to the texts they introduce. The introduction to Nkrumah's book is perfunctory and the translation of the text appears to be quite faithful; as mentioned earlier, even the references to Western publications are translated, and in the few spots where I found excisions in the text, ellipses were used. The Nicolson translation, published the same year, follows a different model: the introduction is substantial and highly political, but the text has been altered relatively little. Perhaps this is the case because the book deals mainly with the past, which is not considered dangerous. There is some precedent for that view in the tsarist censorship. Or is it that in the relatively permissive climate prevailing in 1962, a stringently orthodox introduction was perhaps sufficient to satisfy the authorities even when questionable material was present in the text? (This is reminiscent of the edition of the *Communist Manifesto* I used as a student in the 1950s; the lengthy critical introduction may have been intended by the publisher to soothe the squeamish.) It is also possible, though unlikely, that the two books are handled differently because of differences in the positions of the two publishers, Foreign Literature (Nkrumah) and the Institute of International Relations (Nicolson).

Earlier I mentioned notes that did not appear in the originals but that were added to the translations. These are generally notes of two types, which I shall call "neutral" and "loaded." Neutral notes tend to be purely explanatory to provide Soviet readers with information about some name, term, or event. For instance, Fulbright refers to the saying that "in every woman's secret soul is a drum majorette," which needs no explanation for American readers but for which the translator has added the following note: "In the U.S.A. during festive parades, at the head of every column marches a girl juggling a baton in time to the music. As a rule, beautiful girls are chosen for this. The author wants to say that every girl dreams of being among the chosen."[19] Another kind of neutral note is found frequently in the Nicolson translation, where a term is given by the author in the original Greek, Latin, or other language but is translated for Soviet readers (for example, *koine*, or *Pax Romana*).[20]

Loaded notes are also usually explanatory or descriptive, but the explanation is made from a Soviet standpoint, often with a definite ideological slant. Some of the notes are cited in the discussion of themes, but let me give just one example here. In his radio broadcast of September 7, 1946, called "Future Taking Shape," Nehru referred to "the struggle of the Indonesians for freedom." The translation adds this note:

> The routing by the Soviet Army of the Japanese Kwantung Army in Manchuria in August 1945 created favorable conditions for countries of Asia to gain their independence. In Indonesia a republic was declared on August 17, 1945. The first act of imperialist intervention to suppress the young state was the order by the English command to the Japanese occupation forces in Indonesia regarding "maintaining order" before the arrival of the English forces. From the end of September 1945 English and Dutch troops invaded Java and other islands of the Indonesian archipelago and began a brutal suppression of the independence movement of the Indonesian people. The interventionists received aid in the form of weapons and money from the U.S.A. The colonial war against the Indonesian people lasted four years.[21]

Whatever the accuracy of the account of events in Indonesia, it is certainly presented as incontestable fact, although one suspects that the British, Dutch, and Americans — to say nothing of the Japanese and the Indonesians — might tell the story differently.

Let me turn now to techniques resulting in what I call "textual" differences, by which I mean techniques that alter the meaning of the text and distort the author's intention. Another caveat is in order here: as acknowledged earlier, translation of fiction or poetry is a very delicate business, and as this group is certainly aware, it is not always easy to transfer with accuracy and sensitivity the meaning of a word or phrase from one language to another. In my view it is possible, however — at least in most cases — to render a translation of a work of non-fiction that does reflect accurately both the letter and the spirit of the author's intent. Certainly the translator must occasionally make use of notes, circumlocutions, well-reasoned substitutions, and other techniques — often clumsy, unfortunately — to achieve this aim, but I maintain that it can be done.

With this conviction in mind, I was prepared to give the Soviet translators of these four books the benefit of the doubt. Indeed, I found much that is praiseworthy: solid, professional translation. I also found mistakes, to be sure, or what appear to be mistakes — Nicolson uses the word "conscience," but the translator renders it as "consciousness" [*soznanie*] when he should have used *sovest'*[22] — as well as inexplicable, albeit quite minor, transpositions such as "and"/"or," also in the Nicolson translation.[23] The occasional omission is excusable too. Nkrumah uses the word "formica," but his translator omits it, presumably because there is no formica in the Soviet Union and readers will not know what it is. An explanatory note would have been better, but this is a small transgression.

The significant textual transgressions I found are effected by a number of techniques, some obvious and others more subtle. Examples will be introduced in the discussion of themes to follow; here I will merely enumerate these techniques. Perhaps the most predictable, both on the basis of tsarist practice and because it is so simple, is excision. Words, phrases, sentences, paragraphs, entire pages are excised. There is an important difference between the use of this technique before and after the revolution, however. Before the excision was made with scissors or ink or by pasting paper over the offending passage. It was immediately obvious to the reader that something had been excised. Now there is no such visible sign. The original has been neatly excised in the translation process, as if it never existed. Only in the Nkrumah translation did I find ellipses used to indicate that the translation did not include the entire original.

Changes in meaning are also effected by adding words, or by substituting different words for the ones used by the author. Phrases and sentences are sometimes recast in such a way as to change the meaning or message conveyed. One technique frequently encountered is the translation of statements that the author expressed *conditionally* as if they had been expressed *definitely*. This has the effect of making the author sound more positive or negative than he does in the original; the basic meaning may be the same but the emphasis is very different. Sometimes emphasis is also changed by adding or deleting quotation marks. In Russian, quotation marks can denote irony: "democracy" means *pseudo*-democracy, "leader" means false or self-styled leader. Therefore, these changes are major. Often the translation is an oversimplification, a restatement of the author's ideas that does not reflect the subtlety and complexity of the language with which he expressed those ideas. This may also serve the purpose of omitting the author's caveats, reservations, or opinions, thus constituting quite a serious change.

Some of the textual changes observed might be explained simply by poor translation. However, although there is no way of proving it, I am convinced that others are deliberate and have nothing to do with the translator's command of English. Whatever the intent, there is no doubt that the overall result of these changes, both structural and textual, is translations that differ in varying degrees from their originals. Nor is there any doubt that the variance can be significant. After comparing the introductory section of *The Arrogance of Power* with the translation, I discussed my findings with the author, Senator Fulbright, who agreed that the changes did indeed make the Soviet version significantly different from his original, both concretely and in spirit. He also confirmed my suspicion that he had not authorized excisions and other changes; indeed, he had no idea that any had been made.[24]

Themes

The kinds of changes made in these four translations, using the techniques described earlier, suggest two main areas of concern, each with several facets: the image of the Soviet Union and communism, and the image of the United States and other Western powers.[25] I have already enumerated the main themes in foreign publications that were of concern to the imperial government, but let me repeat them now for purposes of comparison: disrespect toward Russian royalty, opposition to the existing social order, the portrayal of Russians as non-European barbarians, and ideas offensive to religion and morality. Bearing these in mind as we examine the Soviet themes, we will find many similarities and parallels. I have concluded, however, that it is the techniques rather than the themes that really distinguish Soviet censorship from its imperial predecessor.

The Image of the Soviet Union and Communism

Excising the negative   It is common knowledge that the names of former Soviet leaders do not usually appear in print, so it is no surprise that "the Soviet government" is twice substituted for "Khrushchev" in a 1960 speech by Nehru.[26] While in power, however, Soviet leaders may be named; as mentioned earlier, Khrushchev's picture even appears in the Nkrumah translation published in 1962.[27] In general, though, the less attention paid to Soviet change in leadership and the implications thereof the better; an excerpt from a statement by Nehru on March 20, 1956, is called "New Trends in Russia" but is translated "About the XX Congress of the CPSU."[28]

The same rule generally applies to other Eastern European leaders — the name of the prime minister of Czechoslovakia is omitted from a 1958 speech delivered by Nehru at a banquet in the prime minister's honor[29] — but not necessarily to other countries' leaders: President Eisenhower's name is used in another 1958 speech,[30] and Chou En-lai and Mao Tse-tung are mentioned during a debate four years earlier.[31] While relations with China were good, names could be mentioned. Before China was solidly communist, however, positive references to that country had to be toned down; in a 1946 radio broadcast Nehru expressed the hope that China's "present trouble will end soon and a united and democratic China will emerge." This part was acceptable, but the next phrase, that he hoped China would be "playing a great part in the furtherance of world peace and progress," was omitted from the translation.[32]

Communist governments must not be portrayed negatively. When Fulbright describes Cuba's regime as a "communist dictatorship," the Soviet translation calls it a "communist leadership."[33] Nor should criticism of communist activity in Asia or Africa be permitted; a long passage in a 1954 speech by Nehru in which he discusses the disruptive influence of international communism in Southeast Asia is excised,[34] as is Nkrumah's statement that communist ideology does not "have any fruitful set-up in our country,"[35] and Fulbright's mention of a speech by a South Vietnamese Buddhist leader equating the United States with the communists as a threat to his country's independence.[36]

Soviet communist activity is mentioned directly by Fulbright in his explanation of why the United States fought in South Korea— "to defend South Korea against the Russian-inspired aggression of North Korea" — and why he feels that American intervention was "justified and necessary"; the entire passage is cut from the translation.[37] Nicolson also discusses Soviet activity in foreign countries, calling it "formidable, disturbing, compulsive." This is a good example of the technique of "substitution"; in the translation this activity is described as "impressive, assertive, it arouses alarm" [*vnushitel'na, naporista, ona vyzyvaet trevogu*].[38]

Emphasizing the positive Other changes seem to be aimed at setting the record straight regarding the Soviet Union and making sure that credit is given where credit is due. The editor of the Nicolson translation uses notes to add material on anti-Soviet activity by Western powers.[39] For example, Clemenceau is described as one of the chief organizers of intervention against Soviet Russia.[40] Nicolson's statement, "It was the endeavor to reconcile the hopes of the many with the doubts of the few that brought such seeming falsity to foreign policy in the twenty years between 1919 and 1939," is strongly countered by a note to the effect that Nicolson is trying to whitewash the policies of England's leading circles in the period between the First and Second World Wars expressed specifically in the intervention against Soviet Russia, assistance in the revival of German military potential, and the encouragement of fascist aggression in order to turn it against the U.S.S.R.[41]

When Nicolson names international conferences held after 1918, notes are added that describe not only the places and give the dates of the conferences but also provide information related to the Soviet Union; the Cannes Conference was convened "after the complete defeat of the intervention against the Soviet Union," and the Genoa Conference was the scene of "a great victory for Soviet diplomacy."[42]

Soviet support for disarmament, peace, and friendship among nations is stressed whenever possible. A 1958 speech by Nehru entitled "A Gesture" is retitled "On the Decision of the Soviet Government to Discontinue Nuclear Testing."[43] "A Visit to Russia," delivered at Moscow's Dynamo Stadium in 1955, becomes "I Saw an Ardent Yearning for Peace."[44] "Guests from Moscow," a speech given in 1955 at a banquet in New Delhi to honor Bulganin and Khrushchev, is translated as "Friendship and Cooperation." According to the Soviet edition, the speech was given at a reception in honor of "the Soviet delegation"; no names are mentioned.[45]

Changing titles is one way to emphasize the Soviet Union's role, but this end is also achieved by substitution and addition. In Nehru's 1960 press conference statement, "Constructive Approach Needed," he uses pronouns when referring to the Soviet Union and its proposals; in the translation "they" becomes "the Soviet Union," "these proposals" become "Soviet proposals," and "it" becomes "the Soviet program."[46]

The Image of the United States and Western Powers

One must dig a little deeper to explore this theme because it tends to be expressed less directly, often in small and subtle ways. While working I sometimes wondered if I might not be imagining things, and I did discard a number of examples that I considered borderline at best. But many remained that could be considered significant enough to mention, and of those I have selected a few representative cases to present here. I shall be most interested to learn if my colleagues at this conference agree with my interpretation of these changes, or if they believe I have read too much into the translation.

It is also possible that I have leaned too far in the opposite direction and underestimated the significance of some changes. However, I prefer to err in the direction of caution, at least at this stage of my research. It seems that one pernicious effect of the invisible changes wrought by this kind of translation must be to create in the sensitive Soviet reader an overwhelming attitude of suspicion. An entire translated work may be viewed with skepticism and dismissed because of the impossibility of knowing what the author really said. In fact, my comparisons show that the degree and kind of rewriting vary from book to book, and that there is also variation within a single book, but how is one to know this without seeing the original or trusting the publisher? We in the West tend to operate on the assumption that translations of foreign works made available by reputable publishers are indeed faithful to the intentions of the authors. When this is not the case, we hope the reviewers will tell us so, as they often do. The system is by no means foolproof, but its advantages over the system described here need hardly be elaborated.

Criticism of the U.S. Political System and People

The Fulbright translation yields quite a few examples of this subtheme. The senator refers to the American population as "diverse and talented," but in the translation he calls them "talented and energetic." Are Americans not to be portrayed as diverse so that it is easier to make generalizations about them? Or is it the ideas of pluralism that Soviet editor-censors find unpalatable? On the same page Fulbright says America is "fortunate in the institutions devised by the founding fathers and in the wisdom of those who have adapted those institutions to a changing world." In Russian we read that "the founders of the American state devised government institutions that were very flexible and could be skillfully adapted to the needs of a changing world,"[47] which has a rather different flavor, implying that our institutions were designed to be manipulated, and saying nothing about our good fortune in having such institutions or about the wisdom of the designers. (This was one of the first passages I questioned, and I worried that I had read too much into it, but Senator Fulbright confirmed my feeling that the message really was different from that conveyed by the English.)

The technique of excision is used to tone down positive statements about America and Americans. Speaking in general terms but with America in mind, Fulbright criticizes any great nation for forcing itself on other people, for attempting to "make them richer and happier and wiser, to remake them, that is, in its own shining image." The words "richer and happier and wiser" are omitted from the translation;[48] is this done so that the reader will not think of the United States as a place where people are rich and happy and wise? The original statement is hardly a flattering one, but apparently it is nonetheless considered inappropriate for Soviet readers. Another example: Fulbright relates a little anecdote that makes fun of the U.S. military, pointing out that the story is "probably apocryphal"; this disclaimer, however, is omitted in translation, distorting even in a small way the author's intentions.[49] A final example: Fulbright chides his country for neglecting its domestic problems, lamenting that in our neglect we are "denying the world the example of a free society enjoying its freedom to the fullest." The translation deletes "enjoying its freedom to the fullest," as if one should not dwell too much on this image of a free society.[50]

Substitution is employed too. The loaded verb "propagandize" is used twice where Fulbright uses different verbs, "propounds" and "practices".[51] The senator quotes George Kennan's observation that "there is more respect to be won in the opinion of the world by a resolute and courageous liquidation of unsound positions than in the most stubborn pursuit of extravagant or unpromising objectives." The translator renders "positions" as "political principles" and "unpromising" as "uncompromising",[52] which certainly changes Kennan's meaning and, consequently, Fulbright's as well. "Uncompromising" used for "promising" could conceivably have been an honest mistake, given the similarity in spelling, but it is difficult to justify the replacement of "positions" with "political principles" on the grounds of accident.

Changes that put the United States or other Western countries in a bad light are not limited to Fulbright's book. Nkrumah maintains that while there are indeed racial problems in the United States, "it seemed, however, that the racial question in the United States has often been exaggerated deliberately by those who hope to bring the country into disrepute." This passage does not appear in the translation, where his statement simply reads: "Racialism, I said, wherever it existed, obviously should be abolished." A blatant use of substitution is found directly preceding this omission. The passage containing the excised lines just quoted is Nkrumah's answer to a question put to him by an American reporter as to whether "the stories of racial tensions and disturbances" in America are criticized in Ghana. In the translation, "stories" is translated as "facts."[53]

A note in the Nicolson translation points out that while the Soviet Union signed the Geneva Protocol of 1925 banning the use of germ warfare, the United States did not.[54] At the end of his last lecture, Nicolson writes: "I know that the Americans possess more virtue than any giant Power has yet possessed." In translation the last three words are missing;[55] apparently it is permissible to acknowledge American virtue but not to make too much of it! Earlier in the same lecture, Nicolson criticizes the American method of diplomacy because, he maintains, it "weakens certainty." The Soviet translator has gone one step further than the author, and the passage reads that the American method "increases uncertainty."[56] This is an effective technique: the meaning is essentially unchanged, but the reversal alters the emphasis. Increased uncertainty strikes me as stronger and more dangerous than merely weakened certainty.

Some interesting changes have been made in Nicolson's section on diplomacy in ancient Greece, the net effect of which seems to be that Greece, that model of democracy glorified by the West, emerges looking bad; Nicolson himself is critical of Greek diplomacy, but the translation makes him appear to be even more so. The author says Greeks were "universally condemned for their diplomatic unreliability"; the translation calls it "perfidy" or "treachery" [*verolomstvo*], a considerably stronger word.[57] Nicolson says the Greeks were "woefully indiscreet," translated as "they were noted for extreme arrogance" (or "insolence," *zanoschivost'*).[58] He calls their diplomatic system "inefficient," rendered in the translation as "faulty" (or "pernicious," *porochnyi*).[59] Speaking of Demosthenes, Nicolson maintains that he "was certainly not wrong in his indictment of the diplomatic method which that great democracy evolved." The translator modifies "diplomatic method" by the adjective "unskillful" (or "clumsy," *neumelyi*).[60] The translation is certainly stronger than the original, and the Greeks less admirable.

The United States and Western Powers as Imperialists

Not surprisingly, this subtheme is well represented in the translations under consideration. Again, what is especially interesting is not so much the fact that imperialism is stressed as the ways in which the text is altered. Fulbright's book provides numerous examples of a variety of techniques. As mentioned earlier, it is important to bear in mind that the author is himself highly critical of U.S. policy. In fact, when I first read the book I thought I might find no changes at all in the Soviet translation because the original, while not in any sense anti-American, could certainly be seen as a portrait of the United States that the Soviet authorities would want their readers to see. I was wrong. Dozens of changes were made, both blatant and subtle, involving not only simple excisions but also extensive rewriting. The resulting translation strikes me as a quite different book from the original — darker and cruder, lacking its balance, subtlety, and essential sympathy.

With an air of light irony, Fulbright relates some of our history as imperialists, writing of our liberation of the Cubans from Spain only to bring them under an American protectorate. The translation places quotation marks around the word "liberated," as if Fulbright's irony needed to be emphasized still further. The author refers to Theodore Roosevelt, Henry Cabot Lodge, and Admiral Mahan as "'those imperialists of 1898' who wanted America to have an empire just because a big, powerful country like the United States *ought* to have an empire"; this is translated as "those imperialists of 1898 who wanted to transform America into an empire simply because such a big and powerful nation as the U.S.A. should have its colonies." Note the absence of quotation marks around "imperialists of 1898" and the substitution of "colonies" for "empire." Fulbright used those quotation marks deliberately to set off the phrase, the implication being that there was a discrete group of American imperialists in 1898. The translation loses this distinction. As for the use of "colonies," if Fulbright had wanted to use the word, he would have; this goes a step further than he intended.[61]

Nor is it faithful to the author's intentions to translate "American companies may dominate large sections of a country's economy" by the much more definite "American companies control a significant part of the economy of other countries."[62] And this may be a small point, but it seems to me that "save the world for democracy" is not an acceptable translation of the phrase Fulbright quotes, the well-known slogan "making the world safe for democracy."[63] The latter is, of course, imperialistic, and Fulbright uses it to describe what he considers this unfortunate aspect of the American character. The phrase used in the translation, however, has a different feel to it, an active messianism that sounds somehow less grandiose but more aggressive and dangerous than the original.

Some changes in the Nkrumah translation might be seen as strengthening the image of Africa freeing itself from imperialist masters. The title of Chapter 2 is changed from "The Campaign Begins" to "The Struggle Begins"; Chapter 3 is "Organization for Freedom" in the original and "Organization for the Struggle for Freedom" in the translation.[64] Incidentally, Nkrumah refers several times to "a distinctive 'African Personality'"; this is translated as Africa "speaking on her own behalf" or "Africa's own face."[65] I wonder if this wording is preferable because it implies freeing oneself from one's masters and having a voice of one's own but does *not* concede the existence of a distinct "African Personality" that might turn out to be anti-Soviet.

A change that might be worthy of note is found in the Nehru and Nicolson translations: "the United Kingdom," "Great Britain," "Britain," and "British" in the originals appear as "England" or "English" in the translations.[66] This is not a consistent pattern — "Great Britain" is also used in the Nicolson translation[67] — and may not be significant, but it did occur to me that the reduction of "Great Britain" or "the United Kingdom" to "England" might have the effect of downgrading that great power to a mere small island.

The United States as "Arrogant"

I single this out as a separate subtheme to emphasize a peculiarity of the Soviet translation of Fulbright's book. The title itself uses the word *samonadeiannost'*, which might be translated as "presumptuous" or "self-sufficient." That is only the beginning, however; it seems the translator felt it necessary to come up with a different word each time Fulbright used "arrogance." "Intoxication with power" [*op'ianenie*]; "presumption and haughtiness" (or arrogance) and "arrogance (or insolence, or presumption) of power" [*vysokomerie i zanoschivost'*], "haughtiness" (or superciliousness or arrogance) and "intoxication with power" [*nadmennost' i opianenie*]: all are used to render Fulbright's phrase "the arrogance of power."[68] The English language is rich in these words too, but the author chose to stick with a single one, "arrogance." Was the choice of so many different words in Russian dictated by stylistic considerations, or was it perhaps intended to overwhelm the reader with the many varieties of American arrogance?

The United States Behaves Badly toward Other Countries

This subtheme, closely related to the preceding two, appears in all four translations but is most prevalent in *The Arrogance of Power*. Fulbright observes that the United States "may be drifting into commitments which, though generous and benevolent in intent, are so far-reaching as to exceed even America's great capacities." This conditional statement is translated as a definite one: "The U.S.A. is taking on itself even greater commitments that may exceed even the enormous potential of America."[69] Note too that we are no longer credited with generous and benevolent intent. According to Fulbright, we intrude on other societies and "uproot" traditional ways of life; in translation "uproot" becomes "liquidate,"[70] without doubt a stronger and more final word. "Americans as well as Europeans have had a devastating effect in less advanced areas of the world," says Fulbright, but the translation omits "as well as Europeans," leaving America to stand alone as devastator.[71]

An interesting set of changes serves to emphasize the differences in size and strength between America and the countries it devastates. For example, Fulbright says that Americans "have been strikingly successful in breaking down the barriers to change in ancient but fragile cultures"; the translation adds to this "of small countries,"[72] as if to stress our role as bullies. Fulbright is quite explicit about the harm we do despite our good intentions, but the translation goes further still; speaking of Vietnam, Fulbright comments, "What they resent is the disruptive effect of our strong culture upon their fragile one." "Disruptive" is translated as "destructive."[73] Granted the two words are similar, but can this be a mistake? On the next page Fulbright observes, "Sincere though it is, the American effort to build the foundations of freedom in South Vietnam is thus having an effect quite different from the one intended." The translation substitutes "exactly opposite to" for "quite different from,"[74] which is certainly not what the author meant to say.

Conclusions

My study, although limited, does suggest some tentative conclusions. It is clear that substantial qualitative differences exist between at least some Soviet translations and the foreign originals on which they are based. The changes made in the texts of translations, both structural and textual, are evidence of an *active* rather than a *reactive* censorship, a process sufficiently different from the traditional one in Russia and elsewhere that a new term might be required to describe it. These changes seem to be aimed primarily at altering the images of the Soviet Union and the United States (and other Western powers) presented by the authors, with the result that the Soviet Union appears in a more positive light while the West looks worse.

The themes of concern to the imperial and Soviet governments are, at least in a general sense, comparable; that is, the Soviets are still concerned about the treatment by foreign authors of their leadership, their form of government, the image of their country, and the role of the state religion (Russian Orthodoxy in imperial Russia and Soviet orthodox doctrine in the USSR). These are not allowed to be treated with disrespect in foreign writings to be published in Russia, imperial and Soviet alike.

The significant and interesting difference between the old and new regimes lies not in the themes but in the techniques employed to deal with them. Translation Soviet style would seem to be infinitely more effective than "covering over with caviar," as 19th-century Russians used to describe the inking out of offending passages. Now the ink itself, as well as what it covers, is invisible.

Notes

1   Marianna Tax Choldin, *A Fence around the Empire: Russian Censorship of Western Ideas under the Tsars* (Durham, NC: Duke University Press, 1985).

2   Much of this material can be gleaned from the excellent bibliography and notes in *The Soviet Censorship*, edited by Martin Dewhirst and Robert Farrell (Metuchen, NJ: Scarecrow Press, 1973).

3   *Webster's Third New International Dictionary of the English Language* (1961), s.v. "censor."

4   An interesting and recent article on this subject is "The Game of the Soviet Censor" by Tomas Venclara, a Lithuanian poet and former Soviet citizen now teaching at Yale University (*New York Review of Books*, March 31, 1983, pp. 33–35).

5   See Maurice Friedberg, *A Decade of Euphoria: Western Literature in Post-Stalin Russia, 1954–64* (Bloomington: Indiana University Press, 1977), p. 21.

6   See Friedberg, *A Decade of Euphoria*; Marianna Tax Choldin, "The New Censorship: Censorship of Translations in the Soviet Union," *Journal of Library History* 21 (Spring 1986): 334–49); and Henry Glade, "Aspects of Soviet Censorship of West German Belles-Lettres, 1974–1980: An Overview," *Germano-Slavica* 4 (1983): 151–57.

7   J. William Fulbright, *The Arrogance of Power* (New York: Random House, 1966), p. 4. Soviet translation: *Samonadeiannost'sily* (Moscow: Izdatel'stvo Mezhdunarodnye otnosheniia, 1967).

8   Harold Nicolson, *The Evolution of Diplomatic Method* (New York: Macmillan, 1954). The identical Collier Books Edition (1962), entitled *The Evolution of Diplomacy*, was used for this study. The Soviet translation: *Diplomaticheskoe iskusstvo* (Moscow: Izdatel'stvo Instituta Mezhdunarodnyekh otuoshenii, 1962).

9   Kwame Nkrumah, *I Speak of Freedom: A Statement of African Ideology* (London: Heinemann, 1961). Soviet translation: *Ia govoriu o svobode: Izlozhenie afrikanskoi ideologii* (Moscow: Izdatel'stvo inostrannoi literatury, 1962).

10   Jawaharlal Nehru, *India's Foreign Policy: Selected Speeches, September 1946–April 1961* (Delhi: The Publications Division, Ministry of Information and Broadcasting Government of India, 1961). Soviet translation: *Vneshniaia politika Indii: Izbrannye rechi i vystupleniia 1946–64* (Moscow: Izdatel'stvo Progress, 1965).

11   An interesting and fairly recent article on Soviet publishing, including a section on "Progress," is "The Soviet Way of Publishing" by Herbert R. Littman (*Publishers Weekly*, September 18, 1978, pp. 101–18). Two books to note are Boris I. Gorokhoff, *Publishing in the U.S.S.R.* (Bloomington: Indiana University Publications Slavic and East European Series, 1959, vol. 19) and Gregory Walker, *Soviet Book Publishing Policy* (Cambridge: Cambridge University Press, 1978).

12   The Nehru volume may actually have straddled the two regimes: Khrushchev was deposed on October 15, 1964, and the translation went into production in July 1965; the translators, editors, and whomever else were involved might well have begun their work under Khrushchev and completed it under Brezhnev.

13   Nkrumah (Russian), facing p. 279.

14   Nehru (Russian), p. 27.

15   The selections under "Hungary" (one speech) and "Yugoslavia" (two speeches) were omitted, almost certainly because the former is entitled "The Tragedy of Hungary" and discusses the abortive uprising of 1956; and the second speech in the latter category contains references to Tito's relationship with the Soviet Union, stressing his independence.

16   Three selections — "The Way We Function," "On Speaking from Strength," and "U.N. Resolution on Co-Existence" — are combined into one selection in the translation, "Nash obraz deistviia." See Nehru (English), pp. 73–77, 203, 102–04; Nehru (Russian), pp. 189–99.

17   One such quotation, on p. 8, is from the 1955 Russian translation of Nehru's book *The Discovery of India* (translation, p. 24; original, p. 13).

18   Original, Calcutta: Signet Press, 1946; translation, Moscow: Izdatel'stvo inostrannoi literatury, 1955.

19   Fulbright (English), p. 8; (Russian), p. 15.
20   Nicolson (English), pp. 17, 25; (Russian), pp. 38, 43.
21   Nehru (English), pp. 17, 25; (Russian), pp. 38, 43.
22   Nicolson (English), p. 117; (Russian), p. 101.
23   Nicolson (English), pp. 119, 122, 123; (Russian), pp. 102, 104, 105.
24   A quick comparison of the Spanish translation (provided by Senator Fulbright) with the original indicates that this Mexican edition conforms to the usual expectations for a translation; that is, it appears to be a faithful rendition of the author's text in another language. See J. William Fulbright, *La Arrogancia del Poder* (Mexico: Fondo de Cultura Economica, 1976).
25   A third area, little represented in this study but still worth noting, has to do with religion. An example is a quotation from George Bernard Shaw excised from the translation of *The Arrogance of Power*. Religion, Shaw says, is "the only real motive force in the world" (Fulbright [English], p. 18; [Russian], p. 25).
26   Nehru (Russian), p. 236; (English), p. 214.
27   Nkrumah (Russian), facing p. 128.
28   Nehru (English), p. 578; (Russian), p. 178.
29   Nehru (Russian), p. 200; (English), p. 550.
30   Nehru (Russian), p. 210; (English), p. 208.
31   Nehru (Russian), p. 139; (English), p. 92.
32   Nehru (Russian), p. 32; (English), p. 3.
33   Fulbright (English), p. 13; (Russian), p. 21.
34   Nehru (English), pp. 92–93; (Russian), p. 139.
35   Nkrumah (English), p. 139; (Russian), p. 154. This is the excision referred to earlier, which is preceded in the translation by ellipses.
36   Fulbright (English), p. 15; (Russian), p. 23.
37   Fulbright (English), p. 14; (Russian), p. 21.
38   Nicolson (English), p. 121; (Russian), p. 103.
39   No notes are thought to be necessary, however, when correcting mistakes made by the author. Nkrumah refers to the 18 republics of the Soviet Union; the translation simply substitutes the correct number, 15. Nkrumah (English), p. 221; (Russian), p. 239. In a June 1960 speech, Nehru mentions a disarmament conference now meeting in Paris. Again without a note, the translation gives the precise name of the committee and changes the location to the correct one, Geneva. Nehru (English), p. 214; (Russian), p. 235. But a note *is* added in this very interesting instance. Near the end of Chapter 4, "Constitution Making," Nkrumah quotes from one of his own speeches:

> Mr. Speaker, for my part, I can only re-echo the words of a great man: "Man's dearest possession is life, and since it is given to him to live but once, he must so live as not to be besmeared with the shame of a cowardly existence and trivial past, so live that dying he might say: All my life and all my strength were given to the finest cause in the world, the liberation of mankind."

Nkrumah does not identify the passage, but in the Soviet edition it is properly cited as a translation from the Soviet writer N. A. Ostrovskii's well-known novel *Kak zakalialas'stal'* (How the Steel Was Tempered). (1) Nkrumah (English), p. 32; (Russian), pp. 44–5. One of the Soviets involved in the translation must have recognized the passage.
40   Nicolson (Russian), p. 100.

41 Nicolson (English), p. 118; (Russian), p. 117.

42 Nicolson (English), p. 119; (Russian), p. 117.

43 Nehru (English), p. 208; (Russian), p. 210.

44 Nehru (English), p. 572; (Russian), p. 152.

45 Nehru (English), p. 576; (Russian), p. 173.

46 Nehru (English), p. 214; (Russian), p. 235.

47 Fulbright (English), p. 3; (Russian), p. 11.

48 Fulbright (English), p. 3; (Russian), p. 11.

49 Fulbright (English), p. 7; (Russian), p. 15.

50 Fulbright (English), p. 21; (Russian), p. 28.

51 Fulbright (English), pp. 15, 18; (Russian), pp. 22, 25.

52 Fulbright (English), p. 18; (Russian), p. 25.

53 Nkrumah (English), pp. 139–140; (Russian), p. 155. Here, too, ellipses appear in the translation, followed by "abolished."

54 Nicolson (Russian), p. 107, note 9.

55 Nicolson (English), p. 124; (Russian), p. 106.

56 Nicolson (Russian), p. 105; (English), p. 123.

57 Nicolson (English), p. 20; (Russian), p. 40.

58 Nicolson (English), p. 20; (Russian), p. 40.

59 Nicolson (English), p. 23; (Russian), p. 42.

60 Nicolson (English), p. 24; (Russian), p. 43.

61 Fulbright (English), p. 6; (Russian), p. 14.

62 Fulbright (English), p. 10; (Russian), p. 18.

63 Fulbright (Russian), p. 27; (English), p. 20.

64 Nkrumah (English, Russian), tables of contents.

65 Nkrumah (English), pp. 135, 146; (Russian), pp. 150, 162; title of Chapter 15.

66 Nehru (English), pp. 75, 200; (Russian), pp. 193, 183; Nicolson (English), p. 106; (Russian), p. 94.

67 Nicolson (Russian), p. 99; (English), p. 114. "United Kingdom" appears in the Nkrumah translation too: (Russian), p. 298; (English), p. 277.

68 Fulbright (Russian), pp. 13, 30, 17, 18; (English), pp. 5, 22, 9, 11.

69 Fulbright (English), p. 4; (Russian), p. 12.

70 Fulbright (English), p. 19; (Russian), p. 26.

71 Fulbright (English), p. 12; (Russian), p. 20.

72 Fulbright (English), p. 18; (Russian), p. 27.

73 Fulbright (English), p. 16; (Russian), p. 23.

74 Fulbright (English), p. 17; (Russian), p. 24.

Soviet Censorship: Discussion

John Glad (University of Maryland) opened the discussion, noting that Soviet efforts to control what is being published in this country have not been entirely ineffective. In addition to controlling visas for scholars and journalists and providing information preferentially to those journalists who are cooperative, control is also exercised in other ways. Glad cited the cases of Shalamov, whom he translated, and Father Dudko as very interesting examples if not of censorship, then of an attempt at least to minimize harm once something has been published abroad. In an earlier era, Pasternak emerged as a semi-saint thanks to the efforts of the KGB. Neither Dudko nor Shalamov was allowed to go that route; instead, they were both forced to sign rather odious statements. Dudko signed a statement, undoubtedly not written by him: *Vsiakaia vlast' ot Boga, v tom chisle i sovetskaia vlast'* — All power is from God, and that includes Soviet power, the Soviet Government. Shalamov also signed a statement that he did not write, but he still spent 17 years in the camps. No one criticized him, but many people stopped supporting him; Glad views that as a rather effective ploy on the part of the authorities.

Speaking as a translator, Glad observed that it is often very difficult to establish a text from which to work. He cited as an example a work by Vyacheslav Shishkov called *Ugrium reka* (Grim River) published in 1933 and probably the most popular novel in Russia in the 20th century. Four million copies of each volume were sold in the ten-year period between 1955 and 1965 alone. Although it was published in 1933, Shishkov continued to work on it, partly because he wanted to improve it and partly to appease censorship. The final authorized version contains improvements, new pages, even whole chapters of added material. In many other cases new versions appear — not just cut-down versions but also versions with new material added after the author's death, after the appearance of the last authorized edition. The problem of which text the translator is to use is thus a genuine one.

Admiral Mott (American Bar Association) mentioned a booklet, *Soviet Media and Their Message*, prepared by Leonid Finkelstein for the ABA's Committee on Law and National Security, and another publication in which Finkelstein was involved: the only social science textbook, to Mott's knowledge, used in every high school in the Soviet Union, called *Social Science*. Since Soviet accession to the Universal Copyright Convention, he noted, translations can no longer be published in the West without permission (Friedberg pointed out that it is legal if a work is published for scholarly use only and in a limited number of copies). Mott found this restriction ironic in view of the fact that this book illustrates so clearly points made by Finkelstein and Friedberg. In successive editions the names of people like Khrushchev are completely eliminated; in edition after edition the nonpersons are struck from the text. Mott recalled that it had been very difficult to convince the Board of Governors of the ABA to make this translation available to teachers — censorship, observed Mr. Finkelstein! — but when it finally was made available, it revealed more to our social science teachers than any American publication could have done.

Mott then posed a legal question regarding Soviet reporting of U.S. Supreme Court decisions. He cited as an example the case of the long-shoremen who struck against handling all cargo coming from the Soviet Union. The Supreme Court decision went against them on the grounds that one of our laws had been violated, but the Court was very sympathetic to what the longshoremen were trying to do. How would that case be reported, if at all, in the Soviet Union?

Finkelstein responded that he was unaware of how it had been reported in the Soviet Union, or whether it had been reported at all, but assured Mott that there are many ways to handle such a problem, the simplest, of course, being to say nothing: any news that is not suitable is to be erased from memory, simply to be barred. However, it is not as simple as that nowadays, he observed, because there are what they call in the Soviet Union "voices" — that is, The Voice of America, BBC, Radio Liberty, Deutsche Welle, and others — so the Soviets usually try to offer their own versions. He maintained that this is done very skillfully indeed; for example, any decision of the U.S. Supreme Court could be not rephrased, exactly, but presented with minor alterations, in such a way as not to raise unpleasant suspicions. So although he did not know whether this particular incident had been reported at all, he felt sure that they could have reported it, if they wished to, in a way harmless to them.

Finkelstein added that the more crude propaganda emanating from the Soviet Union translated into English, the better; in his view it should be given straight, without any commentaries at all because none is needed. Unfortunately, he observed, this material is often unreadable by Western standards — tedious, boring, and long-winded — but on the other hand, these very qualities might have a strong impact on Western audiences, and the material might even become popular because of its entertainment value!

Eric Willenz (U.S. Department of State) asked Finkelstein and Friedberg to comment on one aspect of censorship that is particularly interesting because of its effects over time on artistic expression: self-censorship. To what extent do they feel it is not only the *substance* of any forms of expression that is subject to censorship but also the *form*? Is it fair to argue that because of this kind of censorship, Soviet artists, whatever their creative area may be, are increasingly unable to be experimental not only in the substance of their works of art but in the form as well? If so, should we assume that those who come out of the Soviet Union do so not always because of the suppression of the substance of their work, particularly writers and poets, but also because of the suppression of form, affecting artists, musicians, dancers? What has been the effect over time? Has this suppression had a depressive effect not only on the state of art but on the artists themselves? Are they deeply aware of an inability to learn to express themselves? He added that monarchical systems also have censorship but that great works of art have nonetheless been produced under these systems.

Friedberg responded first, with a definite "yes." Socialist Realism, he noted, is a universe that rests on three whales: *ideinost'* (and its derivative, *partiinost'*), *narodnost'*, and *tipichnost'* — ideology and Party spirit, popular character, and typicality. *Narodnost'* is commonly interpreted as something accessible to the people, but instead of lifting the people up to the level where they could understand complex works of art, this is interpreted to mean that the artist should descend to the lowest common denominator; in effect, to pop art (or near-pulp fiction).

Having said this, however, Friedberg observed that the penetration into Russia of Western literary works, Western paintings, Western cinema and theater has been used with a degree of success to resist this kind of pressure from the ideological authorities. For instance, someone might write experimental poetry and get dressed down for it. He might then say, "Well, I'm just following the example of such progressive poets as Pablo Neruda and Paul Eluard." Or someone might produce a painting that does not meet with approval, and he might say, "Well, the great progressive figure and fighter for peace Pablo Picasso paints canvases infinitely more abstract," and so forth. In the theater one would invoke the name of Berthold Brecht. Writers, painters, and musicians have been known to use this ploy occasionally — and with some success — as a weapon in the struggle against those who would totally suppress the freedom of the artist to forge ahead.

Finkelstein also responded to the question, noting first that one of the foremost living Russian writers, Vassily Aksyonov, could certainly elaborate on this subject much better than he, because Aksyonov himself had struggled for new forms in Russian literature for decades with great success. His efforts earned him many bruises, and Finkelstein observed that Aksyonov was probably here today because of those efforts. He advised Willenz to ask Aksyonov the same question after his own contribution later in the conference; he would certainly add much more.

Finkelstein made a general observation on the subject of form. In the past, even the recent past, when people like Aksyonov and other young writers started publishing works in unorthodox forms, when the young artists started painting unorthodox canvases, when young musicians started composing unorthodox pieces, these developments were, of course, met with a counterattack from the conservatives. Time, however, does not stand still. In Finkelstein's view the issue of form has taken on a rather different shape. On the one hand, there are genuinely talented people in literature, music, and art who are concerned with new forms. Iurii Liubimov and the Taganka theater must also be mentioned here, he added.

On the other hand, there are opportunists who use new Western forms, especially in graphic art. Finkelstein maintained that if one were to open any Soviet art magazine now, one would find many things painted and drawn in modernistic style, but mainly according to Western fashion. He saw this as an interesting shift: the Soviet authorities, the censors in the broadest sense of the word, are not opposed to innovation in form per se. Sometimes they will let it slip through for the sake of a more attractive appearance. The form is the jar, and the wine in it must be our Soviet wine, but the jar may be jeans and rock music. The authorities are more sophisticated now.

Friedberg commented that there are limits to what Finkelstein described: sometimes it works and sometimes it does not. In 1982 he made a bet with himself (because no one else was willing to bet with him) that someone in the Soviet Union would have the bright idea to announce that "as a token of the Soviet peoples' solidarity with the oppressed nation of Ireland now fighting for its independence [*natsional'no-osvoboditel'naia bor'ba irlandskogo naroda*] we will publish on this centennial of James Joyce his novel *Ulysses*." No such publication has appeared, he noted wryly.

James Billington (Woodrow Wilson Center) wondered how censorship affects the internal communication of the elite — the rather more extensive form of translating and internal communication, the internal transmission of material from the West, and so forth. Finkelstein mentioned a famous instance that occurred in December 1966, when Kosygin was in Britain on an official visit: while chatting with (now) Sir Harold Wilson, Kosygin took up one of Wilson's hints. Wilson said something about all animals being equal. Kosygin smiled immediately in response and said, "Yes, but some are more equal than others!" Obviously, then, the Soviet authorities are, or at least try to be, *au courant*, familiar with the modern, with the *real* literature in the West, with the literature they do not allow people to read.

Yet despite that, Finkelstein continued, all of Soviet society is affected by censorship, and the area hardest hit is not literature, art, or even politics. It is the realm of technology and science, because restrictive censorship and overall secrecy prevent the dissemination of scientific information. Despite the fact that the Soviets created new instrumentalities, new institutions for the dissemination and exchange of information, these cannot function in conditions of secrecy. He noted that he could cite numerous, absolutely ludicrous examples in which he, a science writer, was carrying scientific information from one science institution to another in the Soviet Union. He was really thankful because without that his publication would have spent six months trying to obtain access to a particular document. In America, he observed, there is a great thing called "spin-off"; for example, spin-off from space research. There is little spin-off in the Soviet Union, he said, because of the barriers that surround space research, as is the case with any other militarily significant research.

Censorship, he concluded, takes its revenge; its severe effects can be seen throughout Soviet society, and it dooms many undertakings to failure that might otherwise have succeeded. One must always bear in mind, however, that if censorship were to be eliminated from the Soviet system, it would no longer *be* the Soviet system: it is that well entrenched. Censorship will continue to exert an effect, and Soviet leaders can do nothing about it.

Mikhail Agursky (Hebrew University of Jerusalem) commented on censorship as a political institution, pointing out that we must distinguish this from censorship as a political process. Glavlit as a manifestation of Soviet censorship as a political institution is, in his view, a more formal organization, responsible mainly for maintaining, for example, a list of sources to which one is or is not allowed to refer. The bulk of censorship intervention is made by editorial bodies. Glavlit as a political institution is not responsible for the ideological orientation of Soviet publications. This must be kept in mind; otherwise one cannot understand occasional inconsistencies, such as when one Soviet source permits itself some kind of expression and a second does not. This is not controlled by Glavlit.

He cited one example. In 1965 he published a technical book in the USSR and was struck by an interesting demand from his editor, that he cut out a reference to *Pravda*. When he asked why — the reference was to some critical remarks published not in an editorial but in a feature article in *Pravda* — she told him: "Listen! A book will go abroad, it will sit on a shelf. Nobody will ask for a newspaper, but a book will serve as a reference for many Western scientists for a long time." So what is permissible for the Soviet daily press, even the central press, is not permissible for books. (Friedberg added that this phenomenon had been noted nearly 25 years ago by Leszek Kolakowski, the Polish dissident philosopher. In his famed essay, "What Is Socialism?" he said that "socialism is not a system that objects to the reading of old issues of newspapers.")

Agursky commented further on why Soviet censorship systematically rejects writers such as Herman Wouk, Saul Bellow, and Bernard Malamud. He maintained that we must understand the concept of the Soviet anti-Zionist approach. According to the Soviet view, Zionism is every manifestation of Jewish identity. Long before the publication of his book *To Jerusalem and Back*, Saul Bellow was regarded as a Zionist (Agursky first heard him referred to this way in 1972). He noted a recent article confirming this attitude by the Soviet literary critic Vadim Kozhevnikov published in November 1982 in a literary monthly in Moscow; the author called Bellow the main pillar of Zionist oppression of the American people. Agursky noted that only one story by Bellow, *Gonzaga's Manuscript*, had been published in Russian some time ago, in a collection of American stories. He concluded that *To Jerusalem and Back* is not the only reason for Soviet treatment of Bellow, and that *The Dean's December* is certainly not to blame.

Finkelstein responded to Agursky's comments on Glavlit, claiming that it is only partly true that Glavlit is entirely formal. Finkelstein dealt with Glavlit staff personally for six years on a monthly basis and maintains that while, indeed, their main concern is the "Talmud" — the compilation of censorship rules and regulations — they are also very watchful regarding the ideological side of the text. On many occasions, he recalled, the censor would put a blue question mark next to a paragraph and would say, "Leonid Vladimirovich, now, this, really! Why should you include that?" Finkelstein would always play the fool, asking "Why should I excise this? Explain!" They never did explain, he said; instead, they would say, "But you are an adult, Leonid! Don't you see for yourself?" If you insisted they might back down, as in the case of Kosolapov, the editor of *Literaturnaia gazeta* and the censor when Yevtushenko's poem *Babii Yar* was published. Kosolapov insisted, and the censor reported him to the Central Committee and put a stop to it. This does happen occasionally, he noted, but they keep a watchful eye.

Yuri Elagin (U.S. Information Agency), editor of the Russian-language magazine *Dialog USA*, added a few interesting details on the problem of censorship in the Soviet Union from an entirely different angle. He observed that he, as editor of the Russian-language magazine for the Soviet Union, and his colleagues who edit *America Illustrated* constantly encounter the problem of censorship. In his view they are not as fortunate as their colleagues at Voice of America, whose mistakes will not endanger the very existence of the VOA. If the *America Illustrated* people make a serious mistake, he noted, it could mean the end of the publication, which is not and never was protected by the cultural agreement.

Mr. Elagin indicated that sometimes it is very easy to determine what the Soviets will not like. He gave as an example one issue of an exhibit brochure specially published for the bicentennial exhibit in Moscow in November 1976. An old article from *America Illustrated* was included that discussed the 1930s in America and mentioned the rise of some extremist movements, the Nazi Bund and the Communist Party. Not surprisingly, Moscow did not like to see those two organizations named on the same line; that entire brochure was withdrawn and a new one had to be published.

In other cases, however, he noted that it is not so easy to look ahead and to realize what they will object to. He cited the case of a photo published in *America Illustrated* depicting a ballerina reading an American dance magazine with Baryshnikov on the cover; the Soviets had raised a serious objection to this photo. He mentioned also an article in the magazine by Harold Schoenberg about styles of musical performers, in which famous names were mentioned, including Rostropovich. That name had to be replaced, of course; Elagin used Richter instead. The protest or objection on the highest level ever, Elagin recalled, was made by the Soviet government about three years ago. Despite their sensitivity to such matters, he conceded that he and his colleagues at *America Illustrated* had not predicted this one. On the last page of the text there was a very small photo, postage-stamp size, of a *Readers Digest* cover. If one examined it through a strong magnifying glass, one could read the table of contents, and among the articles was "After Brezhnev, What?" Elagin recalled that Gromyko's deputy came to see the American ambassador because of that photo.

Finkelstein added another example: The censorship cut Arthur Miller's short play *Incident at Vichy* from the March 1965 issue of the magazine *Inostrannaia literatura*, but neglected to remove from the end of the magazine a brief statement to the effect that Arthur Miller's play *Incident at Vichy*, staged in Warsaw, could be found in this issue of the magazine. Of course it was an acute embarrassment, but in the end it had a good result: in three months' time they were forced to publish *Incident at Vichy*!

Albert Todd (Queens College) asked a question that had bothered him for many years. He had posed this question at the London conference in 1969, and although he had received some answers then, he wanted to raise it again here. It is the question of self-censorship, but not as practiced by an author; rather, this is self-censorship of quite a different form. In perhaps half a dozen volumes he has collected from the Soviet Union published in the 1920s, 1930s, and 1940s, he noticed that the name of a responsible person — perhaps the editor, the author of the introductory article, or a member of the editorial board — had been carefully removed from the printed text, seemingly by some process of ink eradication or even more crudely, by the use of a razor blade. For example, in a set of the works of the 19th-century writer Lavrov, a figure whose works were considered worth maintaining and obviously were not themselves the subject of censorship, the name of the author of the introductory article — someone named Teodorovich, he recalled — had been carefully scratched out in each volume of the set he owns. Where, he wondered, does this act of self-censorship take place? Is it in the private home of the owner of the library, Teodorovich having become an unperson? Is it uncomfortable to show his name? Does the act occur in the second-hand bookstore from which the book is obtained, where the proprietor does not wish to be selling something with an unperson's name associated with it? Or does it occur at some other level? Todd had heard various suggestions and was not sure whether he was satisfied that there is a single answer to this question; he wondered if anyone at this conference might comment.

Finkelstein responded that although he could not answer directly, any librarian in the Soviet Union could tell many horror stories. Every month, or perhaps even more frequently, they receive lists of books by, for example, authors who recently emigrated, and those books are to be taken out of circulation. Regarding things that are to be excised, he mentioned the notorious case, known all over the world, of the *Large Soviet Encyclopedia*: when Beria was executed, the publisher circulated extra pages to be added to the volume, accompanied by a notice, "Please cut out with a razor blade such and such a page and replace with the enclosed page," the enclosed page being a long article about the Bering Sea. There are many methods, he concluded, and this is a continuous and painful process, especially because many people are emigrating now and thus relegating themselves to the category of unpersons.

Todd added that he had raised this question because the instances he was thinking of were somewhat different from this classic example of "Bering Sea" substituting for "Beria." The cases he had in mind seemed to be on a private, personal level, perhaps taking place within a personal library or a local bookstore. This is the imposition of the requirements of self-censorship. The author, editor, or publisher is not in control at this level; rather, the owner, or perhaps the purveyor of a book, finds it obligatory to remove a reference to an unperson. In the case of Teodorovich's introduction, he noted, the introduction itself is intact; only his name is removed.

Finkelstein responded that he would not assume that this is self-censorship; precisely how it was done he did not know, but he felt certain that it was done in response to instructions. Glad added that he had seen similar instances in the Lenin Library in Moscow; in one case, he recalled, three copies of a 1925 almanac had all been treated in a similar fashion and had then been rebound, so evidently it had been an official policy of the Lenin Library.

Yuri Yarim-Agaev (Fremont, California) commented on the question of censorship of foreign literature, which he considers particularly important.

Censorship, he observed, is based on psychological compromise between author and censor; some kind of negotiation always takes place, and in his view it is based on the principle of "better something than nothing." How does this work in the Soviet Union? This principle is a destructive one, as we know from the 16th century, when such a compromise could not be reached. He sees the existence of the journal *Novyi mir* as the last step of a possible compromise. Many Soviet authors decided not to compromise at all and to publish their books only as they wrote them; this group is represented by such people as Siniavskii, Aksyonov, and Voinovich, who pioneered this new approach.

In Yarim-Agaev's view, the problem is that many foreign authors know that their books are censored by the Soviet censorship bureau as they are translated, yet they do not protest at all or refuse to allow such books to be published. The same question comes up with Yuri Elagin's publication and with such magazines as *America* and *US–USSR Dialogue*: to what extent can they be compromised? When is compromise still positive and when does it becomes negative; that is, when does this principle of "better something than nothing" start to become simply destructive? At what point is compromise serving bad ends rather than helping people to get information?

In Yarim-Agaev's opinion, we go too far in many cases. In general it would be better if many American authors refused to publish their books at all in the Soviet Union rather than allowing them to be published in a form acceptable to the Soviet censorship system. He emphasized that we must keep in mind, especially in the case of political books, that if the Soviets want to translate such books, they have very serious political intentions in doing so. It is not Americans or other foreign authors who distribute their books in the Soviet Union; rather, it is the Soviets who do so, with specific interests in mind.

Regarding Friedberg's suggestion that we should enter subscriptions to American magazines for people in the Soviet Union, Yarim-Agaev noted that he has conducted this experiment numerous times. It worked very badly, in his experience, and in very strange ways. He chose different types of magazines but no exceptionally conservative ones: *Newsweek*, for example, and *Time*, and some that seem neutral, such as *National Geographic*. At first people in the Soviet Union received some issues, which surprised him: it would have been more consistent, he thought, if the recipient of the subscription had not received any issues at all; if every time he came to the post office, he were simply told, "We don't know anything about it." Yarim-Agaev has not been able to discern any clear pattern. The person for whom he subscribes to the *National Geographic* has not received any issues, but every month or two the person to whom he sends *Newsweek*, a more political magazine, receives an issue, thus demonstrating that he does actually have a subscription. Twice while in the Soviet Union he himself received *Commentary*, which is rather more conservative than the other two titles. In Yarim-Agaev's view these results simply demonstrate that we may reach some general theoretical conclusions and they may be correct, but if we want to know details, if we want to know how this real system really works, we shall have to do more experiments. In any case, it certainly appears that the censorship works badly and that it is an imperfect system—one that could not, in fact, ever be perfect.

Finkelstein responded that Yarim-Agaev was describing the weak link in the Soviet censorship chain, postal censorship, which he sees as not 100 percent effective nowadays. He pointed out that foreign radio stations such as the BBC receive a lot of mail from the Soviet Union that falls through the net; in this same haphazard fashion some of Yarim-Agaev's friends receive their magazines. It has nothing to do, he maintains, with the system of censorship itself; postal censorship is simply unable to cope technically with the task. He agreed with Yarim-Agaev, however, that Western authors and publishers could be considerably more vigilant with regard to Soviet translations of Western works.

Alfred Friendly (Washington, D.C.) commented briefly on some points raised so far. Regarding the presence and absence of self-censorship noted by Professor Todd, he mentioned the one example of censorship purely on orders that he has heard about: in high school and even elementary school texts of the 1930s one had to paste pieces of white paper over the pictures of Marshal Tukhachevskii and anyone else who happened to be appearing in the trials at that time. A schoolchild arriving at that page of the textbook left the page in but blotted out the photograph. Regarding American censorship to fit Soviet demands, he mentioned the example of Muhammad Ali's autobiography: the American publisher refused to sell the rights to the Soviets because the Soviets insisted on removing from the text any reference to the amount of money he had won. (Friedberg added that above all the Soviet authorities did not like Ali's conversion to Islam.)

Friendly raised the technical question of who the "Glavlitchiki" are and how well they work, speculating that there must be a training school for censors. How does one become a censor, how does one stay a censor, and, particularly, how does one learn to go beyond the "Talmud" and to insist on the inclusion in manuscripts of the required positive outlook? Finkelstein responded that although very little is known about the recruitment and training of censors, he could convey some personal impressions. In his view, censors are recruited among the editorial failures — especially Party zealots, Komsomol zealots — who merely show some interest in literary work. He estimated that he probably saw 20 censors at most, perhaps even fewer. They impressed him as youngish people, mainly in their 30s, very seldom in their 40s, moderately well educated. All had probably received Soviet higher education and, in addition, some kind of "institutional higher education" whereby they were specially trained for the job.

Finkelstein doubted that there is a special school for censors but noted that a regular feature of editorial life at his magazine was censors' seminars. Whenever you phoned the censor, he recalled, you reached someone else, who would say, "Oh, Comrade Kirova is in a seminar." His magazine had a censor named Kirova for a long time, and she and others were always at some seminar — they seemed to be endless — and he supposed that this is how they received what in Britain is called "in-job training." Indeed, it was necessary because trends change and the censors always had to be up-to-date.

Finkelstein emphasized that one never discussed with a censor the fate of one's colleagues. He mentioned one Potamirov, whom he described as an eager and very agreeable fellow; Potamirov once divulged to him that he had been a Komsomol official before becoming a censor. Finkelstein and his colleagues rather liked him — he was mild and not terribly nasty. One day he just disappeared without a trace, and Finkelstein found an attractive woman sitting in his chair. Quite naturally, he asked her where Igor was. "Now *I* am Igor," she responded. When he persisted, she said "Oh, he was transferred." So Potamirov was simply transferred, and she materialized from nowhere, and from that day on she was their censor.

The air of mystery is probably deliberate, Finkelstein speculated. The only censor whose background Finkelstein knew about was a special censor, the person who was entitled to censor all writings about space: Mikhail Galaktionovich Kroshkin, whom they used to call "the manager of the moon" because he censored everything connected with space. He was a *kandidat* of technical science; he had defended his dissertation at some scientific institute and then the Party probably assigned him to that responsible post. In Finkelstein's estimation he was very good, as censors go; very liberal and hardworking.

Boris Zaks added a few words about the places censors come from, observing that one must not assume that there is any consistency in this respect. He objected to the suggestion that all censors are trained in one particular way. For instance, someone might graduate from the journalism faculty of Moscow University and then be given a job in the censorship department; he knew of two young women who were assigned to this kind of work, did not like it, and ultimately left. One of them became a member of a journal's staff, and the other worked for another magazine.

No specialized training is required in order to become a censor, Zaks maintained. One does not have to demonstrate any special intelligence; on the contrary, the most important thing is to follow instructions as strictly as possible. One must not be afraid of doing anything silly because if one follows the instructions rigidly, to the letter, one is in the right. Every censor has a manual: he consults it and works accordingly. In addition, he has a number of secret instructions; should there be any changes in policy, such instructions will introduce appropriate changes. As a result, the censor is not the arm that crosses something out but merely the pencil.

Gene Sosin (Radio Liberty) mentioned a friend in the Russian colony in New York, Mark Klionskii, who emigrated in 1974. When he was a beginning artist Klionskii was a follower of the conformist Socialist Realist style, and in that genre he gained quite a reputation. Some of his works were printed in Soviet books, such as the painting of the Party comrade repentant after having been dressed down — after his *kritika* and *samokritika*. Since his emigration art books including Klionskii's paintings have been printed in the Soviet Union but his name no longer exists; no name is ascribed to those paintings.

Sosin also returned to the subject of postal censorship, observing that for many years he has opened scores of airmail envelopes from the Soviet Union sent to various friends in the United States. He noted that if you open up the airmail envelope with the red, white, and blue borders, lay it down flat, and examine it, you will find—without exception, in his experience—a five-digit number stamped on the inside by some kind of a press like that used in this country by a notary public. The numbers vary from city to city. Sosin reported a little experiment: he and friends asked an American, a Vassar graduate who went to the Pushkin Institute for four months of study in 1982, to buy one of those envelopes at a Moscow store, open it up, and see if the numbers were there. He did and found no numbers. The student's next letter, which included a coded message reporting that the envelope he had bought in Moscow did not have those numbers, arrived in an envelope that did have the numbers. Is this censorship, Sosin asked, or something else? Glad was reminded of the story told by the linguist Boris Unbegaun about a man who included with his letter to a friend a note saying "I hope the censors won't take out the rose I'm putting in this letter," but did not enclose a rose; the letter arrived with a rose!

Finkelstein observed that during the war every letter one received had a stamp on it, *Provereno voennoi tsenzuroi*, checked by the military censorship. In his view that was honest and open. He added that he had been told by a reliable source that a great many of those letters were never actually read by the censorship; they simply stamped them and sent them on. There is no question that there was such a stamp; he was unaware, however, of any mark such as that described by Sosin. Glad noted that he had on occasion received letters from the Soviet Union that had obviously been resealed: the glue had made the letter stick to the inside of the envelope, which could not happen if one were simply licking the flap.

Igor Birman (editor, *Russia* magazine) also commented on this question, noting that he had seen a piece in *Pravda* or *Izvestiia* to the effect that this mark — three or four digits, he recalled — is a standard one produced by the brigade that made the envelopes; he did not know whether or not this was true. As for the career patterns of censors, Birman agreed with Zaks. He mentioned a woman he had known for many years — young at first, later not so young anymore! — a good student of his in the Economics Institute. After graduation she was assigned to Glavlit, where she worked, he thought, for two and a half decades. She was either the chief or the only censor of a huge Soviet publishing house, Ekonomika; his own books published there were censored by her. On two occasions, when his books were published by other Moscow publishing houses, he used his connection with her to expedite publication.

Birman disagreed with Finkelstein about the number of censors in the Soviet Union: he found the figure of 70,000 to be impossibly high. In the first place, he pointed out, the censorship of district (*raion*) newspapers is carried out in the districts. Second, based on his own knowledge and experience he maintained that the main, if not the sole, concern of Soviet censorship is to prevent the publication of materials enumerated on a special list.

Ideological censorship is implemented by editorial boards, not by censors, Birman claimed, although efficient censors usually do voice their opinions. Censors have the right to demand that some figure, or the name of a particular factory, be deleted. For example, in one of his books the name of a plant was crossed out because it appeared on the list of secret enterprises. They have no formal right to demand any ideological changes: they can recommend, and then the editor and the director of the publishing house can choose to take the risk of disregarding the recommendation. Usually, of course, they choose not to take the risk. In some cases they do; Birman agreed with Zaks that risks were indeed taken over Yevtushenko's poem *Babii Yar*.

Birman maintained that none of the censors receives any special education. Economic censors graduate from economic institutes; a censor from the publishing house Mysl' graduated from the historical faculty of Moscow University. He personally did not remember any censors going to special seminars and wondered whether that might have been simply an excuse.

George Kolt (National Intelligence Council) brought the discussion back to some of the questions raised earlier, but in a slightly different fashion: he asked the panelists to address the possible dysfunctional aspects of censorship. He wondered whether Glavlit or editorial boards worry because some people do not believe anything they read in the press, while others know the rules extremely well and see them as so institutionalized that they can read right through the censorship. Still others are completely confused by the opaqueness of the message. If this is indeed seen as a problem, is it getting worse?

Friedberg recalled speaking with some people who left the Soviet Union in recent years who told him that one reason so many Soviet Jews did not attempt to flee the advancing Nazi armies was that they took it for granted that they had been misinformed by the Soviet press about the nature of Nazism, especially about Hitler's anti-Semitism. That is, if the papers write such and such, then obviously it must be the other way around; it could not be so bad — and so they stayed behind. He was also told that some people came to the United States with inflated expectations because the Soviet press featured stories of woe — America is a miserable place where everyone is starving and unemployed people live in slums — and they just read it upside down, assuming that everyone in America has a great job and a marvelous apartment.

To close the discussion, Andrei Siniavskii contributed an illustration of how the censors operate, a story about a little book on Picasso that he had written with his friend Igor Golomshtok in 1960. A woman who worked at the popular publishing house Znanie (knowledge) had been thinking about quitting her job for a long time, but before she did she thought she would, as a farewell gesture, do one good deed. She turned to Golomshtok, an art specialist, and commissioned a little book about Picasso, for which Golomshtok enlisted Siniavskii's help.

They completed the manuscript and delivered it to her, and she sent it for review to two outside readers. One was a liberal scientist and an art lover; the other was the writer Ilya Ehrenburg. Because she had reviews from two such authoritative readers, no one else read the manuscript. Ehrenburg also wrote an introduction to the book and subsequently wrote to his old crony Louis Aragon, the French communist writer, with the news that the first Soviet book on Picasso was about to appear. He also shared the joyous news of the forthcoming appearance of the book on Picasso with the exiled Spanish communist leader Dolores Ibarruri.

The book was set to appear when suddenly, on orders from the Central Committee, they just stopped the book and would not issue permission for it to be rolled off the presses. Golomshtok and Siniavskii were told that the entire printing of the book was to be pulped. They asked that they at least be given one author's copy each but were turned down. Siniavskii recalled that luck was with them, however, because Picasso was awarded a prize — he thought it was for the struggle for peace — and as a result the ban was lifted and the book actually appeared in the bookstores. There was not much written about it, but after that Golomshtok found himself unable to work on modern Western painting. He had been forbidden to pursue that topic despite the fact that he was an employee of and a researcher for the museum of modern art. Nothing ever happened to Siniavskii, however; he was only a writer and thus unaffected by instructions relating to the visual arts.

PART II

The Scientist's Laboratory

5

Coping with the Censor: A Soviet Scientist Remembers

Yuri Yarim-Agaev

I shall speak about censorship in Soviet science. I am a physicist; in the Soviet Union I worked with a team of physicists. I was also a member of the Moscow Helsinki Watch group, and thus I had other contacts with Soviet censorship as well.

Censorship can be managed in two ways. You can control the product of creativity or you can control this creativity itself by not allowing people to create something. To me, the fact that in the Soviet Union there does not exist any privately owned photocopying machine or any other technical means to publish something is no less important than the existence of Glavlit and other censorship organizations. If people owned their own printing facilities, they could bypass much of the official censorship.

The degree of impact of censorship differs from field to field. An author can still *write* his novel (though not *publish* it), and a composer *write* his score, and a mathematician or theoretical physicist produce his paper. But in such areas as cinema or theater, or in most fields of science, research itself may be proscribed. There will be no question of publication because there will simply be nothing to publish.

Let us consider what happens when a person wants to conduct his research, to write his papers, to publish them in any way. He does not care how dangerous this may be, or how unusual in his society. In such fields as literature, if he cannot publish inside the country he can, in principle, publish abroad. This is one way to avoid censorship. We know very well from the bitter experience of recent years that such actions are punishable by imprisonment. There exist articles of the criminal code of the

Soviet Union — Articles 190 and 70 — that are designed to punish people who try to bypass censorship.

In science the situation is somewhat different. In the first place, scientists are in principle officially allowed to publish abroad. That is not typical of other people in the Soviet Union. Soviet scientists have the right to publish their papers in international and American scientific journals. However, there are difficulties to overcome. The first is to obtain permission to conduct specific types of research. Then, prior to submission of the paper to a Soviet or a Western journal, it is subjected to much the same kind of censorship as literary materials. There are special commissions in every institute that must scrutinize the scientific paper to see if it contains any information forbidden for publication. Members of such scientific commissions are not special censors. They are scientists from the same research institute where the author works. Hence there is no need to have special censors and to pay them salaries; they do not receive additional pay for this work.

If a scientist wants to publish his paper abroad, he has to submit to this procedure. Many refuse to do so, but I also know of numerous cases of people who decide to avoid the procedure altogether: they simply stick English translations of their papers in envelopes and send them off to foreign scientific journals, where they are published. I do not know of any authors who got into serious trouble for such publications; in most cases the incidents were simply ignored by the Soviet authorities (or perhaps they just pretended not to know about them). Only people who work in absolutely nonsecret, open areas — scientists who conduct unclassified research — can afford this kind of publication.

The main tool of the Soviet censorship in science is secrecy. Censorship is effected in Soviet science through the simple stratagem of declaring the area of research secret. This stratagem is resorted to more and more frequently, and the number of laboratories declared secret is expanding rapidly. I am not referring to special military research institutes or institutes of the Department of Defense but, rather, to civilian academic institutes; to universities that are, in theory, supposed to be absolutely open. If a person associated with this kind of "secret" research publishes without authorization, he will be charged with divulging state secrets and can even be charged with espionage. The tendency to classify more and more researchers in academic institutes and universities as secret is no trivial matter. You will not find any mention of secrecy on any level in Soviet law. For example, the labor code of the Soviet Union — there is a big book of labor laws, including all kinds of Soviet institutes, universities, and the like — contains no mention of secrecy at all.

My situation was a specific one, of course, but it is a good illustration of what happens when one's research is declared secret. At the end of 1979, while I was working in the Institute of Chemical Physics, which is one of the largest academic institutes in the Soviet Union, it became clear that the administration had decided to fire me. The real reason was that I had become a member of the Moscow Helsinki Watch group. They did not want to give this as a reason for my dismissal, however; they chose a different way. One day they told me that my research was to be classified as secret. In fact, it was absolutely open research — I never dealt with any secret information — but they knew that I would not wish to apply for a security clearance and that if I did so, I would be refused such clearance; they could then simply tell me that I could not work in this area. I refused to apply for clearance, and they decided to transfer me to another laboratory, where I was not able to work because I lacked professional competence in the area.

Having lost my old job and been transferred against my will, I finally appealed to a regular district court which, according to Soviet law, is supposed to consider such cases. This court accepted my appeal; the judge told me that what had happened was counter to Soviet law and scheduled a hearing of my case. However, when I came to the hearing the judge told me that the institute in which I worked was subject to special courts. I said that I had never heard of the existence of special courts in the Soviet Union, but the judge gave me an address and told me to go there. He said, "I cannot tell you anything about it: go to this court and you will find out what it is."

I went to that address. It was a two-story building with an ordinary door, but nothing was written on that door. I entered and saw that it did indeed look like a real court. The secretary told me this was special court number 12, and because my institute was a "special regulations" institute, we were subject to such a court. I asked if I could bring my lawyer to this court. No, she said; "we have our own lawyers." I asked whether hearings in this court were open, and she said that I could submit a list of people I wanted to be present at the hearing; they would then check this list. If the people worked at my institute, there should be no problem.

I was a little surprised and decided to meet with the judge and ask him about his court. He refused to answer any questions and told me that if I wished I could leave my case in this court and there would be a hearing. I refused and appealed to the Moscow City Court because the district court refused to consider my case. Then I received a unique document — a decision of the Moscow City Court that my case must be considered by a special court. It is an official paper with the seal of the Department of Justice (I have several copies of it). This document is very important, I think, because the existence of such special courts is never mentioned. Indeed, the chairman of the USSR Supreme Court, Smirnov, states in his book that no special courts exist in the Soviet Union.

So you see, the existence of censorship is simply not mentioned at all. Censorship, and everything connected with it, simply contradicts all Soviet laws and Soviet constitutions. Subsequently I learned that the special courts deal with enterprises, research institutes, and even entire cities engaged in classified work. All hearings are secret, as are all decisions of such courts. This is important, because it demonstrates that secrecy is more important in the USSR than even the Soviet constitution.

The Scientist's Laboratory:
Discussion

Ellen Mickiewicz (Emory University) addressed a question to the first two panels, as well as to forthcoming panels. She noted that various examples had been cited drawn from each decade beginning with the 1930s, and that parallels had been made between the tsarist and Soviet regimes, some of which were criticized as inappropriate. She sensed an implicit question underlying the whole conference: What is the role of evolution, of change? How, she asked, should we treat these data, these stories from different periods? Certainly we know that there have been changes internal to the Soviet Union. What is our philosophy and our understanding of all these changes, even technologies — communications, for example — with respect to the particular instances of censorship with which we are dealing? In other words, how do we fit them into some kind of developmental trend? Or are we saying, philosophically, that in this area we are change-free?

Friedberg noted that some sort of definition seemed to be emerging of censorship's influence on the evolution of particular modes of cultural or social expression. Does censorship influence not only the direction but also the manner of development, of articulation, of the role of these modes in society? Does censorship suppress certain modes and certain values embodied in that expression? Does it promote others? What are the parallels between observance of unwritten social taboos, social conformism, observance of certain etiquette, and censorship? Censorship cannot be violated with the degree of impunity with which social etiquette can be violated, whereby one would be punished only by the usual ostracism that society may impose on one for committing such violations.

In Friedberg's view, participants in this conference were trying to project how censorship is likely to affect Soviet cultural and intellectual life in the next decade or so, assuming (as he suspected most would agree) that these controls will persist to some extent. Perhaps they will be enforced less stringently, perhaps more so, but he would very much doubt that the moment will arrive in our lifetime when the Party would relinquish the right to impose its will, to intervene in these processes. In other words, he concluded, the thaw was precisely that: it was a warmer temperature that melted some of the ice, but it was not spring and it was not summer. In fact, the thaw resulted in what thaws very often result in: namely, it brought into the open the dirt and decay of old life that was hidden under the majesty of snow and ice during the total freeze. At no time was the very principle of the Party's right to intervene in cultural, artistic, and intellectual life openly questioned.

Linda Lubrano (American University) made an analogy between the Soviet Union and a corporation, and commented on the use of secrecy as a means of control over science in the Soviet Union. In the ensuing discussion Friedberg noted with regret that so far no use had been made in this conference of that goldmine of information on the Soviet Union that is contained in Soviet folklore; he was thinking particularly of the story about the little child who asked why the Kremlin is surrounded by a tall wall. The *babushka* says, "Well, this is to prevent the criminals from crossing over the wall." The child asks, "Which way?" Ultimately, said Friedberg, one could conclude that it does not really matter because what the wall does is isolate the Kremlin from the outside world.

Boris Zaks took issue with Lubrano's comments, objecting sharply and categorically to any kind of analogy between the Soviet system and corporations and denying any similarity. Corporations exist side by side with one another, he observed, and treat their neighboring corporations accordingly. In the Soviet Union censorship accomplishes the task of protecting the monopoly of the dictatorship. In his view such analogies with Western corporations are inappropriate.

Lubrano responded that her comments had not in any sense been meant as a whitewash of the Soviet censorship system. She had merely referred to a concept widely used in American literature on the Soviet Union and on science: the concept of corporation writ large as a way to describe the Soviet Union. In her view this concept is quite consistent with the observations made by Zaks. The Soviet Union as an entire country is viewed as one huge corporation in competition with other countries and other multinational corporations around the world; that is the extent of the comparison. She noted that within corporations in the United States industrial secrecy is indeed practiced: there is open communication within that corporation to a certain point, but not between corporations. Similarly, the Soviet Union does not consider it desirable (nor does the United States) to divulge certain scientific and technical information that is potentially damaging to its own national interest. That is as far as the analogy goes.

Agursky observed that based on his own considerable experience of Soviet secrecy — described in his book about the Soviet military-industrial complex — he was not sure that it is possible to describe all Soviet secrecy in science (industrial and scientific secrecy) only in terms of totalitarian control over the society. He suggested that a great deal about Soviet secrecy can be explained by the internal dynamics of the Soviet bureaucracy responsible for secrecy, which has a vested interest in maintaining secrecy. He gave an example from his own experience that had nothing to do with the interests of the Soviet state. In 1969 the Soviet authority responsible for secrecy in several secret and completely isolated military-industrial complexes — not public organizations — issued instructions that all Soviet scientific reports about visits of Soviet delegations to a completely open international exhibition be made secret. This cannot be explained in terms of any reasonable interest of the Soviet state; rather, it is in the vested interest of the bureaucracy to keep secrecy intact. He noted that there is a huge mass of people in the Soviet Union who work within this system and that any move toward making secrecy less drastic, toward weakening it, is regarded by them as a challenge to their own organization.

The Soviet Union, Agursky concluded, is probably a corporate state but not one single corporation: it consists of very different corporations with interesting and complicated mutual relationships. We are still prisoners of the concept of totalitarian society. The Soviet Union is a totalitarian society only in intention. In fact, it is a corporate body made up of different corporations, or whatever one wants to call them, with very complicated interplay. We must not exaggerate, for example, the planning capability of the Soviet system; we must not picture some kind of power at the very top that can control every-thing from above and below.

Denis Mickiewicz (Emory University) raised the question of the natural — one might even say cosmic — interest of people in having a flow of informa-tion: is this true of the sciences as well as of the arts? It seems that writers in the Soviet Union know the game very well, he observed, and so do the readers; they have developed a system of communicating between the lines, *mezhdu strok*. He asked whether that system exists as an actual definable and distinct apparatus, and if so, what censorship does with this apparatus.

Finkelstein responded that this notion is indeed very well known in the Soviet Union: it is known as *nekontroliruemyi podtekst*, uncontrollable subtext. Censorship is very intent upon hunting it down and diminishing it as much as possible, but, of course, it is a "hare and hound" situation. He noted that writers grow increasingly impertinent in using that uncontrollable subtext skillfully, especially because the area is boundless. One might hint at Nicholas I; or it might be *Boris Godunov*, the most recent wonderful exam-ple: *Boris Godunov* was banned from staging in the Taganka Theater. Why? It was Pushkin, after all, was it not? But of course it was Pushkin interpreted by Liubimov, so it is the interpretation that was at issue. One is aware of a kind of shadow-boxing between the author, who tried to use various ruses to convey the message, and the censors — not necessarily Glavlit censors; rather, editors and the whole machinery of censorship — who tried to eliminate the message.

In Finkelstein's view this is one of the most tragic aspects of the present state of spiritual life in Soviet society. It has reached the stage where everything looks a bit suspicious, no one trusts anyone, and people are trying to communicate by what might be called transcendental means. This all points to the extremely bad condition of the whole society and its current mentality; to the great cynicism that is growing inside the society. This is in itself significant. The uncontrollable subtext is only one of the manifestations of this general condition.

Friedberg added that the problem with such a subtext is that it may greatly enrich a literary text but may mislead people who are reading a nonliterary text, where one is not conditioned to be wary of metaphor, allegory, and so forth. For example, he could easily see that a reference in a Soviet text to the book by Vladimir Nabokov's brother, the composer Nicholas Nabokov, entitled *The Diary of a Cosmopolitan*, would make people believe that he is obviously Jewish, because the word *kosmopolit* acquired this connotation in the Soviet Union. It is not in the dictionary, but most would confirm this, Friedberg maintained.

Albert Todd remarked that this was not merely a conference on censorship but a conference on Soviet direction, which is itself subject to various interpretations. Does it mean "direction" in the sense of *napravlenie* or *rukovodstvo*? (Friedberg suggested *tvorcheskoe rukovodstvo*, creative direction in the sense of "control.")

Todd recalled remarks made during the 1969 London conference on Soviet censorship by Arkadii Belinkov, who made a very strong point that the distinct difference between Soviet censorship and perhaps all others, certainly earlier Russian forms of censorship, is that in addition to being a proscriptive kind of censorship, denying and forbidding, it is also a prescriptive censorship, giving direction and guidance. The latter is inherent in the title here, Todd observed, and with that in mind he raised a question about the prescriptive character of contemporary censorship. We are all familiar with its influence in the literary world: the positive hero, the love affair between girl, boy, and tractor. We know too about the tragic consequences of censorship in the realm of science, the consequences of which are still being felt and perhaps forever will be in the Soviet Union.

The question was addressed particularly to scientists present: what is the character, the degree, the form of prescriptive direction that is not to be separated from, but is also part and parcel of, the proscriptive forms of Soviet censorship in the fields of science today? Yarim-Agaev responded that since 1982, no scientific project can be conducted before receiving the approval of the institute's Party committee in addition to the approval of a scientific council.

PART III

Literature and Intellectual Life

6

Censoring Artistic Imagination

Maurice Friedberg
Vassily Aksyonov
Vladimir Voinovich
Andrei Siniavskii

Introduction

Friedberg opened the session devoted to literature with the comment
that although censorship is a method of influencing the expression of all
artistic and intellectual life, barring none — including the nonverbal ones,
such as painting, symphonic music, ballet — when we speak of censorship,
we think first and foremost of literature. Censorship of literature has a long
tradition in Russia, and the tradition is neither quite as simple nor as entirely
negative as one might think. A case may be made for the proposition that the
existence of certain limitations on freedom of expression in belles lettres may
even benefit the creation in certain traditions and in certain genres. This can
be seen, for instance, from the fact that the total abolition of all restrictions
on what used to be called smut has resulted in the total disappearance of
the old and venerable genre of the bedroom farce. Those of us who are old
enough still remember with a degree of nostalgia the off-color joke, which is
now totally inaccessible to the young.

He noted that the three writers about to speak were among those
in the forefront of Russian literature of the post-Stalin period. Ultimately
the restrictions of censorship in the USSR proved too much in their case
and, far from benefiting their work, resulted in their emigration. They now
find themselves in Germany, France, and the United States. Friedberg added
that emigration is not an entirely negative phenomenon. The literature of

Poland, for instance, rests above all on the work that was created by the great 19th-century émigrés: Mickiewicz, Norwid, and many others.

Friedberg introduced Vassily Aksyonov with the observation that many critics, including himself, had proclaimed Aksyonov the most American of young Soviet writers when he was still in the USSR ("not a compliment," interjected Aksyonov). Friedberg recalled speaking of Aksyonov as the writer who managed to assimilate creatively the best in the tradition of such older, by then almost classical authors as Hemingway, as well as of the more promising younger writers, his contemporaries. He noted some similarities between Aksyonov's work and the better work of J. D. Salinger. Friedberg considers Aksyonov the one Russian prose writer now an émigré who is sustained not exclusively by memory but also by new impressions of the New World.

Introducing Vladimir Voinovich, Friedberg recalled that in 1952 the man who might have been groomed for the job of Stalin's successor, Georgii Malenkov, said it was time the Soviet Union produced its own Gogols and Shchedrins. This was on the occasion of the Gogol centennial; Friedberg remembered saying to a friend, "Boy, are the Soviets going to be sorry!" He did not know that his words would prove prophetic a few years later.

In the person of Vladimir Voinovich we have a worthy modern successor to Gogol and Shchedrin, Friedberg noted; since Bulgakov there has been no writer in Russia working in a comic vein who could compete with him for first place in that category of writing. Everyone knows Voinovich's masterpieces: the *Ivankiad* is, among other things, a perfect introduction to the housing situation in the Soviet Union; and Friedberg suggested that those interested in the Soviet army can do no better than to read the *Extraordinary Adventures of Private Ivan Chonkin*, a modern combination of *Don Quixote* and *The Good Soldier Schweik*.

In introducing Andrei Siniavsky, Friedberg observed that he really needs no introduction; the only question is whether he is more Andrei Siniavsky or more Abram Tertz. He noted with real satisfaction that Siniavsky continues to use this schizophrenic combination of names, sometimes one and sometimes the other. He recalled the excitement in 1963–1964, when the Paris Polish monthly *Kultura* began to bring out Siniavsky's early work. Then the Soviet embassy began to spread through its disinformation agency rumors that no *Soviet* author could write in this vein, that Abram Tertz was really a counterrevolutionary Hungarian or an anticommunist Pole. He recalled too how, during Siniavsky's trial, the judge expressed genuine indignation because Andrei Donatovich Siniavsky, a Russian, had assumed the Jewish-sounding *nom de plume* of Abram Tertz.

Friedberg characterized Siniavsky as far and away the most important Russian literary critic writing today, and at the same time definitely one of the most important prose writers writing in any language. He observed that Chekhov's statement about his own writing applies to Siniavsky as well: he has written everything except poetry and denunciations to the police.

The following are the papers presented by the three writers, Aksyonov, Voinovich, and Siniavsky.

Vassily Aksyonov

After all that has happened, it seems a bit bizarre to give way to reminiscences of socialist realism, finding oneself in the District of Columbia between the innocent states of Virginia and Maryland. When you tell students here about this creative method there is always animation in the classroom, for some reason a lack of seriousness. Examples of this literary trend, such as the novels of Vsevolod Kochetov, *The Province Party Secretary* (*Sekretar' obkoma*), and of Arkadii Perventsev, *The Olive Branch* (*Olivkovaia vetv'*), always inspire an uproar.

"'Sonia, Sonia,' " I read from the novel. "'We lived all our lives under him. In him we loved Lenin. Do you remember *The Problems of Leninism*? In him we loved our flesh-and-blood Party. I can't judge him. Only the Party can.' Sonia wept with him." This is from *The Province Party Secretary*. And now from *The Olive Branch*: "'Look, there goes Budennyi.[1] And what a marshal he is! Do you hear the strains of the *Bandera Rossa*? How good it is in our country for the foreign proletariat!' " I read and the students shout with laughter.

The liveliest show of the semester was the lecture on the no-conflict theory of literature, the struggle of the good with the excellent, the abolition of the battle of good and evil. The play was *The Cavalier of the Golden Star*; the dramatist, Aleksei Surov: "A golden age, when boundless kolkhoz fields swayed in the wind, and in the center of the country was erected a monument on the top of which a four-ton truck could make a u-turn." That is true. That is not an exaggeration, believe me.

A grand move made with giant steps, the aesthetic still has not yet been given the recognition it deserves. Only of late are they beginning to really appreciate it. It brings forth laughter, an outpouring of émigré wit. But socialist realism is not just funny: it is a very serious matter indeed. Even from here, from the shores of the Potomac, the ominous seriousness of the doctrine is evident: the sum total of master's and doctoral dissertations; the billions of squandered rubles; the army, the navy, the air force; the education of the young – the heirs and themselves teachers of ensuing generations. The centuries-old clouds of socialist realism hang over the serious brow of our unsmiling homeland.

Here school years come to mind. Socialist realism, the formula went at that time, was indisputably linked to the Russian realistic tradition and to revolutionary romanticism. Along with Pythagoras' theorem, with Michurin's watermelons,[2] Darwin's little beasts, and Engels' albuminous bodies, arose a kind of shapeless amalgam of Ivan Sergeevich Turgenev and *Poor Liza*.[3] The ardent heart of Dante was transplanted into Pavka Korchagin.[4] One can indulge in metaphysical speculation and ask oneself once more — Why does socialist realism need literature at all? Can it not really do without literature and show life in its revolutionary development — that is, not as it is but as it should be in the 66th dream of Vera Pavlovna?[5]

Socialist realism needs literature so that it may replace it with something else by the same name — that is, so that literature may be replaced by literature of socialist realism. And therein, in its metaphysical aspect, is the chief goal — truly the chief goal, and not a secondary one — for the replacement is accomplished not for the sake of something else but precisely for the sake of the replacement itself.

In this way we can now speculate to our hearts' content on the shores of the Potomac or the Seine. Then, during the "thaw," on the shores of the Neva, the Moscow River, and that same Seine, such dissident ideas did not even occur to us. We all tried to adapt the ancient teachings to the contemporary cause of the 1960s. I say "ancient" because it seemed that in the three decades that had elapsed since the 1930s, when the formula was born, until the 1960s, there passed time equal to the Tatar occupation of Russia — with a year counting for ten, like time served in the uranium mines.

To disavow socialist realism right away is impossible, as it was impossible, for example, to disavow the 1812 Battle of Borodino. One could, it is true, consider this battle our victory and not enlarge on the fact that as a result of this battle the city of Moscow was surrendered and burned down by Napoleon. This very battle in the tradition of socialist realism led us to a conclusive victory over the occupying French forces and to the establishment, in the language of Molière, of the splendid Russian word "bistro."

In the 1960s, without disavowing Party liberals, the "Dubčeks" [*dubcheki*][6] of many hues tried to make use of it to affirm positive principles for these new times, to broaden, as it were, the creative limits of contemporary art. "And after all, this is not difficult, comrades, not hard at all," the Dubčeks said to each other, "because at the base of our remarkable socialist realism lies a profound philosophical optimism, at the base of which lies, as everyone knows, profound philosophical pessimism."

And so carry on as you like, go all the way — as long as philosophical optimism lies at the base of your work. Even tragedies are permissible if they are optimistic.[7]

Historical optimism turned into a kind of battering ram for breaking open the stronghold of Stalinist conservatism. Let us imagine that the dogmatists descend on young writers and filmmakers. They accuse them of "felliniism," of deviating from socialist realism, of betraying their education, of sliding down into the swamp of bourgeois formalism and the avant-garde. And in answer they receive the following argument: the controversial Western artist Federico Fellini is, in his deepest being, a real socialist realist.

Panic ensues. There is alarm in the night at the Leningrad Party Regional Committee office. The high-frequency communications wires crackle: "We would like a more precise explanation. You call Fellini a socialist realist?"

We hear you, comrade Leningraders. This is your night shift instructor-on-duty Dubchenko on the phone, speaking for the Communist Party of the Soviet Union on questions of literature and art. Yes, comrade Leningraders, most recent research has established that Federico Fellini, his bourgeois decadence notwithstanding, is, on the strength of his talent, a socialist realist because his work is rooted in the philosophy of historical optimism.

"And where in his work do you find optimism?" asks Regional Party Secretary Tolstikov in a rage.

"At the very end," explains instructor Dubchenko patiently. "In Fellini, optimism is always at the very end. Remember *Nights of Cabiria*? At the end those nice young people appear on motor scooters. . . . Remember *8 1/2*? At the end there's the little boy with the optimistic trumpet. In this way socialist realism manifests itself. Such is the power of its enormous influence on the intellects of the decadent West."

"We won't tolerate it!" growls Tolstikov. "Let Moscow go to pieces. Here in Leningrad, the cradle of the revolution, the question of Fellini is decided!"

The argument, to everyone's surprise, is decided not in favor of the prior of the Smol'nyi Monastery — I beg your pardon, Institute. He was sent on a "trip to China."

Suddenly there was a great demonstration of dubčekist support from the banks of the Seine. A member of the French Communist Party's Central Committee, Comrade Roger Garaudy,[8] came out with his views on "realism without shores." There was great rejoicing. The boundless expanses of socialist realism summoned the courageous: "Sail on where you will . . ."

And here the Party sounded the alarm, sounded it in earnest, and became truly concerned: "How can one proceed without shores? After all, if you sail without shores you will not get anywhere!" It became necessary, gently, to expose the perfidious Roger Garaudy. The discussion dragged on for many successive years before reaching the conclusion: shorelessness is prohibited.

Abolition of shoreless realism was entered into the treasurehouse of Marxism as immutably as the law of surplus value. But the Dubčeks would not give up. All right then, in socialist realism one cannot do without shores. That much is obvious to every Marxist. But the question, comrades, is what kind of shoreline should socialist realism have: set in concrete, or drawn according to an administrator's rule; or indented, mysterious, full of magical adventures, resembling Norwegian fjords, straits, gulfs, archipelagos? Come to think of it, there was no mention of archipelagos.[9]

Through the 1960s, yes and even later, debates continued with varying intensity. Sometimes for reinforcement of a particular argument they brought in columns of tanks and made airborne landings. The Czechoslovak campaign of 1968 was, it turns out, a purely literary action.

Well, so once while walking along the Smithsonian Mall in Washington, I gave myself up to reminiscences about socialist realism. It is a funny thing to do, is it not, especially for a person whose very presence in Washington is also something of an argument in the controversy among Marxist theoreticians. But after so many years the soul somehow yearned for some generalizations. Numerous and random memories tried to assume the shape of an answer. "No, no," I said to myself. "It's not that simple, and everything isn't so absurdly complicated either. Look, it's not only people without talent who work there. After all, within the system of socialist realism there sometimes appear some important novels, for example; and now even with existentialist dressing."

Take, for instance, Chingiz Aitmatov. Really profound, that he is. In his last book he even uses quotations from the Holy Scripture, and human loneliness even oppresses him, and there is not quite that much cant about the pride of the Soviet man living in our grand epoch — or however the cliché goes.

Take a look at Chingiz Aitmatov. Does he not really demonstrate intellectual independence? These are the sorts of thoughts he expresses on the pages of *Literaturnaia gazeta* (*The Literary Gazette*).

In human history there are temporary, unhealthy periods, when somehow the intolerable is tolerated. But the intolerable must disappear, if only because it impedes the normal relations of people on earth. A system cannot long endure if it brings suffering to millions of people. Nothing can save it, or, what's more, perpetuate it. Civilization is ringing the sound of alarm, the battle intensifies for lofty moral heights, for ideals and noble goals. That is a universal problem. It is impossible to consider the problem an internal affair, and remain indifferent.

Open your eyes! This was written by a Soviet writer in a Soviet newspaper. Has socialist realism not once more sailed too far? No, ladies and gentlemen, not too far, for the reason that what is under discussion is simply the racist regime in South Africa.

So everything is under control. No sore spots were touched. One can, it turns out, be a great writer even in socialist realism if only one pretends that the sensitive spots do not exist. Class genocide does not exist, nor does Stalinist butchery, nor the Gulag, nor dulling propaganda, nor rampant alcoholism, nor the robbery of the people, nor the degradingly low quality of life or of food, nor forced "psychotherapy" for dissidents. Well, one could continue with "minor" things: neither is there anti-Semitism, nor contempt for the Kirghiz and their like, nor mockery of religion. So do not brush against these sore spots — and there are two dozen others, very tiny ones — and you will remain within socialist realism and will develop your talent, which in this case does exist.

So, then, socialist realism means — it is very simply . . . Somehow one does not dare simplify the question that much. At this moment, from a passing school bus bearing the legend "Springfield Iowa Elementary School" (this was here on the Smithsonian Mall), out of the window protruded the head of a boy with a familiar appearance — is he not the one from the Hans Christian Andersen fairy tale who made those inappropriate remarks about the Emperor's clothes?

"Mr. Aksyonov," he says, "socialist realism is merely a system of censorship."

What? Can it really be so simple? And a thousand dissertations have been written only as a smoke screen? And merely to put up a smoke screen they have jousted at endless conferences on Eurocommunism, debating shorelessness and indispensable optimism? Is it only then as a smoke screen, only so as not to detect that the Emperor is in fact naked and that all of this vast Soviet literature, as it turns out, exists only as a smoke screen, as a pretext for the system of censorship, the name of which is socialist realism, with its mixture of realistic traditions and revolutionary romanticism?

Vladimir Voinovich

I heard an interesting story related to our present topic. It seems that Soviet television had arranged to present a film version of *The Memoirs of Sherlock Holmes* by Conan Doyle. Work on the project began before April 1979 (you will understand later why I specify this date). Before my departure I heard that the film had been completed. Viewers were already getting ready to watch it on their TV sets when the rumor spread that the film had been banned, or its release postponed; someone had been reprimanded, and so on.

What happened? It seems that in the first part of the film Sherlock Holmes meets Doctor Watson. Holmes says, "I see that you have just come from Afghanistan." Watson, of course, is very surprised and asks, "How did you guess?" Sherlock Holmes answers, "It's very simple. The fact is that you are limping on your left leg, you have been recently wounded, you could be so injured only in a war, and there's a war going on in Afghanistan. It's all very simple." After some delay the film was indeed shown, but with the uncalled-for reference to Afghanistan replaced: Said Sherlock Holmes, "Oh, I see you have come from some Eastern country."

This episode tells a great deal and merits examination. It is an example of how a book by an author who is not at all anti-Soviet — a foreigner to boot, and one who has been published many times in the Soviet Union — can suddenly, for no special reason, become anti-Soviet, and this without any such intention on the author's part. Besides, when those words were replaced, we no longer had Sherlock Holmes, who would have known precisely where someone had been and why. He would never say, "from some Eastern country" — even I could have guessed that much!

Here we see how censorship perverts; it interferes not only with a book's ideological direction but with its creative fabric. I could cite many examples of older writers, authors of literary classics, who somehow managed to write anti-Soviet pieces. For example, last November I had the pleasure of quoting a line of Gogol's: "There once lived and died a public prosecutor." Gogol wrote of this prosecutor that he was a loyal son of the fatherland, that he wept for widows and orphans and did a great deal for humanity; to tell the whole truth, it turns out that with all his virtues, the only problem was that he had thick, wide eyebrows. This line was omitted by the censor when the opera of *Dead Souls* was performed at the Bolshoi Theater.[10]

Much has been said today, and will be said tomorrow, about censorship as an institution that removes various political or military information or certain names, allusions, and so on. Censorship removes the names of Trotsky or Sakharov, Gumilev[11] or Beria.[12] One can select the most diverse group; it does not matter because all of them are eliminated. At first censorship sought to combat concealed meanings, the "subtext." Then came the concept of the "unverifiable subtext"; that is, a subtext about which it is even difficult to say that it is a subtext. People also spoke of allusions; it was important that no allusions occur. When a director was asked what an allusion is, he said, "You see, that's when you sit in the movie theater watching a travel film; they show the mountains of the Caucasus, and you think, 'Still, Brezhnev is a son of a bitch.'"

I would like to tell you a little about my own experience. The fact is that it is incorrect to call censorship "censorship" because the real censorship is all of the Soviet state, not only Glavlit or whatever they call it now or called it in the past. That is only one part of the system, which controls literature and art. Writers learn that censorship means not only that things are removed but that things are inserted (or you are made to insert them yourself). In this sense all of Soviet society works against the writer: the censors, editors (and I have in mind all sorts of editors), publishers, and others who meddle in literature as well.

If, for example, you write a book about geologists, it is sent to some geological administration, and this administration offers its opinion. Officially, it is sent so that the geological administration can say that from a technical point of view everything is accurate. In fact, however, if you have written that the geologists sit in their tent drinking and playing dominos, the head of the geological administration will write that you have slandered Soviet geologists, who never play dominos and work hard all the time, and so on; the book may not be published. This geologist too, then, can prevent publication of a book.

I have not talked yet about the KGB. It plays a peculiar but specific role as an institution to which any type of novel is sent. If you write a novel about Dzerzhinskii,[13] it will be sent there and appropriate comments will be made.

In addition to political requirements, there are also purely aesthetic ones. An aesthetic has been developed: literature must be uniform, nothing should exceed the limits of the permissible. The struggle for quality is a separate matter. Let me present to you what starts out as a trivial example. At one time in the Soviet Union I was known as the author of a very well known song. (Actually, I was not known, but the song was!) This song contained the following words:

> I believe, my friends, that a rocket caravan
> will rush us on from star to star.
> On the dusty paths of distant planets
> we will leave our tracks.

I wrote this song without the slightest malicious intent, and I was not trying to say anything bad about the Soviet state between the lines. The song was recorded on tape and broadcast on the radio every day, sometimes several times a day, and then it was decided to release a recording of it.

The editor at the music editorial office handling the recording phoned me and said, "You know, we want to record your song, but we have to take out one word." "What word?" I asked. She answered, "We have to take out the word 'dusty.'" "What do you mean?" I said. "Well, you see," she responded, "you're calling the cosmos and the planets dusty." "They have cosmic dust," I retorted, "and they don't have janitors — nobody swept it up." She insisted: "This is not quite right. It makes the image less lofty." In short, we had a long argument. Then she said to me, "Look, maybe we could write 'the first path.'" "No," I said, "we won't write 'the first.'" "'The new'?" she countered. "What do you mean, new?" I said. "If there had been old . . ." In the end, she refused to record the word and I refused to change it.

I know, of course, that this text is not of great merit, but "dusty" was nevertheless a word of some vitality, originality. She took aim precisely at that word to kill it. Such editors have a very precise viewpoint and feel acutely what they cannot explain. The word really was not anti-Soviet, but nevertheless the song was not recorded for a long time, not until about a year and a half later. Then suddenly some cosmonauts sang it in space, and Khrushchev sang it from the dais at Lenin's Mausoleum.

The editor called me after that and said, "We're recording your song tomorrow." "Good," I told her; "I have only one request." "What's that?" she asked, startled. "I would like to take out the word 'dusty,'" I said. "Are you joking?" she shrieked. "No, I'm not joking — you know, it isn't quite right; it makes the image less lofty. The dust just doesn't fit in." "But you know that Nikita Sergeevich sang it from the dais of Lenin's Mausoleum," she reminded me. I said, "Well, Nikita Sergeevich is not the author. I am the author, and I want to change this word!"

They would not let me change it. (It is true that I did not try very hard.) Then there was a big ceremonial reception, with television cameras, and the cosmonauts appeared. All of a sudden one of these cosmonauts, Popovich, said to me, "I have something to say to the author. You know that line, 'Let's have a smoke before we take off' — but we cosmonauts don't smoke." That was the last straw: I lost my temper; I made a scene; I swore. I said that I had not written it for them but for someone who was simply having a smoke, hanging around, flying — all to no avail. That word was removed, and they began to sing, "Let's sing before take off." "Let's sing" — that sounds like when the police say "let's go."

After the song was so widely broadcast, I succeeded in publishing some of my old verses that I had not been able to get printed until then. The newspaper *Moskovskii komsomolets* (*The Moscow Young Communist*) asked me for them. I gave them the poems, they printed them, and suddenly there was a tremendous uproar — even worse than with the Sherlock Holmes film. Someone was fired, someone was reprimanded. It seems that the poems had been read personally by Comrade Malinovskii, minister of defense and marshal of the Soviet Union. The marshal said these poems were a stab in the back of the Soviet Army.

Once again, the poems contained nothing anti-Soviet — in any case, the Soviet Army could survive such a blow — but there was a poem about a dance attended by soldiers and officers, and the girls at the dance preferred the latter to the former. That was all — in short, a very ordinary occurrence. This, by the way, was shortly after the Cuban missile crisis because I remember thinking that if the Minister of Defense could devote so much attention to some poems printed in *Moskovskii komsomolets*, then the defense of the country was in bad shape. At the same time, however, it shows what an important position the writer occupies in Soviet society, if the marshal himself takes such an interest. Here in the U.S. I doubt that a single young poet could really expect Caspar Weinberger to come down on him for his poems, although some poets, I suspect, would not mind if he did.

Of course censorship interferes with Soviet literature, eliminating some things and adding others — but it should be said most emphatically that the overwhelming majority of books in the Soviet Union are in no way harmed by this. Even with something crossed out and something else inserted, these books remain exactly as they were before. I do not want to name names, but I know a poet who in the Soviet Union was very Soviet and then became very anti-Soviet here, but the quality of his verse, in my estimation, did not change at all. He is the same as he always was.

There is another literature, though, that the Soviet state does not accept — none of it, period. That literature, by the way, often does not fit the rubric of anti-Soviet, so they must come up with something to say about it, and they ask who needs it, and why, and what does it teach?

Take Bulgakov, for instance. His work offers a very good example of how Soviet censorship works a book over. All you need do is compare the first Soviet journal version with the one published by Possev,[14] in which the censored passages are italicized. At Princeton recently I discussed with my students a number of writers, including Bulgakov. I looked carefully for some meaning in these aborted passages and have read many different conjectures. In some cases, such as the scene at Torgsin,[15] it is understandable why it would be censored. In other cases it seems difficult to understand but is in fact quite understandable. They simply tried to tame the book, to groom it, to smooth it down, so that it would be, to the extent possible, more ordinary. They did not succeed because the book overstepped the limits. But certain words, certain sentences, certain paragraphs were eliminated to make the book less striking. This is a very important goal of Soviet censorship, Soviet editors, and the entire Soviet system.

I must tell you another funny incident. I once wrote a book set 120 years ago. The book begins with a father in the country writing a letter to his son in Kazan'. Among other instructions, he writes, "I have one more request —

send me Zilberling's book, *No More Hemorrhoids.*" (There was such a book 120 years ago.) My editor edited it in front of me; she looked down bashfully and simply crossed it out. I said, "What are you doing? Why are you doing this?" She replied, "You know very well." I said, "No, I do not. Explain to me what the problem is." "I can't explain it to you," she said and blushed. I tried to explain to her that "hemorrhoids" is a completely printable word, that even such a puritanical literature as the classical Russian used this term; even Gogol mentions "hemorrhoidal color of face." In short, I had to argue with her at great length to make my point.

Here is another incident from my own experience, this time as a writer of prose. I wrote my first story in 1960. It was called "We Live Here." I meant no harm. I looked at things as many of us did, perhaps out of naïveté. I cannot say that I was a great admirer, a conscious admirer, of the Soviet system: I was not. It was just that in 1960 it seemed to me, as it did to many others, that everything somehow was getting better, and that was just fine with me. When I wrote my first story, I wanted to stay within the rules. I wanted to describe country life but within the limits tolerated by Soviet literature, and for this reason I chose for my heroes' home the virgin lands. This may well be an example of self-censorship. Still, in addition to tractors and other machines, my story also featured something about human relationships. I gave the story to a certain old writer to read — this was, after all, my first story. He read it and said, "You know, someone will probably print this story, but you will take a beating." "But why?" I asked. "Because what is described in it resembles real life too much."

This is, I think, the main point. What is important is not that you name someone or allude to someone between the lines. If worse comes to worse and the censor crosses something out, you can insert it somewhere else. I had such problems, especially with my songs. But it sometimes happens that a writer writes something altogether unacceptable. I once wrote a story, "A Half Kilometer's Distance" [*Rasstoianie v polkilometra*]. It got printed eventually, but first I took it to the Sovetskii pisatel' (Soviet Writer) Publishers. The editor, himself a writer, called me into the corridor and we had the following conversation:

> Editor: "Listen, what were you thinking of when you wrote this?"
> Voinovich: "I was thinking that I would write this story."
> Editor: "And you seriously expect to publish it?"
> Voinovich: "Why not publish it? There's nothing objectionable in it."

The story concerns the death of a man in a village. It describes his funeral: how they drink vodka, how they argue about the number of columns at the Bolshoi Theater. Life is not very happy there, but as a matter of fact I in no way blamed the Soviet state for any part of this life. It was ordinary village life. It is true that the Soviet state claims that it has changed everything, and therefore life should not be like this. The editor simply did not know what to tell me about my story. Of course he returned it to me. When what they call the thaw came, and with it the heyday of *Novyi mir* — this was a very brief period — the story was published in the journal along with some others.

When I wrote the first part of the first book of *Chonkin*,[16] I had no illusions that it would get published. I had illusions that it might happen in ten years or so. For this reason I tried to soft-pedal certain things. When this piece ended up in the West and it was discussed in the Writers Union, one writer quizzed me: "Who are you? Were you born in the Soviet Union?" "Yes, in the Soviet Union," I replied. "Were you raised in the Soviet Union, or were you educated abroad?" he continued. "Did you serve in the Army?" "Yes," I said, "I served in the Army." "And have you really seen something like this somewhere?" he challenged me. I told him what I had seen, and we clashed about it, but that is an altogether different story. The man really looked at me as at a maniac. The reason was that this piece completely exceeded the limits. They wanted to charge me with having written an anti-Soviet book. I asked what in the work was anti-Soviet. Then they changed their formulation and called it hostile to the people (*antinarodnoe*). They rejected it outright.

I feel that all of this was Soviet censorship. The man whom I just mentioned was a Soviet censor, as was another, whom I will now name: Viktor Tel'pugov. During the discussion of how the manuscript got out of the country, he said: "It is not really important how it got out of the country; it is not important how it came to be published there. What is important is that it was written. If I learned that it merely had been written — or not even written, but merely conceived by the author — then I would feel that the author deserved a prison term or even to be shot. I myself would petition the appropriate authorities to punish the author accordingly."

This is Soviet censorship in action. First the editor plays his part, then the censor; and if they make a mistake and the work somehow appears, then our model factory workers take part, the heroes of socialist labor, generals, admirals, marshals; and if this does not help, the Union of Soviet Writers is included as well and uses all its punitive possibilities. If not, then the matter will be handed over to the Committee on State Security (KGB), who will handle it their way.

In conclusion, I would like to say that although people believe that the majority of Soviet writers suffer from censorship, in reality this is a great delusion. The overwhelming majority of Soviet writers simply could not exist without censorship because they could not withstand competition. They can write only what they are told to write. Take Mednikov, for example: he would be very glad to write pornography instead of writing about the working class, but he knows that in pornography there would be much more competition. Writing about the working class places him outside the competition. This is an interesting point: censorship benefits not only very poor writers but also those who are not very good, like Chingiz Aitmatov. In his case, too, one might say that if there were no censorship, his novel (about which Vassily Aksyonov spoke) would attract no attention.

Andrei Siniavskii

Before coming here I decided to find out — just to be sure and to avoid making mistakes — what the word "censorship" means, the term itself, in Soviet usage. I took a look at the 1955 edition, I believe it was, of the *Dictionary of Foreign Words* and found there a full description of censorship in ancient Rome, and of tsarist censorship. And at the end, after tsarist censorship, it says the following: "In the capitalist countries censorship protects the interests of the ruling exploiting classes and is directed first and foremost against the working class and the toilers, against the dissemination of revolutionary, democratic ideas and views." That was all; not another word.

Thus the word "censorship" itself was censored, and appears, as it were, in censored, adulterated form. This one small fact demonstrates the scale of censorship in general, its engulfment of everything that is written and spoken, and even, I would say, of silence.

In my youth I had the following experience. In 1949 I was accepted to Ph.D. candidacy, and as such I was expected to attend faculty meetings, in this case of the Soviet literature department of the School of Philology of Moscow State University. One of the first departmental meetings, right at the beginning of the school year, was devoted to the problems of upbringing of the young students. The lecturer — this was Evgeniia Ivanovna Koval'chik, already quite an old, venerable lady, the head of the Soviet literature department — said that there were, comrades, different types of students. Some students argue with the instructor, take part in a dispute, or even, on occasion, ask provocative questions. One keeps tabs on such people. But there is a special category of students to whom you must pay particular attention. These are the students who study well, do well on their examinations, but never ask questions, and, apart from examinations, keep silent completely. And suddenly, quite hysterically, raising her finger to the ceiling, she exclaimed, "And what are they thinking about in their silence?"

In short, in the Soviet situation for the majority of cases, apparently, one may no longer apply that classic formula of Pushkin's from *Boris Godunov* — in response to the authorities' proclamation, "All hail the new Tsar, Dmitri Ivanovich!" — "the people keep silent." It seems to me that in a broad sense the word "censorship" is first of all standardized Soviet language. In this sense censorship becomes, to an extent, a serious enough factor in the historical development of the Soviet Union.

Let us imagine that I open the *Large Encyclopedic Dictionary*, published in 1980. The dictionary is very complete, but in this edition, for example, one already finds that Malenkov[17] is missing; or, more precisely, there is a Malenkov but a different one — a worker, a participant in the October Revolution, who died in combat in 1918. And of course many others are missing. We can even recall the progression of historical changes name by name. First of all, Stalin suddenly disappeared from print without any explanation — his name has simply vanished. Then, as we know, Khrushchev disappeared, also without explanation. Now, quite recently, Brezhnev has disappeared: his name can no longer be found in Soviet newspapers.

For example, not long ago a resolution of the Central Committee was published on the 80th anniversary of the second congress of the Russian Social Democratic Workers' Party. Therein is provided a survey of 80 years of Russian and Soviet history. Only two names are mentioned there: Lenin at the beginning and Andropov at the end. There is no Stalin, no Khrushchev, and now no Brezhnev either. Another example: not long ago I bought a certain book on the Orthodox Church, an antireligious book. There on the first page, to be seen even at a glance — apparently it had been done in haste — Brezhnev's name had been removed and in its place was simply a reference to the report of the 26th Congress, something of that kind. A gap remained in the line where Brezhnev's name had been.

I would like to talk a little about language, about this Soviet language. Another side of it is explanation, or perhaps direction, of people by means of some conditioned code words, some sort of agreed-upon clichés. Sometimes it is clear what is hiding behind these; sometimes it is not entirely clear. I am referring to such locutions as "cult of personality" or "voluntarism."

For example, this is how they spoke of Khrushchev, in such a rigid formulation: "His activities were marked by manifestations of subjectivism and voluntarism." It is really quite impossible to understand fully what is hidden behind this. Or, we all recall another cliché, a sinister one, even though outwardly it appears quite inoffensive. The term was "cosmopolitan." It implied anti-Semitism, struggle with the West, and so on. Simply by means of this one word — which suddenly made its appearance and then began to be seen everywhere — cosmopolitans suddenly multiplied. By the way, here is an amusing analogy. Recently, in the anti-Soviet Russian-language émigré press there has appeared the word "Russophobes," used more and more in relation to Americans, to the Jews, apparently, and to liberals: Russophobes are multiplying everywhere. All this also demonstrates, of course, certain changes in the realm of émigré social thought.

Such a tendency exists as well in Soviet society: the striving to modify reality by means of language itself. For this reason language frequently, as it were, overtakes reality, anticipates reality. Often it is also at variance with reality. We know that from the beginning the Soviet state engendered a very stormy, rapid process of changing names and titles of institutions, cities, and so forth.

Indeed, this elemental force of renaming so ate into our consciousness, our psyche that, for example, two years ago when the splendid writer Solzhenitsyn, while being interviewed by the BBC, spoke of Leningrad, he was determined not to use this word because it is so offensive. He said, "I was in a city — what can I call it — after all, I don't want to call it Petersburg, either, although I know that this is not to honor Peter the Great, whom I do not particularly admire." He explained, "I know it is in honor of the apostle Peter. The city is called Saint Petersburg. Still, it is an unfortunate word, a Dutch word." He suggested that the city be renamed and proposed the name "Nevgorod," along the lines of Novgorod. But in the first place, Nevgorod sounds strange in Russian, as with a simple shift of accent from the first to the second syllable it becomes "neither in town nor in the country."[18] In addition, it is too close to Novgorod.[19] Finally, what of the argument about a Dutch word? "Kazan" is a Tatar word, and we would have to rename everything Russian-style. This psychology was, of course, operating in the creation of "Volgograd" or "Leningrad," although somehow to another end.

The Soviet language, changing reality, as it were — or in any case its outline — is, of course, first and foremost politicized language. Therefore, for example, the very word "Soviet" has become widespread to an unprecedented degree. Everything has become Soviet; and although it is clear anyway that everything is Soviet, the word will still be used for some reason: *Soviet* industry and not just industry; not just women but *Soviet* women; not just a person but precisely a *Soviet* person — from which it is clear that a great deal depends on this epithet and on the valuation of this person. This is not a person like all people but a special, Soviet person — the best, and so on and so on.

Or take a word that long ago began to penetrate everywhere and is still in use: *gosudarstvennyi* — "state" — although *everything* is operated by the state. The stores are all state-owned, but nevertheless the name is, for instance, The State Department Store (GUM). All the universities are state-operated, but they are invariably called Moscow State University, Leningrad State University, and so on. There is even the State Circus (Gostsirk). It would be understandable if there were also some private circuses — but as it is, all circuses are state circuses. (I have forgotten where I learned this, but sometime in the early 1920s a phony magician traveled around a Soviet province with a sign proclaiming "State Fortunes," *Gosfortuna*.)

Here one is reminded, of course, of the obligatory, honorary names: everything must be in someone's name, Lenin's or someone else's. Often these additions are nonsensical. Take Pushkin's name, for example. Why is the Museum of Fine Arts named for Pushkin? And why, when the Chamber Theater was closed, was another theater opened in the same place under the name of the Pushkin Theater? They never performed any Pushkin there. Of course there is a great deal named for Gorky, so much that there was even a witticism about "the Gorky Monument to Pushkin."

All this attests to a tendency of this censored language to be, in general, a mannered, resplendent, inflated language. I will cite but one example. In Paris, where I live, we had a movie theater with what I think was a very fitting and lovely name for a movie theater: Harlequin. This movie theater began to show only Soviet films, and, specializing in Soviet films, it thus fell into the sphere of Soviet influence, as it were. Could the Harlequin show Soviet films? No! They simply had to rename it, and now it is called the Cosmos.

Still another aspect is the profusion of euphemisms. Censored language is such bashful language, to the point of being quite strange sometimes. I remember that I — and not only I but Soviet readers in general — were surprised when in 1953, after Stalin's death, there was suddenly a report that "slowdowns" had occurred in the GDR, under the influence of imperialist agents, of course. What kinds of slowdowns? It was strikes that were taking place. But "strikes" is not a good word to use, because "strikes" has certain associations. A strike is the doing of the proletariat, both the international and Russian proletariat. It is an honorable word, "strike," a proud word. And here it was replaced with "slowdowns."

There is also the tendency to replace the word "prison" with another word, "isolator" [*izoliator*]. In Lefortovo Prison, for example, where I served time, the name Lefortovo Prison was not used. The official name was Lefortovo Isolator. The Lefortovo inmates, *zeki*,[20] had always been called "prisoners" [*zakliuchennye*]. Even in submitting an official document — a complaint, for example, or a request for something — the inmate was obliged to write "Prisoner Siniavsky." As I remember, while I was in prison a strict resolution suddenly appeared prohibiting the use of the word "prisoner" and requiring the use instead of the word "convict" [*osuzhdennyi*].[21] The word "prisoner" was identified with a great number of prisoners and with the Stalin era, so it was decided to change it somehow. Furthermore, when a person writes "convict" he is acknowledging, as it were, that he was tried and for a good reason; that is, that he was sentenced justifiably. A person is not permitted to change this formula: he must write "convict."

From here, from the West, one will encounter every kind of difficulty in arriving at the truth through the Soviet press. Often one may reach this truth by either reading or thinking in inverse terms. For example, not long ago I saw the following headline in a Soviet newspaper: "U.S. Prepares for Chemical War." Reading no further, I surmised that apparently they had begun to write somewhere in America that gas was being used by the Soviets in Afghanistan. Here, you see, one must surmise from the inverse. But you cannot always figure it out, and for this reason strange and sometimes even terrible things can happen.

I had a friend, Anatolii Iakobson — many of you have probably heard of him; unfortunately, he is no longer living. He was a historian, a teacher, and agreed to give a history examination to a young man completing the requirements for a high school diploma. This was sometime in the 1960s. The young man had not witnessed the Second World War, or, in any event, did not remember it. He was asked a question concerning the coalition of the Great Powers during the war. The young man was silent. Iakobson guessed that he may not have been sure of the meaning of the word "coalition." "Well," he said, "the Allies — who were our allies?" The other was silent. Already shaken, Anatolii said, "All right. America — on whose side did she fight? Was she our ally or Hitler's ally?" "Hitler's ally," said the young man.

Why did this happen? Because, you see, he had no recollection of the events themselves but did recall seeing in the papers again and again all sorts of things about "warmongers," "imperialists," even "fascists." All of it rearranged itself in his mind, and everything in the world was turned upside down, including history itself.

In the prison camps I sometimes would meet people — true, not many, but I did meet a few — who did not believe that the Soviet Union launched rockets and sputniks into space. They said that this was all nonsense, that it was just published in the newspapers for propaganda purposes, and that in fact there was no such thing, no such thing at all.

So here we see two mistakes at once, two terrible mistakes, resulting from Soviet censorship. Both under the influence of this censorship and by thinking inversely, a person acquires a kind of distorted understanding. Here is another example. Everyone knows the two mistaken points of view about the Western world that are fairly widespread among the Soviet public. One point of view, stemming from some kind of belief in Soviet newspapers, is that the West is an utter horror. Take Leonid Pliushch's mother, for instance. She is a simple woman and has now joined him in Paris, but when he first asked her to come she wrote to him and said, "How will I live there? Where you are, in Paris, there is hunger, unemployment, and terrorists are everywhere, shooting people . . ." In other words, here you have the terrible West, the hellish West, the image of Hell.

On the other hand, there is the completely opposite, also mistaken view that the West is simply sheer paradise. There is no unemployment here. I have met people who thought that it was sufficient for a person in the Soviet Union to spend 10 years in prison for some political crime; then, if he emigrated to the West, he would be guaranteed a pension for life, as if in appreciation of his martyrdom, so to speak. The West is rich, after all: they have money to burn.

Two days after the October Revolution a decree was issued on the closing of private newspapers, signed by Lenin. This venture was accompanied by one curious reservation. I quote: "Constraint of the press, even at critical times, is permissible only within limits of absolute necessity. The present decree is of a temporary nature and will be rescinded by a special law upon the resumption of normal social conditions."

There has been no such law. And even when normal conditions did resume — in 1921, the beginning of the New Economic Policy — it was also Lenin who said, "In wartime we act in a military manner. We promise no freedom and no democracy of any kind." I think that censorship is related to the fact that Soviet society still finds itself in a permanent state of war — with varying degrees of intensity, perhaps, but a permanent state nonetheless. Censorship is one form of war.

I have heard some views on the benefits of censorship. I was told that one censor said that on the whole, censorship is better both for readers and for writers because it trains them to create a subtext in the work and also to penetrate the subtext. Furthermore, it is said to be because of censorship that readers value so highly such authors as Pasternak and Babel. It is as if you love them because you are surrounded by censorship, and then suddenly you come upon something of value. Another view was expressed by the fine poet Joseph Brodsky, who (apparently out of snobbery) spoke at the Venice Biennial on the great benefits of Soviet censorship. These benefits are, he said, that it cuts off the hacks right away, and it promotes metaphorical language.

I could add something myself on the benefits of censorship if I were to rummage around in my head long enough. Right now I can think of only one: there are few misprints in the press. They are afraid of misprints, especially in political documents. On the other side, however, for some genres — anti-Soviet anecdotes and uncensored songs, for example — censorship is particularly beneficial.

Finally, there are situations in which censorship strengthens some people. It forces them either to deceive censorship or to appear in samizdat. It tempers the character of the writer; it educates him in resistance to censorship. But then, war also tempers.

Notes

1 Founder of the Red Cavalry; appointed marshal in 1936.

2 Ivan Vladimirovich Michurin, theoretical and experimental geneticist, then much in vogue in the USSR.

3 Popular sentimental novel (1792) by Nikolai Mikhailovich Karamzin.

4 A steadfast young communist protagonist of Nikolai Ostrovskii's *How the Steel Was Tempered* (1935).

5 Heroine of Nikolai Chernyshevskii's programmatic revolutionary novel *What Is to Be Done?* (1863).

6 Alexander Dubcek, a leader of the attempted liberalization in Czechoslovakia, headed the Czech Communist Party from January 1968 to April 1969.

7 An ironic reference to Vsevolod Vishnevskii's staunchly Stalinist play, *An Optimistic Tragedy* (1933).

8 Political Department, French Communist Party, 1956–1970. Subsequently broke with the Party.

9 Because of associations with Aleksandr Solzhenitsyn's *Gulag Archipelago* (1975).

10 Leonid I. Brezhnev, then the head of the Soviet state, had conspicuously thick and wide eyebrows, the subject of a number of jokes.

11 Nikolai Gumilev, a Russian poet (1886–1921), was executed by a Soviet firing squad.

12 Lavrentii Beria, Stalin's last head of the secret police, was executed in 1953 after the dictator's death.

13 Feliks Dzerzhinskii (1877–1926), founder of the Soviet secret police.

14 Russian émigré publisher in West Germany.

15 The All-Union Association for Trade with Foreigners, or forerunner of modern Soviet "Berezka" hard-currency stores.

16 *The Life and Ordinary Adventures of Private Ivan Chonkin*, a lampoon of the Soviet military, begun in 1963, published in the West in the Russian journal *Grani* (1969), then by YMCA Press (Paris, 1975), published in English by Farrar, Straus and Giroux (1977).

17 Georgii Maksimilianovich Malenkov served on Stalin's State Defense Committee during World War II; as deputy premier 1946–1953; premier 1953–1955.

18 *Ne v gorod, ne v derevniu*, or *ni k selu ni k gorodu*: inopportunely or inappropriately, neither here nor there.

19 That is, Leningrad and Novgorod are little more than 100 miles apart.

20 Abbreviated, commonly used form of *zakliuchennye* (z/k).

21 Related to the Russian *sud*, meaning court of law, trial, and to the Russian words for judge, to judge, to try, and so forth.

Literature and Intellectual Life: Discussion

Friedberg opened the discussion by agreeing with Voinovich's remarks about writers in emigration. He added that the émigré writer abroad often finds himself in a tragic situation: arriving in the West, the writer tries to find an American, French, German, or Italian publisher for his work and suddenly discovers that the work that caused a great deal of commotion in the Soviet Union evokes indifference abroad. The reason for that is simple, Friedberg noted. In part, it was interesting over there because everyone was excited about the ability of that particular writer to get around the censor on this or that issue; but, of course, this ability does not evoke any great excitement in the West. Listening to Voinovich, Friedberg remarked, he could think only with sadness about what has happened to the institution of Russian censorship. The censors have grown mediocre and unimaginative. Compare them with such distinguished writers of the past as Ivan Goncharov, Fedor Tiutchev, even Valerii Briusov, all of whom were censors. *They* would not have had any problems with allegory or metaphor; they knew literature!

Ludmila Foster (Voice of America) continued the discussion by asking Siniavsky to share with the group some recollections from the time of his trial. She recalled, for instance, that the Italian newspaper *Il Giorno* described how the judge asked Siniavsky's "accomplice"[1] why he had failed to explain the reason for setting events he wrote about not in ancient Rome but in the Soviet Union. Foster asked Siniavsky to comment on such pearls as these — censorship in action.

Siniavsky responded with an example, a passage about Lenin that had particularly incriminated him. In his story *Liubimov* he had written — without malice, incidentally — the following about Lenin: "Lenin howls at the moon at night." Of course, this aroused indignation and was taken as an extreme expression of anti-Soviet feeling, but neither the judge nor the prosecutor, who routinely quoted abundantly from his work, dared quote this particular passage. "Now, there is censorship for you!" Siniavsky concluded.

Igor Birman commented that much had been said about censorship as a negative phenomenon; the point had been made that authors are resourceful people who generate Aesopian language and somehow know how, by means of allusions, to get around the rules of censorship. But, he noted, nothing had been said about those infrequent opportunities that occur when the party line changes, providing unexpected chances for writers to drive a point home. He had in mind situations such as when, during de-Stalinization, Solzhenitsyn was allowed to publish *Ivan Denisovich*.

Birman observed that under Andropov the Party was coming out against corruption, offering an opportunity for an enterprising writer to compose something along the lines of a new *Inspector General* on the subject of Soviet corruption and thus to reflect something new: to tell some kind of truth, or at least a portion of the truth, about Soviet conditions. He asked whether anyone knew of cases in which an author was able to seize a favorable moment and do something creative. This is a situation in which, in his opinion, censorship may provide some new opportunities; or, at the very least, this might be one of those rare chances to make some new contribution to Soviet literature within the framework of Soviet conditions.

Aksyonov responded that this was a broad question. Birman was speaking not about censorship but about the different campaigns, as it were, that are launched in Soviet society on signals from above. To be sure, during these campaigns there is always some animation, and attempts are made to "push through" some controversial or courageous idea. Aksyonov recalled an incident when he began to write all kinds of satirical, unpleasant things. One of them was staged in Moscow by the Sovremennik theater; there was such harassment of everyone involved that those responsible for the article's appearance, the editorial staff, beseeched him: "Now, tell me, what is it aimed at? Whom is it aimed at?" They needed formulations so as to be able to report higher up. He and Oleg Efremov said, "But at the petty bourgeoisie, of course," and then the person was completely happy: it had been aimed at the petty bourgeoisie, and he had a formulation, and furthermore there was a formulation also for the critics: "the sharply anti-bourgeois direction of the presentation . . ."

Such practices are common, Aksyonov observed. He went on to discuss the case of Viktor Rozov, a leading playwright. In the early 1960s and even in the 1950s he wrote youthful, rebellious plays, all of which were staged and performed. He was criticized, of course, but somehow he became a very placid and successful Soviet dramatist, part of the "literary set." Not long ago, however, there was another row; Aksyonov had just received a letter from Moscow about it. Rozov wrote a play about the corrupt Soviet elite, *Gnezdo glukharia* (*The Nest of the Woodgrouse*).[2] It would seem to have been very timely for the campaign Andropov's people were leading, but it turned out that it was not suitable after all. The play was banned and declared to reflect the Djilas heresy.[3]

Aksyonov explained that the authorities saw immediately that this play was not merely criticizing local conditions. They want such criticism to be local because a writer is, after all, the Party's helper and should reflect such criticism. To the assertion that there is no criticism, the government propagandists have a ready answer: should Aleksandr Borisovich Chakovskii be sitting here now, Aksyonov suggested, he would say, "Show the doubter *Literaturnaia gazeta*, and you will see how much criticism there is in my paper. Even *Pravda*, our foremost paper, and *Komsomol'skaia pravda* dare to criticize. This is public control in action, the searchlight: we criticize all our shortcomings."

Aksyonov recalled how, when they were chiseling away at his "Ticket to the Stars,"[4] the secretary for ideology of the Young Communist League Central Committee called him in and asked, "Why are you writing about this? After all, we are not pressuring you. We don't force you to write only about the good. Look, take a disgrace such as the one in the 12th Trucking Fleet. You know, all the trucks are operating illegally. This is what needs criticism. These are the kinds of things you should write about, and not all these incomprehensible ideas the young people have." In Aksyonov's view, when things operate on that level, they are allowed. Sometimes something manages to sneak through, but when they sense that there is something else involved, they react immediately in a completely different way. Thus Rozov's play was seen as a reflection of Djilas.

Aksyonov cited another example of something "slipping through": a Soviet *Inspector General*, also known as "Dublenka" ("The Fur Coat"), by Boris Vakhtin, from the *Metropol* collection.[5] He noted that it is always easier for plays of average artistic merit to get through; high artistic quality always attracts suspicion. He mentioned the rather sharp criticism of a play by the Belorussian playwright Makaenko, which was performed in the Theatre of Satire. People said, "Just think about what it is he dares criticize." When criticism really goes too far, then they are very quick to put a stop to it. They react very quickly when they sense real danger.

Friedberg observed that when a writer has more innocent purposes in mind, he can use a device: for instance, with all the Victorian standards of prudery in Soviet literature, some erotic literature does get published, provided the writer can use the excuse that it really satirizes the Roman Catholic Church. It can go all the way back to François Villon, Rabelais, and Boccaccio and all the way forward to modern Latin American literature. This might go through, whereas something like what Aksyonov described would not be permitted.

Aksyonov made an additional comment on pornography, referring to a recent interesting article in the *Washington Post* that demonstrated how American journalists sometimes have the wrong idea about Soviet literature. It was a dispatch from Moscow; at the time he reacted very strongly to it and wrote a letter to the *Washington Post*. But the *Post* too dislikes criticism on its home ground and did not print the letter. The dispatch dealt with the subject of the erotic in Soviet literature. The headline, he recalled, was something like "A New Strike against Young Soviet Writers Daring to Broach Erotic Subject Matter." This was a complete misunderstanding, Aksyonov asserted. In the first place, some hint of the erotic is tolerated in Soviet literature. It gets by even more easily if it is of poor literary quality, rendered in an amateurish way, he noted; if it is knowledgeably and well written, it is forbidden.

The dispatch discussed an article by Sergei Chuprynin, whom Aksyonov acknowledged as one of the more interesting critics now writing in the Soviet Union. The piece was an attempt not so much to suppress the subject as to erect some kind of flimsy dam against the terrifying flood of hack writings. None of the writers mentioned in this article — including Chuprynin himself — was very young. They were all middle-aged people of average gifts, absolutely obedient, absolutely conformist, who were now being given some leeway. They described how "bare breasts, full of vital juices, quivered." They wrote, "She stood before the mirror and examined her noble, naked body," and so forth. From this sort of thing, Aksyonov asserted, one can see the kind of misunderstandings that sometimes arise.

Siniavsky addressed the question of Solzhenitsyn's *One Day in the Life of Ivan Denisovich*: It was a miracle, he noted, that a work on such a scale, of such perfection, and on such a delicate subject did appear. In Siniavsky's view, a series of coincidences was necessary. The piece had to excite Tvardovskii. A journal like *Novyi mir* had to exist, as well as a person like Tvardovskii, who had to take it all the way up to Khrushchev; and in deciding the question Khrushchev had to go against the opinion of the Politburo. However, Siniavsky added, the good fortune of *Ivan Denisovich* was of short duration, as we know. And before Solzhenitsyn had time to succeed in completing any of his later works, the official attitude toward *One Day in the Life of Ivan Denisovich* changed abruptly.

Siniavsky recalled an amusing episode in which he was involved during the inquest, which often consisted of arguments with the investigators on theoretical, literary points to see who would have the last word. In discussing *One Day in the Life of Ivan Denisovich*, the investigator said that it was a disgraceful piece of work. Siniavsky said, "Why disgraceful? It's wonderful! Why, not too long ago *Pravda* nominated it for a Lenin Prize!" The investigator replied, "Yes, Andrei Donatovich. *Pravda* expresses the official point of view. But it is, after all, necessary, Andrei Donatovich, to have one's own opinion."

A question was addressed to Voinovich concerning the village writers: how do they fit into this whole picture, and why are they allowed more or less free rein? Might not some real talent arise here and express itself? Voinovich responded that he personally regards the village writers without particular rapture. He does not deny their talent — on the contrary, he considers them gifted people who really do rise above the common level — but he does not see them rising above the level permitted in Soviet literature. They write a little something on a permissible topic. They also took advantage of that time.

Voinovich added that during his presentation he had forgotten to mention censorship not only of books but of behavior as well. He noted that the village writers get away with much because of their model behavior, but in fact they strive only for what is possible in Soviet literature. They may write about something that once existed in village life, but not one of them can describe collectivization as, for example, Grossman described it in his book, *Forever Flowing* (*Vse techet*).[6] Not one of them is able to describe such events with the force with which an unofficial writer describes them. (Aksyonov pointed out that Voinovich is himself also partly a village writer, and that he was sitting here, and not in the Writers Union of the USSR.)

Agursky disagreed with Voinovich — he does not consider it trivial when a book such as Rasputin's *Farewell to Matyora*[7] (*Proshchanie s Matëroi*) criticizes several principles of the Soviet system and condemns the entire industrial program; that is, the Soviet industrialization of Siberia. Voinovich rejoined that the industrial program is a trivial subject for literature, not to be compared with the relations between two people, a great subject for literature. Unconvinced, Agursky cited descriptions of collectivization, urging consideration of Mozhaev, Abramov, Belov's *The Eves* [*Kanuny*], Zalygin's book *On the Irtysh* [*Na Irtyshe*].

Voinovich retorted that he does not like Zalygin's *On the Irtysh* at all – he simply finds it boring – and maintained his position that what he calls Soviet censorship is aimed entirely at preventing literature from rising beyond the forbidden level of artistic investigation. An important theme is not enough for him; he personally likes books he can pick up and read, unable to tear himself away; books that make him cry; books that, ten years later, he wants to read again. He read Zalygin's book but cannot remember what was in it and does not want to read it again.

Aksyonov commented that he is not at all against this type of literature: let it continue, he urged. But if this literature intrudes itself as the only possible kind — and this is what has happened — then it has only one goal: to break off the tenuous, fragile ties with European, Western culture and civilization; to be submerged once again in the provincial seclusion of contemporary Soviet culture. We see this aim clearly even now, he warned; even in some of the works discussed in these polemics.

Friedberg intervened, noting that to one who has read Agursky's study (published in the Hebrew University Monograph Series) and the books of both Aksyonov and Voinovich, it is clear that they are talking at cross-purposes. He pointed out that Agursky was essentially trying to prove the social and political significance of that literature; Voinovich was expressing a lack of special enthusiasm for the aesthetic merits of these writers; and Aksyonov was making the rather astute observation that this literature, albeit important in the sense that it fosters patriotic values, attachment to Russian traditions, and especially attachment to Siberia as the quintessential Russia, does objectively foster a certain parochial quality in Russian literature. There is no denying that this literature tries to divorce itself from the mainstream of Western writing.

Denis Mickiewicz observed that this important argument has to do with texts and subtexts. Having grown up at the end of the first emigration, he remembered that in such arguments there was always, among the émigré community, a rather negative attitude toward the appearance of any kind of Soviet literary work. The reasoning was that if the Soviet censorship approved it, then the author must be a scoundrel and his work is no good. Now, he commented, we are accustomed to finding many excellent pieces of work; indeed, Aksyonov, Siniavsky, and Voinovich would not have been well known had the Soviet censorship, in its time, not permitted it — for which we are grateful.

In Denis Mickiewicz' view, it would be correct to say that self-censorship warns all authors in the Soviet Union against printing texts that are overtly seditious. They send those to samizdat or to tamizdat. Consequently, in his opinion censorship has more to do with subtexts. If one considers that, as Voinovich said, the aim of censorship is a leveling, then one can say that it is truly desirable, from the point of view of censorship, to break that slender thread that ties contemporary Soviet literature to the West. By the same logic, however, one could say that it would also be in their interest to cut the ties to prerevolutionary Russian classics, which they have long been trying to do.

Denis Mickiewicz suggested that one may also ask this question: Is it not simply the authors' personal conduct, rather than their subtexts, that prompts the censors not to print their work, and even to punish the authors? Whether the subtext becomes a sufficiently conventional apparatus, against which censorship has developed its own machinery, is another problem. Does the authors' subtext — what in this discussion was termed an "unverifiable subtext" — serve as a conventional apparatus known to authors themselves, and not just to writers but even to musicians, artists, and the public? Is such an apparatus a challenge to censorship for it to put its machinery into action, to battle with this apparatus? If this is so, where is this machinery and how does it work?

Aksyonov noted that this comes close to the question touched on by Siniavsky regarding the so-called blessings of censorship. Claims of censorship's beneficial effects contain an element of snobbery, he observed, adding that there was, however, a reason for it. He cited as an example the late Iurii

Trifonov's work. Trifonov developed this mechanism precisely, to the point of consummate craftsmanship; Aksyonov emphasized that this craftsmanship was not invented; rather, it arose spontaneously. He described Trifonov's method as an involved system of the finest brushstrokes and the most subtle of allusions. He stressed that the author must still work a great deal with the reader, who develops a tremendous sensitivity. Aksyonov could not recall another instance of the use of censorship for growth of a personal style as productive as in the case of Trifonov.

Aksyonov mentioned a paper by Lev Losseff, entitled "The Blessings of Censorship,"[8] presented in Washington at the October 1982 convention of the American Association for the Advancement of Slavic Studies. Losseff cited an example from the two versions of Solzhenitsyn's *The First Circle*. Aksyonov had not been aware of this, but according to Losseff, *The First Circle* had originally been intended for publication in *Novyi mir* and the journal had wanted to publish it. The central hero, Innokentii, calls his family doctor — the traditional Russian doctor, who used to come with his black bag and cured him of scarlet fever, and so forth — to warn him that he (the doctor) is under threat of arrest. *Novyi mir* did not publish it, and Solzhenitsyn, finding himself in the West, started work on a second version of the novel in which he repudiated what seemed to him to be this toned-down version. Now, according to Losseff, Innokentii calls the Americans to pass on some nuclear secret. The political significance of the novel is thereby increased, but artistically, in Aksyonov's view, it is somewhat diminished.

Aksyonov agreed with Voinovich that Soviet censorship does not cut. He has explored this idea repeatedly with his students: Soviet censorship is preoccupied mainly not with the extraction of anything but with augmentation. This is a creative process. Censorship makes additions to an opus. What does it add? It adds love, and it is always concerned when there is a leakage of love. To whom does the leakage of love flow? We need not say to whom; everyone knows to whom it flows. When there is little love, censorship becomes anxious and preoccupied with this augmentation of love. Concerning the form of all the various avant-garde pieces in the Soviet Union, Aksyonov maintained that the problem is not that they interfere with anything. They do not carry any anti-Soviet charge, as it were. But they are lacking in love.

The censors, the authorities, get the impression that life is going on without them, and they are anxious because people out there are still occupied with something, they still experiment, they act in an unbusinesslike manner, comrades. The avant-garde is a form that at times becomes even more undesirable than original thinking or individuality: sometimes individuality irritates more than dissidence. Individuality is the mark of a person who lives his own life, as it were, and the heck with the rest of you; this inspires wild indignation. Furthermore, in general they have a low tolerance for all of these formalistic tricks.

Nevertheless, Aksyonov noted, we know that in different periods of the history of Soviet literature—and there have been different periods—something always did manage to slip through. Thinking about form one need only look at the issue of *Novyi mir* with a story by Andrei Voznesenskii called "O" — simply the letter "O," that sleek, round little letter and nothing more. One must understand, Aksyonov insisted, that at the height of Brezhnev-Andropov — mature socialism — to publish under the title of "O" a story in which the central hero is a black hole is truly from outer space! Some people get away with a great deal, he observed.

Toward the end of his stay in the USSR, Aksyonov recalled, they excused his form. "Go ahead," they said; "do what you will." He remembered Feliks Kuznetsov saying to him in their last conversation, "Can't you really mind your manners? We allow you everything, and you give us nothing in return." They published *In Search of a Genre* [*Poiski zhanra*], which Aksyonov characterized as containing nothing special in terms of form but not entirely neutral prose either. He mentioned another curious example, having to do with village prose. When *In Search of a Genre* — his last book published in the Soviet Union — came out, a young writer showed up from Irkutsk and said, "We were astounded by your book." Aksyonov asked him why, seeing no quality there that might astound. "We didn't know that it is still permitted to write a book like this," the writer said. "They told us long ago that it is not permitted; that we have to write like Rasputin."

Friedberg observed that the difference between the purely negative function of censorship and what we might call the constructive creation function is something that he illustrates to students by means of a short story by Il'f and Petrov, a team of Soviet humorists whom he generally does not admire because he finds a great deal of self-serving hypocrisy in their work. One is expected to laugh when, in *The Little Golden Calf*, a man in the madhouse says that unlike elsewhere in the USSR, there is freedom of speech in a madhouse. The madman is right, Friedberg asserted: *try* shouting in the street, "Down with communism, long live free parliament!" and you know what will happen. He also has his students read the story *How Soviet Robinson Crusoe Was Created*, containing a million and one suggestions on how to improve the novel: get rid of the romance with the young woman who was shipwrecked together with the hero (overly erotic) and include references to meetings and membership dues and so forth. Ultimately what results is a classic socialist realist story, and the editor says "Get rid of the name Robinson Crusoe — who needs him?"

Glad asked whether it is not also censorship when writers are forced to emigrate; that is, when it is not some paragraph or book that is eliminated but the author himself. For émigré writers censorship is a historical fact. In principle it no longer exists. Glad wondered how it would be in the future for writers such as those assembled at this conference: If they write about Russia, finding themselves here, then they would have to live on memories, writing about what was before in their other, censored, lives; they would not live and write in accordance with their present lives. If, on the other hand, they write about America or Germany or France, it seemed to him that this too would be strange for their readers. For whom, he asked, are they going to write?

Voinovich responded first, commenting that Glad had translated Shalamov, who, in his time, emigrated from Kolyma to Moscow, lived on memories, and wrote what is on the whole not at all a bad book.[9] Voinovich suggested that he and others, also having emigrated and also living on memories, might also write books that will not be too bad.

Siniavsky spoke next, observing that in his opinion this matter is purely individual. He knows writers who suffer a great deal from the fact that they find themselves in emigration; torn, as it were, from their native soil, from their native language. He sees this emigration as truly a large and, when all is said and done, tragic problem. He personally experienced no difficulties of this kind, he commented; somehow he had always been accustomed simply to inventing things out of his own self rather than describing the life around him. He has always worked on some kind of subjective basis, and as long as he exists within himself, he feels he will be able to extract something. As for the question of for whom one writes, in Siniavsky's view, each writer will have his own response. He himself writes abstractly. He would, of course, like very much to be read in Russia, but he has no need of many readers; it is simply not important to him. He does not seek a wide readership, and for that reason this aspect of the problem does not trouble him either.

On the other hand, he stated that he was much more deeply troubled by the rather serious censorship that exists in the Russian-language press here in the West. Of course, he added, it is different from Soviet censorship and can be circumvented. A writer can, after all, do as Siniavsky and his family did: take over and run his own press, printing everything he writes. What he finds difficult — and expects to continue to find difficult — is the attitude of émigré readers here, and, most important, of certain circles: of the literary establishment.

Siniavsky commented that he feels rather painfully the problem of what he calls Russophobia, noting that he is considered a Russophobe; he added that he finds it somehow awkward and embarrassing to contend that he loves Russia. Another complicated problem he sees arising has to do with literary criticism. Again, he can do as he pleases because he has a journal of his own, but for some other authors it is very difficult at times to publish some sharply worded, unconventional criticism. For example, in his view it is difficult to publish anything critical of Solzhenitsyn, of his ideas. This would be almost unheard of in Russian publishing; and even if it did get printed, it would bring forth a furious explosion of hatred for the author.

Aksyonov did not entirely agree with Siniavsky, maintaining that sometimes one does read articles critical of Solzhenitsyn, and, in fact, in publications that otherwise support Solzhenitsyn's views. He agreed that passions boil and seethe here, but that seemed to him a normal basis for literary life anywhere. If suddenly all of Russia were liberated, he speculated, what kinds of literary passions would well up within its expanses; how many opposing newspapers and groups of various kinds? Aksyonov repeated a funny story told him by Ilya Levin: An émigré in Texas had a little pistol without a license. A policeman found out that he was from Russia and said, "This is not Russia, where you walk around with pistols! This is Texas!"

Concerning censorship and for whom to write, Aksyonov commented that émigré writers, having rid themselves of Soviet censorship, are still left with another kind of censorship, which will continue and even grow stronger. For him this censorship is one of taste: stylistic censorship. This is the only censorship he wants to follow, and it seems to him that it is already showing signs of some kind of moral order; an aesthetic, he observed, becomes to some degree an ethic. As for the reader for whom he writes, Aksyonov noted that the reader changes just as his hero does. A writer basically creates for his reader; he invents not only his hero but his reader as well. Referring to the novel he once wrote about his readers, *Our Golden Hardware* [*Zolotaia nasha zhelezka*], Aksyonov characterized his imaginary reader as a type of person from the 1960s in Russia, an intellectual. Basically, he concluded, his reader does not change, and he maintained that he has never written for a closed circle of readers.

Aksyonov acknowledged that his main readership remains behind in Russia. He has had some confirmations of the fact that despite everything that has happened, they still read him there; somehow his work penetrates and is disseminated. He asserted, however, that he has never limited himself only to a Russian readership. Concerning translations, he commented that while something is lost, sometimes something is also gained. One finds readers in different countries.

Aksyonov sees something elusive in writers of his generation. He spoke of a reading by a Dutch prose writer he had attended recently. He looked at the writer as the man read his prose aloud, and a funny thought struck him. The Dutch writer, who read from an English translation, looked like a person of Aksyonov's own age. It occurred to Aksyonov that even if the Dutchman had plastic surgery and were transformed into a young man, all the same there would remain in him something indefinable, so that Aksyonov would immediately spot him as a man of his own generation. A Dutchman, an Englishman, a Japanese, or an American, no matter: Aksyonov recognizes these people. He is convinced they all have some common feature; their readers even resemble one another somehow.

Friedberg commented that when we speak of writing away from one's native land, we must remember that the life span of a literary work is long. A great many Russian literary works of some importance have, in fact, been written, created abroad. In Rome a Russian lyric poem was written by Tiutchev, a member of the imperial Russian diplomatic service; as well as Gogol's *Dead Souls*, a classic of world literature. Quite a few important Russian novels were written by Russian authors residing for varying periods in Western Europe, and ultimately these novels reached the reader back in Russia.

In Friedberg's opinion, the single most important case in recent years is that of Ivan Bunin, who wrote many of his important works while living in the south of France, far from any Russian surroundings; he wrote novels in Russian that were published in the USSR after his death. Friedberg has heard that on many occasions a beginning writer visiting the editorial offices of *Novyi mir*, *Neva*, *Oktiabr'*, or other journals might get the following advice from the editor: "Your command of Russian is weak. Read Bunin." It is the language of Bunin, the language that he retained for almost half a century after leaving the USSR, that is one of his chief attractions.

One kind of work that cannot be successful if written away from one's native surroundings, Friedberg continued, is demonstrated by the novels of Turgenev: social novels, novels containing important social commentary. However, literature dealing with eternal human problems can be created almost endlessly, and sooner or later that literature reaches its reader.

Aksyonov cited the example of Nabokov; his setting is absolutely alien for Russian readers, yet he achieved great success with them. Friedberg asked Aksyonov how many Soviet writers he would compare to Nabokov as a Russian writer. Aksyonov replied that Nabokov was enormously popular among Russians, influencing a whole generation of writers in Russia. For a long time, he said, a large group of writers was overshadowed by two authors, Nabokov and Platonov; and what a contest that was!

Herman Ermolaev (Princeton University) commented on Solzhenitsyn, noting that it has been said that he politicized his novel *The First Circle*. In the original edition Volodin calls the American embassy and tells them that a Soviet agent by the name of Koval' should be receiving information from an American professor relating to the building of an atomic bomb. Ermolaev noted that this is all based on facts — Lev Kopelev writes about it in *Ease My Sorrows* [*Utoli moia pechali*]. Such a phone call was, in fact, made by the son of a Soviet diplomat, and the agent who was to receive these secrets was named Koval'.

Ludmila Foster added a footnote to Siniavsky's and Aksyonov's comments about censorship in the West, where there is no official censorship. She observed that when Nabokov began to write his books in Berlin, and later in Paris, Russian émigré critics tore into him for all they were worth. They said, "What kinds of books are these, gentlemen, without even the scent of Russia in them? What kind of writer is this?" She noted that it was not the Soviet Georgii Markovs who wrote this, but the émigré poet Georgii Ivanov. He wrote that Nabokov is a nonentity in literature; what can you expect from him? Mikhail Osorgin, a respectable and competent writer, also criticized Nabokov bitterly.

In the end, Foster continued, when Nabokov's most "abstract" novel came out, *Invitation to a Beheading* (*Priglashenie na kazn'*), these people really got after him. Nabokov threw in the towel and stopped writing in Russian. This was an existential tragedy for Nabokov because his readers, his audience, did not accept him, and he started to write in English. Then, after Nabokov had established himself as an American writer, the American critics and critics throughout the world praised him — oh, what a marvelous writer! — and all his older novels were translated into English. The American critics raved about him: What a talent! What a genius! Foster recalled the words of a Russian émigré critic: "Oh, what a genius this Nabokov is! What a shame that his work is not in Russian!" Nabokov did not need Soviet critics like Feliks Kuznetsov and Georgii Markov, she observed; he had émigrés to do him in. This, in her view, was a writer's tragedy.

Notes

1   Iulii Daniel, writer, tried together with A. D. Siniavsky, February 10–14, 1966.

2   The play was performed in Moscow in the summer of 1983, and in New York and Washington, DC, early in 1984.

3   Suggesting the "revisionist" ideas of Milovan Djilas, a Yugoslav Party and government official under Tito, imprisoned in the 1950s and 1960s for anti-Stalinist and liberal articles and books, such as *The New Class* (1957).

4   Story by Aksyonov, published in 1961.

5   *Metropol'*, an almanac assembled by a number of well-known Soviet writers that was refused publication; it included works by Aksyonov, Akhmadulina, Vysotskii, Bitov, Aleshkovskii, and Iskander. Contributors received individual penalties. The book has been published in the West, edited by Aksyonov.

6   Published by London: Collins Harvill, 1986.

7 Published by Macmillan, 1980.

8 Subsequently expanded into a book: Lev Losseff, *On the Beneficence of Censorship: Aesopian Language in Modern Russian Literature* (München: Verlag Otto Sagner, 1984). Finkelstein reminded Aksyonov of an interesting question posed earlier: how censorship not only influences content but also shapes the form of a work and how one may contend with this. He urged Aksyonov to respond, as one of the first who undertook to bend the form prescribed by socialist realism. Aksyonov commented that in order to do so he would have to refer to a great number of examples from his own experience. He stressed that there is a tremendous difference in the understanding of censorship in the West, or in old Russia, and in the Soviet Union. Tsarist censorship, he maintained, was Western-type censorship directed at the cutting of dangerous passages; he noted, for example, the publication of Mayakovsky's poem "A Cloud in Trousers" ("*Oblako v shtanakh*") with ellipses.

9 Varlam Shalamov's *Kolyma Tales*, published in the United States and Canada in John Glad's translation, 1980.

PART IV

The Mass Media

7

Film Censorship in the USSR

Valery S. Golovskoy

The first Moscow film censor, appointed on November 27, 1908, was B. B. Sheremet'ev, a senior assistant for special assignments to the mayor of Moscow.[1] A. Khanzhonkov, one of the founders of the Russian cinema, recalled that prior to that time "there had been no single censorship authority. For a small payment, the local authorities, such as the precinct captain or even a local policeman, would look the other way."[2] However, even the emergence of official censorship had practically no effect on the activity of the filmmakers and distributors; the numerous scandals with which the history of Russian film abounds are the best proof of that fact.

In 1914, Purishkevich, a member of the State Duma, raised the question of censorship in films. At a May 14 session of the Duma he expressed the urgent need to "ban the dissemination in the countryside of *uncensored films* by a legislative act, and to establish for this purpose a mixed commission consisting of representatives of the departments of education, interior, army, navy and the Holy Synod . . . ; and to establish a state monopoly over cinema."[3]

The realization of this alluring idea of complete state control of the cinema was to be achieved, however, only after the October Revolution. On August 27, 1919, Lenin signed the "decree on nationalization of the entire motion picture industry and trade." The decree was preceded by 1918 resolutions on the control over the activities of motion picture theaters and on film censorship that were issued in Moscow and the Ukraine (see appendix A).

A Russian version of this paper appears in *SSSR. Vnutrennie protivorechiia*; see the bibliography for the full citation. – Ed.

Lenin's pronouncements on the need for censorship of motion picture production were marked by some caution. On February 22, 1922, in the course of a conversation with Lunacharskii, he noted: "Of course, censorship is still needed. Counterrevolutionary and immoral films must not be tolerated."[4] Several other of Lenin's fragmentary statements on censorship can be found. For example, in "Memorandum to Comrade Litkens" of January 17, 1922, there was discussion of the increase in motion picture profits and of the role of private investments, "but only on condition of censorship by the People's Commissariat of Education."[5] The same memorandum also proposes the establishment of other forms of control: "Pictures of a propagandistic or educational character must be submitted for review to old Marxists and men of letters."[6] In response to Lenin's directives, P. I. Voevodin, a senior official, wrote on February 20, 1922:

> Concerning the establishment of censorship and control over films being shown, there is such censorship. It will be powerless, however, if we do not succeed in releasing new films. For filmmakers, taking advantage of the dearth of appropriate pictures, will drag up out of their cellars all sorts of "thrillers" and "obscene" pictures that they had hidden away during nationalization.[7]

This declaration is especially noteworthy because it was made a year prior to the organization, on February 9, 1923, of the Repertory Control Committee. Within the Repertory Control Committee a section on film was created under the direction of Pavel Bliakhin, an old Bolshevik and screenwriter.

During the 1920s censorship of films and of cinema was somewhat chaotic. In one of the first books on the cinema to be published in Soviet Russia, Nikolai Lebedev, a leading communist critic, devoted an entire chapter to film censorship. Among the important problems of censorship, he mentioned the banning of films even after their showing in some theaters. As this caused enormous financial losses, Lebedev proposed "further strengthening of the Repertory Control Committee apparatus with competent personnel, so that once a decision was made concerning a particular motion picture, there would be no further change."[8]

Another scourge of the cinema in those years was the banning by local authorities of pictures previously approved by the Central Repertory Committee. A third deficiency of the central censorship apparatus, in Lebedev's view, was the absence of clear-cut criteria for the evaluation of films. On the one hand, there was permissiveness. The censorship "sees its goal only in banning absolutely unacceptable films."[9] On the other hand, censors might impose a ban or demand the remaking of films that the filmmakers themselves considered revolutionary. Even *Little Red Devils* [*Krasnye d'iavoliata*], Lebedev remarked, "was subjected to excision."[10]

Anatolii Lunacharskii, People's Commissar of Education, wrote repeatedly of the rivalry between the censors and Party and Soviet organizations. In a 1926 article he said:

> I consider the present review methods quite wrong. In my opinion, screenplays should not be reviewed by two censorship organizations, the Artistic Council of the Political Education Committee, and the Central Repertory Committee. I have proposed to higher party organs the establishment of a single censorship organization. The Central Repertory Committee insists that it should carry out censorship functions, while the Artistic Council considers it its province, I have no preferences on the choice of organization to be entrusted with this task. Still, I consider absurd a state of affairs whereby one organization approves a picture, a studio works on it, and then another organization cancels the film. I have some doubts also about the editing of films imported from abroad. Apparently, the procedure is accomplished in a totally dictatorial manner by a few editors from Soviet Film. This, in turn, results in the mutilation of the film, in absurd alterations of the subtitles, and so forth. Much must be done to put some order in this activity. A collective of censors must be established that would act with greater care.[11]

In 1928, Lunacharskii again turned to the question of rivalry between official censorship and the supervisory organizations. The fact was that the Repertory Control Committee frequently banned pictures that the Party had approved. "Why, in fact, should the party comrades, sitting on the Repertory Control Committee, be any more competent in this matter than the party comrades whom the Party itself and the Soviet government placed at the head of production? Or why should the Repertory Control Committee of the Russian Republic be able to put itself in the position of higher court over the Repertory Control Committee of the Ukrainian Film Administration?"[12]

In a letter to Shvedchikov, then chairman of Soviet Film,[13] written in the same year (1928), Lunacharskii recommended a more active defense of film interests against censorship and appealed for help to members of the board of the People's Commissariat of Education. "I declare categorically that I will steadfastly defend the principle of the greatest possible freedom of choice."[14] I also wish to recall Lunacharskii's letter to F. F. Raskol'nikov, chief of the Central Repertory Committee, in which he reported that the People's Commissar of Education, by his own authority, had reversed the decision of the censorship authorities banning the film *The Lame Landowner* [*Khromoi barin*].[15] Lunacharskii wrote even more pointedly of this concern in an article, "Film as an Instrument of Mass Propaganda and Agitation" (1930):

> Ideological assistance to them [those in film administration] on the part of the state is reduced in practice to *the incredible severity of censorship by repertory control committees* which bans an enormous percentage of all screenplays submitted . . . and even so fails to avert the occasional release of worthless films. The problems of screenplay censorship — insofar as we have exclusively state production and unlimited opportunity to staff it with people as competent politically as possible (after all, it is not only censors who understand good and evil) — are, in the final analysis, a secondary matter. Of primary importance is the painstaking organization of the leading ideological staff.[16]

Lunacharskii sensed that censorship was becoming an awesome force; that it was becoming ever more difficult to manage even for him, the direct superior of Glavlit and of the Central Repertory Committee, and other Bolshevik leaders. By the end of the 1920s censorship had grown within the body of the bureaucratic party-state machine like a cancerous tumor.

Yet even the establishment of what Lunacharskii called "leading ideological centers" — that is, of a party-state apparatus of control — failed to bring about a desirable change. The party-state organizations fought with the official censors for the right of control. And they gained that right.

In the recently published memoirs of the late film director Kamil' Iarmatov, one finds some interesting depictions of Soviet Film's activities during the 1930s. Iarmatov, who worked in the Tadzhik Republic Studio, brought his new picture to Soviet Film. He arrived to find a screening in progress:

> We entered the room on tip-toe, and felt our way into some seats. They were showing a picture by the Armenian director Barkhudarian, *Two Nights* [*Dve nochi*]. It captivated me immediately. But then the lights flashed on. "Enough," commanded a comrade who was obviously in authority. Subsequently I learned that this was Comrade K. Iukov, head of the Main Committee. "What's the matter? Why didn't they remake this? We won't accept it. You may show it at home in Armenia!" So that's how it is, I thought. But I liked the film! Then an Uzbek picture came on, by Suleiman Khodzhaev, whom I knew well. It was called *Before Dawn* [*Pered rassvetom*]. And it all happened all over again; the screening was interrupted in the third reel. "Nonsense! Who brought this? Who presented it?" The director of the *Shark Iulduz* Studio rose from his seat: "I brought it." And Iukov again, "We won't take it. Entertain yourselves with it, if you like."[17]

The screening of Iarmatov's film *The Emigrant* went off well, and, reel in hand, he took the trolley to the Central Repertory Committee laboratories, which were located at Chistye Prudy. The head of the film section, P. Bliakhin, viewed the picture on the spot, signed the permit, and requested only that the ending — in which the hero spent too long strangling the villain — be cut slightly.

In Iarmatov's memoirs the censors are presented in a more favorable light than the state organizations. Yet, according to official information, in those years (the late 1920s to early 1930s) more than 16 percent of all films were banned each year by the Central Repertory Control Committee because of their low ideological and political quality. This situation prevailed until 1932.[18]

Nevertheless, one must note a certain degree of openness in the work of film and theater censorship in the late 1920s. From 1926 to 1928 the Central Arts Administration published a bulletin that printed articles and reviews with analyses of film and stage productions and that also provided ratings as well as reasons for their ban or audience restrictions. It also published lists of approved and banned films.[19]

Structure and Functions

From the moment of their creation, Glavlit and the Repertory Control Committee were part of the system of the People's Commissariat of Education. Despite the numerous reorganizations of the 1920s and 1930s, censorship remained under the authority of the People's Commissariat of Education for many years. In 1928, in the course of bureaucratic growth of the state and party apparatus, the Central Arts Administration was established within the People's Commissariat of Education system, and the Central Repertory Committee was separated from its immediate superior, Glavlit. However, in the 1930s, despite the establishment of the Central Motion Picture Administration (and also of the Committee on Affairs of the Arts), film and theater censorship remained within the People's Commissariat of Education. The final merger of film production and censorship was not completed until 1962, with the establishment of the Committee on Motion Pictures.

Looking at the structure over time, one can see how supplemental control units in the form of various councils were created within the same structures (the Central Political Education Committee, the Central Arts Administration), in counterbalance to official censorship. Efforts continued to establish an "ideological staff," as Lunacharskii called it, and consequently total control over the country's spiritual life.

Let us turn now to the structure and functions of the Central Repertory Committee itself and of its film section. The February 9, 1923, resolution of the Council of People's Commissars of the RSFSR on the creation of the Central Repertory Committee stated: "The committee for repertory control (the Central Repertory Committee), is part of the Central Administration for Literature and Publications (Glavlit)." Its functions — in relation to the cinema — were defined as follows: "a) authorization of public screenings of motion pictures, b) compilation and publication of lists of pictures approved and prohibited for public screening."[20]

To accomplish these goals, the committee was authorized to control the repertory of all movie theaters and to publish guidelines. In cases of violation of the resolution on repertory controls, it was authorized to make movie theaters and others accountable and subject to prosecution by the administrative (police) and judicial organs. Within individual provinces, according to Glavlit's directives, control fell to the Provincial Department for Literature and Publications and, within individual districts, to District Departments of Education. At that time the censorship authority was called *politkontrol'* and the censors, accordingly, political controllers.

As we see, the goals of the censorship of entertainment were still modest enough. The Central Repertory Committee had no local representatives. In practice, Glavlit functionaries and local departments of education were not in a position to exert control over movie theaters. However, a new statute on the censorship of entertainment performances was promulgated in 1934; it merits closer scrutiny, as the basic principles of this document remain relevant to this time. The resolution was entitled "On the Ratification of a Statute of February 29, 1934, on the Main Administration for Monitoring Entertainment Performances and Repertories of the People's Commissariat of Education of the RSFSR." (This resolution superseded that of 1923.) "The Main Administration for Monitoring Performances and Repertories," the resolution stated, "exercises political-ideological, artistic, and military control, both preliminary and subsequent, over all manner of entertainment presentations and repertories (theater, music, variety shows, film, recordings, and radio features) within the territory of the RSFSR."[21]

Article 2 of the resolution discussed the tasks assigned to the Central Repertory Committee:

a) authorization for production, public performance, and distribution . . . of dramatic, musical, and choreographic works, as well as variety shows and circus presentations, and motion pictures; b) permission to record, produce, and distribute phonograph records; c) subsequent control over public presentations of works and performances enumerated in a) and b).

This article also discusses controls on exports and imports, the mandatory registration of all new places of entertainment, and control over feature shows.

Paragraph 5 (paraphrased here) spelled out the restrictive functions of censorship, forbidding public performances and distribution of theatrical and musical presentations, motion pictures, and phonograph records that contain agitation or propaganda directed against the Soviet authorities and the dictatorship of the proletariat; that divulge state secrets; that arouse national and religious fanaticism; that are of a mystical nature or of a pornographic character; that lack the proper ideological stance; or that are of an antiartistic nature. This paragraph also mandated the withdrawal from circulation of works banned from performance or display and oversight of the repertory of all places of entertainment, and of the public performance of dramatic, musical, and choreographic works, as well as of circus and variety shows and motion pictures.

Thus along with such obvious considerations as divulging state secrets, or pornography, there are also such vague formulations as "lack of the proper ideological stance" and the even vaguer "antiartistic" works. This created a legal basis for direct interference in the artistic process. Party bureaucrats on all levels were given the right to full control over literature and the arts. This condition was maintained and broadened from the 1920s through the 1950s, and in the 1960s and 1970s it became the principal factor in party activities affecting the country's spiritual life.

The resolution of 1934 also provided instructions for the removal of prohibited works. The major objective here was immediate action by the apparatus after receipt of written orders or telephoned telegram. Paragraph 6 directed the following sequence:

> When removing unacceptable film frames or subtitles a report is to be composed in the presence of representatives of the local administration for repertory control and the local office of the Russian Film Distribution Trust. The report is to be compiled in three copies, of which one will be kept in the special affairs (department) of the Russian Film Distribution Office, the second at the Repertory Control Administration, and the third is to be sent immediately to the Central Administration for Monitoring Performances and Repertories. Withdrawn film frames are to be destroyed by the Russian Film Distribution Office in the presence of a representative of the local repertory control administration.

A separate paragraph prohibited any changes in a film or a film advertisement without special permission of the Central Repertory Committee.

One of the most important innovations arising from this resolution was the creation of an enormous *local* apparatus of control. Control administrations, which were local organs of the Main Administration, were established within the people's commissariats of education of the autonomous republics (ASSRs), territories, and provinces. Local administrations appointed their own plenipotentiaries in the districts, as well as in all the major cultural institutions (the theater, phonograph record factories, film studios). These questions were defined more precisely with relation to motion pictures in a special resolution of June 29, 1935, of the Motion Picture Administration of the Council of People's Commissars of the RSFSR and the Repertory Control Committee. The resolution was entitled "On the Establishment of Positions for Plenipotentiaries of the Main Administration for Monitoring Performances and Repertories in the Provincial, Territorial, and Autonomous Republic Offices of the Russian Film Distribution Trust."

Two other important directives issued in conjunction with the resolution of the Council of People's Commissars must be mentioned. One, entitled "On the Ways to Implement Control over Performances and Repertories," consisted of nine sections and 39 paragraphs. This was a joint directive of June 15, 1934, of the RSFSR People's Commissariat of Education, the People's Commissariat of Internal Affairs of the USSR,[22] and the RSFSR People's Commissariat of Justice.

Of its nine sections, three are of particular interest here. Section B, on the issuance of permits, contained an instruction that a screenplay must be submitted in two copies for the preliminary phase of censorship. In order to receive a permit for a film, however, one had to present "a declaration in the prescribed form, certification of the film's acceptance by the supervisory film organization, three copies of all subtitles in the film, three copies of the film proofs, and prototypes of the film itself."[23]

Section H dealt with the rights and responsibilities of officers of the Central Administration[24] and its local agencies. Paragraph 34 specified that such officers had the right to review the repertory of all entertainment performance enterprises and organizations, as well as individual performers; to withdraw prohibited repertory; to prepare reports on the heads of entertainment performance enterprises, organizations, and individual contractors upon discovery of violations of laws on control and instructions of the Central Administration or its local agencies; to close down shows (concerts, stage performances, or film shows) through the appropriate administrative organs, as well as to ban from performance individuals lacking permission of the control organs. Finally, these officers had the right of free entry to all entertainment performance enterprises and organizations.

Section I dealt with responsibility. According to paragraph 36, violations of laws and regulations on control or resolutions and instructions of the Central Administration and its local organs by heads of entertainment performance and production enterprises carried disciplinary and judicial responsibility, depending on the circumstances involved, and in accordance with the appropriate articles on malfeasance of the Criminal Code (Articles 109, 111, 112), assuming these actions contained no evidence of other crimes (Article 58[10] and others).[25] In that case, other persons involved in the same violation were held accountable in accordance with Article 185 of the Criminal Code.[26] The direct enforcement of restrictive measures (by order of the censorship organs) was entrusted to the NKVD (the secret police) and the People's Commissariat of Justice.

No less important is another directive of the Repertory Control Committee dated June 29, 1935, and issued in coordination with the Film Distribution Administration of the RSFSR, Council of People's Commissars: "On Procedures for the Implementation of Subsequent Supervision by Provincial, Territorial, and Autonomous Republic Repertory Control Administrations over the Distribution and Showing of Films." This directive, with its many paragraphs and subparagraphs, is too long to be reproduced here in its entirety, but paraphrased excerpts from paragraph 9 give the general idea.

This section lists the tasks to be performed by local agencies of repertory control with regard to the distribution of motion pictures: supervision of the compilation and implementation of repertory schedules; periodic viewings of locally available films to establish which of them may be unfit (that is, politically harmful, obsolete, or lacking in thematic unity because of wear and tear); systematic checks to establish that the proof and the film being shown coincide exactly; checking for the presence in all film warehouses and Russian Film Distribution offices of a screening permit from the Central Repertory Control Administration; systematic checks in film screening units for the presence of Russian Film Distribution Trust waybills corresponding to official format and bearing the stamp and signature of the film warehouse supervisor. (In the absence of the appropriately formulated stamp, the film was to be withdrawn from circulation immediately, and those responsible were to be prosecuted in accordance with the Criminal Code.)

Subparagraph *f* mandates monitoring of the political and artistic character of film advertisements. Printing posters of a cheap or hard-sell character distorting the political and ideological content of the film was forbidden, as was inclusion of titles and subtitles not approved by the Main Repertory Control Administration and placement in a film of advertisements of photographs and drawings from a film prohibited by the Central Repertory Control Administration. Proofs of all new motion pictures had to be subjected to preliminary viewing and checking prior to their release for public showing, and local organs of repertory control were to maintain a regular check of the storage of prohibited films and to monitor their timely dispatch as appropriate.

Paragraph 11 of this directive warned that actions such as distribution and showing of films not approved by the Central Repertory Control Administration, changing of film titles without the knowledge of the control organizations, retention of a prohibited film at a warehouse, and independent editing of separate parts of a film approved by the Central Repertory Control Administration would result in criminal proceedings against those responsible, brought by the local agencies or by the Main Repertory Control Administration.

I wish to emphasize once again that with almost no exception, the regulatory functions of censorship have not changed up to this time. Close study of these documents is especially important because they were the last public writings on activities related to the censorship of entertainment.

Although an independent state institution charged with cinematic activities was created in 1922 (the Film Administration of the Council of People's Commissars RSFSR, later the Central Administration for the Film and Photo Industry and the Motion Picture Administration), censorship functions remained within the structure of the People's Commissariat of Education and interacted with the film organizations. This situation prevailed for nearly 30 years, until the establishment in 1962 of the Committee on Motion Pictures of the USSR Council of Ministers. An independent Department for Film Repertory Control was created in the bowels of the committee's Central Administration for Film Distribution. This event coincided with the general decentralization of censorship and its organization according to departmental criteria.[27]

Film Censorship Activities in the 1960s and 1970s

Deeply concealed within the structure of the Film Committee (since 1972, Goskino USSR), the Department for Film Repertory Control of the Central Administration for Film Distribution came under the dual authority of the motion picture bureaucracy and Glavlit.[28] How, then, is film censorship carried out now? First, one must note that film productions undergo censorship twice.

A completed and approved screenplay first goes through the Glavlit censors. Before "launching" the screenplay into production, creating the working group, or beginning work on the director's copy, one must obtain the Glavlit stamp (Glavlit itself, and not the Department for Film Repertory Control). The screenplay thus goes through the same censorship process as any other literary work.[29] In the majority of cases the screenplay is approved without difficulty, as the censors know that it is a semifinished product that will go through countless departments and be subjected to a great many alterations.

One screenplay was rejected by the censors for production and for publication in a journal on the grounds that it mentioned a chemical substance that acts on the human body. (The screenplay was science fiction and the name of the substance had been invented by the authors.) The censors claimed that there was a similar substance on their list of products that cannot be mentioned. Mention of the substance invented by the authors could not appear in print or on the screen because Western intelligence might guess that research was being done in this area. Only after several years was the screenplay published and the film produced. Of course, the censors' demands were met.[30] It must be acknowledged, however, that such instances are rare. After all, a screenplay passes through many departments in the film studio and in the committee (it is normally rewritten five or six times) and arrives at the censors' office in "perfect" condition.

The production of a film is no less seriously monitored. (There are numerous screenings of the material by the studio editors, the arts council, the party committee, the editorial apparatus of the Film Committee, the Arts Council of the Committee, and, in individual cases, by the instructor of the film section of the Department of Culture and the Central Committee of the Soviet Communist Party!) At long last the film's production is completed and it is accepted by the studio. The director then prepares the materials required for application for a permit: the certificate of formal acceptance, seven copies of the proofs, seven copies of the text of the subtitles, and a control copy of the film. All the documents must be in perfect condition and absolutely identical: a discrepancy in a comma, not to mention an inaccuracy in a proof, may cause the material to be returned.

The Control Department is located in the same place as the Main Administration for Film Distribution — at the Mosfilm studios (Mosfil'movskaia Street, 1). Censorship of films is part of the centralized system. This means that any film, wherever shot and of whatever nature, must be censored by the Control Department in Moscow and must obtain permission for duplication and for presentation in theaters. (Films released only for local screening in a republic are exceptions.)

The Department's staff examines all of the materials and each frame of the film itself, both on the screen and at the editor's desk, after which it issues a permit in the prescribed form. The example of such a permit shown below in translation is particularly instructive, as it pertains to a publicity film barely more than one minute in length. The small publicity studio, Estonian Advertising Films, was required to present its "mini-reel" to the censors with all the requisite materials.

(SEAL)
USSR STATE COMMITTEE ON MOTION PICTURES
(GOSKINO USSR)

CENTRAL ADMINISTRATION FOR FILM DISTRIBUTION
DEPARTMENT FOR FILM REPERTORY CONTROL
18 November 1980

PERMIT No. 411-R80

The Department for Film Repertory Control approves for screening within the borders of the USSR the advertising film FOR WOMEN AND CHILDREN

Production: Estonian Advertising Films
Type: color
Parts: 1   Meters: 39.1
Requisitioned by: GLAVKOOPTORGREKLAMA (Central Administra-
tion for Cooperative Trade Advertisements)

Head of the Department
for Film Repertory Control   (signature)
                                              F. F. Ivanov
                                              "Mosfilm" Press,
                                              S2 – 10,000

Here is another sample permit, this time for a feature film:

---

film title: *Brief Encounters*
year of production: 1967
film studio: Odessa
DEPARTMENT FOR FILM REPERTORY CONTROL[31]
Permit No. 2138/67

The Department for Film Repertory Control authorizes the showing of the black-and-white sound film *Brief Encounters* within the borders of the USSR for any audience except children's shows for an unlimited period.
classification: feature
genre: film story
number of parts: 10
meters: 2,658
screenplay: K. Muratova and L. Zhukhovitskii
Director: K. Muratova

> Head of the Department
> for Film Repertory
> Control
> A. Vilesov

The permit follows the film to the duplication plant and then to all the locations where it might be screened. Proofs, printed for each film shown, accompany the film and allow the local controller to compare methodically the copy on the screen with the original approved by the censors. The permit is typed on the cover of each set of proofs. As we see, the permit provides many details about the film that will assist its future monitors. Exact indication of the film's length (39.1 meters, 2,658 meters) is especially important, as it allows the film copy to be checked in each new locale. Any change in the number of meters (projectionists like to cut a few frames)[32] will lead to immediate withdrawal of the copy.

The departmental nature of contemporary censorship — its merger, as it were, with the administrative apparatus — has far-reaching consequences.

The prohibitive functions of censorship have been sharply reduced. The large staff of the editorial department, working conscientiously, literally leaves no questionable spots that might raise objections.

The censors use their "lists" in examining, first of all, the visual content: Is some secret site included in a frame — a city, perhaps, or a building? Are people shown in military uniform? The theme, content, and sample text of the future film have already undergone censorship in the screenplay stage, so that part, as a rule, raises no difficulties. When necessary, the Control Department sends a film for approval to military, space flight, and nuclear energy censors. In practice, however, this is a mere formality because in the process of producing a film on the army, space explorations, or the atom bomb, the motion picture authorities remain in close consultation with the Ministry of Defense, the KGB, and sundry committees. The film is authorized with their direct participation. The motion picture censors of these departments are thus reduced to dealing with formalities.

What are the tasks facing contemporary film censorship? Permits must be issued for large-scale duplication of films and their subsequent distribution.[33] The compilation of repertories and the showing of films must be monitored, and prohibited films must be withdrawn and destroyed. As may be seen, only the first of these tasks is concerned with the strictly proscriptive and approval functions. The others are defined by the supervisory character of film censorship activities; they are its executive tasks.

The placement of film censorship within the Goskino structure not only freed it from many tasks that the editorial apparatus had assumed but also provided the opportunity to exercise complete local control wherever movie theaters exist. Instructors from the Control Department and its representative are staff members of the film distribution administrations and departments in provinces, districts, and cities throughout the country. It is they who perform the routine tasks of checking proofs, examining films, monitoring the contents of advertisements, composing documents for the withdrawal of a film when a telegram directing such action is received by telephone from the department, and the like.

There is still one more advantage, of a purely propagandistic nature, deriving from the absence of a central censorship apparatus in the USSR. It seems that it has now become much more difficult than it was, let us say, in the 1920s or 1930s to say with absolute certainty that a particular film has been banned by the censors. One can speak of the banning of a film by censorship only in two cases: when the film is refused a permit and when the film is withdrawn from distribution by order of the Department for Film Repertory Control (which, in turn, acts on orders from Glavlit or from the Goskino leadership).

Whereas the first type of censorship activity (refusal to issue a permit) has been virtually unheard of in recent years, the second is thriving. Thus withdrawal of a film from the film distribution network occurs when its authors emigrate from the USSR for the West or for Israel. This affects, for the most part, directors and actors (the names of screenwriters and technicians merely disappear from the credits, and the pictures continue to be shown), as well as dissidents and people of whom the Soviet authorities disapprove, such as Sergei Paradzhanov. The films of Mikhail Kalik and Mikhail Bogin, Genrikh Gabai and Boris Frumin, films in which Viktoriia Fedorova and Savelii Kramarov acted, pictures produced from screenplays by Viktor Nekrasov and Vassily Aksyonov, Aleksandr Galich, and Georgii Vladimov, have disappeared from the screen forever.

Films no longer consonant with contemporary political conditions may be withdrawn as well. Thus in the 1970s, pictures with a theme relating to Stalin's cult of personality — Grigorii Chukhrai's *Clear Sky* [*Chistoe nebo*] and Vladimir Basov's *Silence* [*Tishina*] — disappeared from the screen. In 1980, a Soviet-Bulgarian comedy, *Just Barely, with Love* [*S liubov'iu popolam*], came out. Within two months it was withdrawn from distribution, as well as from the creative biography of the director, Sergei Mikaelian. The reason: the Bulgarian Party leadership considered the comedy insulting to the dignity of Bulgarians.

These and many other cases of the banning of a film (when there is an order for the withdrawal and destruction of the copies) should be distinguished from the many instances when a film is banned by the administrative-party organs. Meanwhile, complete confusion prevails in this area.[34] I would suggest the following gradations of "work" by the administrative-party apparatus in connection with films to which some objection is raised.

First, a film may not be approved by Goskino. (It is "put on the shelf.") One such case is illustrated by an excerpt from a speech by O. Sharkov, the Party committee secretary of the Lenfilm studio, in connection with the film *Mistakes of Youth* [*Oshibki iunosti*] by the director Boris Frumin, who subsequently emigrated to the West.

It is evident that none of us was altogether a man of principle, if we released the notorious *Mistakes of Youth* — a production that will never see the light of day. Practically speaking, the association fell under his thumb and was unable to compel the director to carry out its recommendations. After viewing the film, the Party committee overturned the decision of the Greater Arts Council, considering the picture not ready for formal acceptance. Consequently, the ideological errors have not been removed, and *by decision of Goskino the picture was put on the shelf*.[35]

Much more frequently the following occurs. A film is approved by Goskino but subsequently put on the shelf. In recent years Goskino has even paid the authors of the film a prescribed minimum honorarium, preferring to keep the ban quiet. The film will not be distributed — in some cases until many years later; in others, ever. In these instances there is both a permit from the censors and a document showing acceptance of the film, but this does not change the essence of the matter. Thus for many years it was impossible to find anyone who had seen the film *Andrei Rublëv*, although it had a permit from the censors. Gleb Panfilov's *The Theme* [*Tema*] has been gathering dust since 1975. Elem Klimov's *Agony* [*Agoniia*] has been in storage in the Special Department of Goskino since 1975. In 1982, it was sold to a number of countries, but so far they have still been afraid to present it in the USSR.[36] The usual explanations for such sanctions are ideological errors, allusions to present conditions, the presentation of Soviet life in dark colors, and so forth.

Another substantial number of films — victims of party authorities — are removed from circulation for one reason or another but are neither banned nor destroyed. Copies of these films are kept in film distribution warehouses, but they are not recommended for screening. Sometimes these films reappear in distribution. A typical case is that of Grigorii Chukhrai's *The Quagmire* [*Triasina*], which, for example, Zhanna Vronskaia included in a list of prohibited films.[37] After its release this film quickly disappeared under pressure from the Ministry of Defense, but some time later it began to be shown again. Following the departure for the West of the director, Andrei Mikhalkov-Konchalovskii, his films disappeared from the screen, but this was a temporary measure — until his return home.

The next most widely practiced form of "work with a film" is restriction of its distribution: a film may be limited in its screening throughout the country, may be released in only one or two copies, or may be approved for screening but only in cities. For five years a talented production by Georgian director Otar Ioseliani was denied a Goskino permit for distribution throughout the country. To be sure, it was then shown in one theater, for all of two weeks.[38]

It should be noted that a number of films that were met at first with "ideological" objections and were restricted in distribution subsequently became Soviet classics and were shown freely, primarily in the cities. Among these were *Andrei Rublëv; Daytime Stars* [*Dnevnye zvezdy*] by Igor' Talankin; and *The Entreaty* [*Mol'ba*] by Tengiz Abuladze.[39]

Although the film's authors and viewers do not really care who banned a film or why it disappeared from the screen, researchers should have this information. In every concrete case they should ascertain the reason and who was to blame. This will help in forming a true picture of the ideological and propagandistic mechanisms of the Soviet system.

APPENDIX A: *Censorship and Control in Soviet Film*

Dates and Facts

1918

February 17. The Department on Arts of the Ukrainian Board of Public Education approved a directive on the introduction of control over the activities of filmmakers.

March 4. The presidium of the Moscow City Council approved a resolution "On the Monitoring of Film Enterprises."

July 17. The presidium of the Moscow City Council approved a resolution "On Censorship of Movie Theaters," establishing control by the Film Committee of the People's Commissariat of Education over the activities of all types of film enterprises and film repertories.

1919

September 11. Following the publication of a decree on the nationalization of the motion picture industry and motion picture trade (August 27), the Film Attestation Commission of the Moscow City Council was reorganized into the Censorship Commission.

1920

November 12. Lenin wrote a decree of the Council of People's Commissars RSFSR on the establishment of the Central Political Education Committee of the Republic (Glavpolitprosvet). The committee was entrusted with the task of ideological control of the arts, including motion pictures.

1921

November. An order was published by the Political Education Committee of the Azerbaidzhan Soviet Socialist Republic on the preliminary review of entertainment repertories created under the auspices of the republic's Political Education Committee on the Arts Control Commission.

1922

December 14. The People's Commissariat RSFSR approved a resolution on the Repertory Control Committee.

1923

February 9. The Council of People's Commissars adopted a decree on the establishment of the Central Repertory Control Committee.

December 24. *Pravda* published a resolution of the RSFSR People's Commissariat of Education on the establishment, under the Political Education Committee, of the Central Repertory Control Committee.

1924

June. A Commission on Film was established under the Department of Agitation and Propaganda (Agitprop) of the Central Committee of the Russian Communist Party (Bolsheviks) and the Central Committee of the Russian Communist Youth League (RKSM/1918–1924).

September 8. The Board of the People's Commissariat of Education approved a resolution on the Arts Council of the Political Education Committee.

1925

August 8. Resolution of the RSFSR People's Commissariat of Education on the transfer to the Political Education Committee of functions of monitoring and control of distribution.

December. The decisions of the Film Commission of the Propaganda Department of the Central Committee of the Russian Communist Party (Bolsheviks) "4. On the Question of Unifying Film Censorship" were published.

1928

July 5. The Board of the Arts Administration adopted a resolution on the establishment of a film department in the Arts Administration.

July 17. The presidium of the Moscow City Council adopted a resolution on the barring of children under 16 years from motion picture theaters (except at special children's showings).

December 17. The USSR Council of People's Commissars adopted a resolution on the creation of a Film Committee under the USSR Council of People's Commissars.

1929

January 11. A resolution was adopted by the Central Committee of the All-Union Communist Party (Bolsheviks) "On the supervisory staff for film industry personnel," marking the launching of a decisive battle for "ideological consistency in film production."

August 26. The RSFSR College of the People's Commissariat of Education adopted a resolution on the political-arts council in the Central Repertory Control Committee.

September 2. Declaration of the All-Russian Central Executive Committee (VTsIK/1917–1936) and the Council of People's Commissars, on the establishment of the Council on Affairs of Literature and the Arts.

1931

December 14. *Pravda* published an article "on a Bolshevik Track" that called for control and vigilance in film production. The article was based on Resolution of the Central Committee of the All-Union Communist Party (Bolsheviks) of December 8.

1933

February 11. The USSR Council of People's Commissars adopted a resolution on the organization of the Central Motion Picture Administration (GUK).

February. The Central Committee of the All-Union Communist Party (Bolsheviks) created a permanent film commission under the Organizational Bureau of the Central Committee. Only screenplays authorized by the Organizational Bureau commission were to be accepted for production.

August 13. A permanent commission on the renewal of film repertory within the Motion Picture Administration holdings and monitoring of film repertory was established.

November 14. The Council of People's Commissars adopted a resolution on the establishment of a trust for film distribution (Russian Film Distribution Trust) under the Motion Picture Administration of the RSFSR Council of People's Commissars. Offices of political controllers (censors) were created within the Trust.

1934

January 14. The Central Committee of the Communist Party (Bolsheviks) of the Ukraine resolved that all screenplays are to be authorized by the Department of Culture and Propaganda (Kul'tprop) of the Central Committee, and completed films by the Organizational Bureau of the Central Committee of the Communist Party (Bolsheviks) of the Ukraine.

February 29. The RSFSR Council of People's Commissars adopted a resolution "On Confirming the Status of the Central Administration for Monitoring Performances and Repertories of the RSFSR's People's Commissariat of Education."

July 4. The Motion Picture Administration decided to create a department of repertory and the mass press with the right of complete control over film distribution and exhibition.

July 15. The RSFSR People's Commissariat of Education, the People's Commissariat of Internal Affairs of the USSR, and the RSFSR People's Commissariat of Justice published instructions "on procedures for the implementation of monitoring performances and repertories."

1935

June 29. The Repertory Control Committee published instructions "on procedures for issuing authorizing certification for the right to show films."

June 29. The Repertory Control Committee and the Film Distribution Administration issued a resolution "On Establishing Positions of Authorized Representatives of the Central Administration for Monitoring Performances and Repertories in Provincial, Regional, and Autonomous-Republic (ASSR) Offices of the Russian Film Distribution Trust."

1938

September 4. The Council on People's Commissars USSR approved a regulation on the Committee on Motion Pictures of the USSR Council of People's Commissars.

1940

January 15. The structure of the Main Administration for Large-Scale Printing and Distribution of Motion Pictures (Glavkinoprokat) confirmed by decree of the Committee on Motion Pictures.

1945

March 20. The Presidium of the Supreme Soviet of the USSR published a decree on the creation of the USSR Ministry of Motion Pictures.

1953

March 15. The Supreme Soviet of the USSR published a decree on the reorganization of USSR ministries. The Ministry of Motion Pictures became part of the Ministry of Culture of the USSR.

March 30. Main Motion Picture Administration and Main Film Distribution Administration were created within the Ministry of Culture USSR.

1963

March 23. Committee on Motion Pictures of the Council of Ministers of the USSR was formed by decree of the Presidium of the Supreme Soviet of the USSR.

1972

August 22. By decree of the Supreme Soviet of the USSR, the Committee on Motion Pictures was reorganized into the State Committee on Motion Pictures of the USSR Council of Ministers (Goskino USSR).

Source: *Sovetskoe kino v datakh i faktakh (1917–1969)*, prepared by Gosfil'mofond (The All-Union State Depository for Motion Pictures) (Moscow: Iskusstvo, 1974), 568 pp. (for official use).

APPENDIX B: *Translator's Glossary*

Included here are most of the names of organizations used in the translation, with the Russian forms supplied by the author, and expansions or additional information. Many of these can be found in *Slovar' sokrashchenii russkogo iazyka* (Moscow: Izd-vo Russkii iazyk, 1977). Translations for some frequently used names (e.g., Repertory Control Committee instead of Main Committee for Monitoring Repertory) have been shortened in the text; complete names are given here. Omitted from the glossary are a few organizations that were mentioned only once, for which Russian equivalents were supplied in the text, and/or the translations of which were obvious.

English Translation	*Original or Definition*
Arts Administration	Glaviskusstvo: Main Administration for Matters of the Arts
Arts Control Commission	Kontrol'no-khudozhestvennaia komissiia
Arts Council	Khudozhestvennyi sovet
Committee on Artistic Affairs	Komitet po delam iskusstv
Committee on Motion Pictures	Komitet po kinematografii (under the Council of Ministers, USSR)
Council of People's Commissars	SNK: Sovnarkom (1917–1946)
Criminal Code of Malfeasance	Ugolovnyi kodeks o dolzhnostnykh prestupleniiakh
Department for Film Repertory	Otdel kontrolia za kinorepertuarom Control (Department for Monitoring Motion Picture Repertories)
District Department of [Public] Education	UONO: Uezdnyi otdel narodnogo obrazovaniia
Film Committee	Komitet po kino (since 1972: Goskino USSR)
Film Distribution Administration	Upravlenie kinofikatsiia (under Council of People's Commissars, RSFSR)

Glavlit	Central Administration for Matters of Literature and Publications; later, Main Administration for the Protection of State Secrets in Printing
Goskino	State Committee of the Council of Ministers, USSR, on Motion Pictures
Central Administration for Film Distribution	Glavnoe upravleniia kinofikatsii i kinoprokata (of the Committee on Motion Pictures of the Council of Ministers, USSR)
Central Administration for Monitoring Performances and Repertories	Glavnoe upravlenie po kontroliu za zrelishchami i repertuarom (under the People's Commissariat of Education)
Central Administration for the Film and Photo Industry	GUKF: Glavnoe upravlenie kinofotopromyshlennosti
Central Committee	Glavka: Glavnyi komitet (e.g., for Repertory Control)
Motion Picture Administration	GUK: Glavnoe upravlenie kinematografii

NKVD	Narodnyi komissariat (Narkomat) vnutrennikh del (People's Commissariat of Internal Affairs)
People's Commissariat of Education	NKP: Narkompros
People's Commissariat of Justice	NKIU: Narodnyi komissariat (Narkomat) iustitsii
Political Education Committee	Glavpolitprosvet: Main Political Education Committee of the People's Commissariat of Education, RSFSR (1920–1930)
Provincial Department for Literature and Publications	Gublit: Gubernskii otdel literatury i izdatel'stv
Repertory Control Administration	Upravlenie repertuarnogo kontrolia
(or in lower case); Main Repertory Control Administration Repertory Control Committee	GURK: Glavnoe . . . . GRK: Glavrepertkom: Glavnyi komitet po kontroliu za repertuarom
repertory control committee	(local committee, in a republic, etc.)
Russian Film Distribution Trust	Rossnabfil'm (under the Motion Picture Administration of the

	Council of People's Commissars, RSFSR)
Soviet Film	Sovkino: Vserossiiskoe fotokinematograficheskoe aktsionernoe obshchestvo (All-Russian Photo and Film Joint-Stock Company)
State Film Depository	Gosfil'mofond (All-Union State Depository for Motion Pictures)
Ukrainian Film Administration	VUFKU: All-Ukrainian Photography and Film Administration

Notes

1   Veniamin Vishnevskii, "Kommentarii." In A. Khanzhonkov, *Perrye gody russkoi kinematograffii. Vospominaiia* (Moscow-Leningrad: Iskusstvo, 1937). See also Richard Taylor, *The Politics of the Soviet Cinema* (Cambridge: Cambridge University Press, 1979), pp. 7–8, 21, 76, 112.

2   Vishnevskii, "Kommentarii," p. 27.

3   Ibid, p. 76, emphasis added.

4   *Lunacharskii o kino* (Moscow: Iskusstvo, 1965), p. 40.

5   *Samoe razhnoe iz rsekh iskusstr. Lenin o kino.* Collection of documents (Moscow: Iskusstvo, 1963), p. 37. [Many organizations of this type (People's Commissariat), given in the Russian text as acronyms, are translated here for ease of reading; consult the glossary in appendix B for Russian originals. — ED.]

6   Ibid.

7   Ibid, p. 81. One could cite many examples of the functioning of film censorship in 1918–1919. The Arts Control Commission operated in Moscow until 1922 under the local departments of public education. See A. Gak, "K istorii sozdaniia 'Sovkino'," in *Iz istorii kino* (Moscow: Izd-vo AN SSSR, 1962), no. 5, p. 133. Censorship functions in Petrograd were performed by the Petrograd Film Committee. A resolution of March 21, 1919, stated: "The regional motion picture committee sets itself the task of cleansing the region of the films now inundating it that run counter to the basic principles of this committee. Such films include: 1) counterrevolutionary pictures; 2) presentations unfit for public viewing from a political point of view; 3) films with contents designed to inspire criminal and base passions in human nature." With this goal, a censorship board was established under the administrative and control council of the Film Committee. See A. Gak, "Kinoorganizatsii Petrograda v 1918–1925," in *Iz istorii kino* (Moscow: Izd-vo AN SSSR, 1961), no. 4, pp. 63–64.

8   N. Lebedev, *Kino* (Moscow: Krasnaia nov', 1924), p. 188.

9   Ibid, p. 189.

10   Ibid, p. 190. *Krasnye d'iavoliata* (1923) — Ivan Perestiani, director; Pavel Bliakhin, screenwriter. This first Soviet adventure film was a tremendous box-office success.

11   *Lunacharskii o kino*, p. 63. See Esfir' Shub, *Zhizn' moia — kinematograf* (Moscow: Iskusstvo, 1972) on the practice of reediting Western films in the 1920s.

12   *Lunacharskii o kino*, p. 131. VUFKU: Vseukrainskoe Foto-Kino Upravlenie (literally, The All-Ukrainian Photography and Film Administration).

13   Soviet Film (*Sovkino*) is the central state organization governing the motion picture industry. It was formed in 1924 within the People's Commissariat of Education.

14   *Lunacharskii O Kino*, p. 278.

15   Ibid, p. 281–82. Letter of January 21, 1929.

16   Ibid, p. 175, emphasis added.

17   Kamil' Iarmatov, *Vozvrashchenie* (Moscow: Iskusstvo, 1980), p. 189. The incident described here occurred in 1934.

18   TsGALI (The Central State Archive of Literature and Art, USSR), *f.* 645, *op.* 1, *ed. khr.* 381, *ll.* 16–17. TsGALI, *f.* 2497, *op. ed. khr.* 39, *l.* 213. (Russian abbreviations: *f.* — depository; *op.* — inventory; *ed. khr.* — storage unit; *l., ll.* — leaf, leaves.) Cited according to A. I. Rubailo, *Partiinoe rukovodstvo razvitiem kinoiskusstva (1928–1937)* (Moscow: Izd-vo MGU [Moscow State University Press], 1976), p. 19.

19   *Repertuarnyi biulleten' Glaviskusstva*, 1926–1928. A complete set of this publication can be found in the New York Public Library.

20   *Kinospravochnik za 1926 god* (Moscow: Kinopechat', 1926), p. 29.

21   Here and subsequently I cite the texts of resolutions and directives from *Kinofotopromyshlennost'. Sistematizirovannyi sbornik zakonodatel'nykh postanovlenii i rasporiazhenii* (Moscow: Kinofotoizdat, 1936), pp. 134–43. See also *Sovetskaia kinematografiia. Sistematizirovannyi sbornik reshenii* (1940); *Resheniia partii i pravitel'stva o kino*, 3 vols. (Moscow: *NIITIK*, 1979) (internal publication).

22   Bulletin *NKP* RSFSR 1934, no. 31, p. 13. The NKVD was also the commissariat comprising the secret police, then known by the same initials. — ED.

23   For more detail, see "Instruktsiia GUK ot 29 iiunia 1935 g" (in coordination with the Film Distribution Administration of the Council of People's Commissars [SNK] RSFSR, "On the Ordinance on the Issuance of Permits for the Showing of Films"), *Kinofotopromyshlennost'*, p. 142.

24   The Central Administration for Monitoring Performances and Repertories. — ED.

25   Article 58 and its subsections are a catchall for such political crimes as slander of the state. — ED.

26   Article 58[10] of RSFSR Criminal Code: anti-State activity. Term: up to 25 years. Article 185 (excerpt): "(For) violation of the laws of photographic and film censorship — imprisonment for a term of up to three months or a fine of up to 300 rubles."

27   The present Ministry of Culture, USSR, contains a Repertory Control Committee (Glavrepertkom: Central Administration for Repertory Control), which censors the theater, circus, variety shows, music, fine arts, and phonograph records. The censorship of radio and television was transferred to the Committee on Television and Radio.

28   For a recent look at censorship in the 1960s and 1970s, see my article, "Sushchestvuet li tsenzura v Sovetskom Soiuze? (o nekotorykh metodologicheskikh problemakh izucheniia sovetskoi tsenzury)," *Kontinent* (Paris), no. 42 (1984), pp. 147–73.

29   If a screenplay is published in a journal or book, the text undergoes Glavlit censorship again.

30   The screenplay *Ivantsov, Petrov, Sidorov* (by E. Grigor'ev and O. Nikich) was

published in the journal *Iskusstvo kino*, no. 7, 1977, and later produced at Mosfilm studios.

31 Later the name changed slightly: Department of Film Repertory Control (Otdel po kontroliu za kinorepertuarom: Otdel kontrolia za kinorepertuarom). It was headed for many years by A. Vilesov, who was then replaced by F. Ivanov.

32 Presumably in order to sell them as transparencies. — ED.

33 Foreign films accepted for distribution in the USSR are also censored. This takes place after the dubbing and preparation of the copy for duplication. The selection of foreign films is carried out by a special commission of Goskino, with participation of representatives of the Central Committee of the Soviet Communist Party but without participation of the censors.

34 See the list of prohibited films in *Vestnik russkogo studencheskogo khristianskogo dvizheniia*, no. 100, (1971), pp. 204–05; Jeanne Vronskaya, *51 Suppressed Films, Index on Censorship* 4/81, pp. 14–15. Some believe that all copies of withdrawn films are destroyed. This is not so. Copies are kept at the State Film Depository (Gosfil'mofond), as well as at the Photograph Library of the Motion Picture Institute (VGIK). Examples are *A Vile Anecdote* (*Skvernyi anekdot*) by A. Alov and V. Naumov and *Assia's Luck* (*Asino schast'e*) by A. Konchalovskii.

35 Cited according to the Lenfilm studio journal *Kadr* (published in large editions), December 4, 1978 (no. 21), emphasis added by editors.

36 All were finally released for general distribution by 1986. — ED.

37 See Vronskaya article in *Index on Censorship*.

38 There is one more type of ban: that of the local administration. Thus the Ukrainian director Iurii Il'enko's film, *The White Bird with the Black Spot* (*Belaia ptitsa c chernoi otmetinoi*), was screened in Moscow but was banned in the Ukraine. Andrei Tarkovskii's *The Mirror* (*Zerkalo*) could, for a time, be seen in Leningrad or Riga but was not distributed in Moscow or Kiev, and so forth.

39 These films, too, were eventually released in the mid-1980s. — ED.

8

Censoring the Journalist

Ilya Suslov

Not long ago I was invited to speak on the radio here in Washington. It was an hour-long nighttime program, from midnight to one a.m., in which the moderator asks questions, the guest answers, and the audience then calls in with more questions. The well-known critic John Corcoran asked me about life in the Soviet Union, and then the audience phoned in, interested in the same thing. They were amused by my terrible English pronunciation as I tried to answer their queries. This was all so natural and normal that it was only later, after the broadcast, that I came to realize that without any preparation, without any preliminary discussion, I had gone directly on the air, without any censorship. I was reminded then of an appearance I once made on television in Moscow. I am a practitioner, not a theoretician, and so will simply tell you about that experience so you can understand how the system works.

Veselovskii and I, co-editors of a column on the last page of *Literaturnaia gazeta* called the Twelve Chairs Club, were phoned by the late Aleksei Kapler, whose name may be familiar; he was a screenwriter who had the misfortune to fall in love with Stalin's daughter. For this Stalin banished him for many years to the most fearsome places in the north. Then he married another woman, a poet — but that is another story. Kapler was a very nice, very intelligent man who for many years ran perhaps the most popular radio show in the Soviet Union, "Kinopanorama" ("Film Panorama"). He talked about new films that were no longer banned and about the actors, who then joined in the discussion. Kapler wanted us, the administration of the Twelve Chairs Club, to introduce some new comedy films that were just being released.

We were, of course, delighted to oblige. After all, who would not like to appear on the screen in the company of famous directors and actors? We wrote the script for the "Kinopanorama" program, allocated the jokes and quips, shaved (or, more precisely, I did — Veselovskii spruced up his huge red beard), and off we went to record our program. They had warned us that we would be filmed on the new videotape that had just been received from abroad — special, very expensive tape that cannot be cut or edited. For this reason the filming would be accomplished nonstop, using several cameras: without pauses, without stuttering, and please, be sober.

"This is some kind of anti-Soviet tape," I said. "I mean, what do you mean, you can't cut it? What if the management doesn't like it?" "Follow the approved script," said the broadcast director. "All of your wisecracks have been approved, and you know how to act. The main thing is speed of delivery. Get ready, let's go." And we did a wonderful "Kinopanorama." Kapler beamed. Our actor friends joked and improvised, and Veselovskii and I recited our adages with hidden meanings, published in the *Literaturka*.[1]

The next day I gathered my friends at my house in order to give, over a bottle of cognac, a running commentary on the program. But no matter how we strained, we could not see a thing; that is, "Kinopanorama" was on, but Veselovskii and I were not. They had cut us out of a videotape that, by all the laws of technology, cannot be cut. My friends drank cognac and taunted me: "So, you thought you'd deceive our beloved Soviet government," they said. "But, you see, it was all recorded," I muttered. "Everything had been approved."

The next morning Kapler called and explained what had happened. It seems that after the program was recorded on that foreign and somewhat anti-Soviet tape, Comrade Lapin, the chairman of Gosteleradio,[2] asked to see it. Comrade Lapin was very unhappy with our little jokes with their hidden meanings. Kapler and his crew tried hard to convince Comrade Lapin that it had all been typed up beforehand and therefore had all been authorized for presentation, but Comrade Lapin said: "What is permitted to Jupiter is not permitted to the bull. The *Literaturka* is read by a handful of intellectuals, but we on television are watched by millions and millions of Soviet people. It's bad enough that these scoundrels corrupt the ideologically unstable intelligentsia with their dubious jokes, but now they are raising their hands against our entire people. They will not get away with this."

Kapler's group began to talk to him about the tape, which could not be cut, about the fact that the entire broadcast was at stake; but Comrade Lapin said, starting to laugh, "What do you mean, it cannot be cut? If the Party needs it, anything can be cut. There weren't any that the Bolsheviks didn't cut — surely you must know that. So bring me the people who know how to cut." And they cut up the tape. They extracted from it my freshly shaven face and the flaming beard of Veselovskii and then they spliced up the foreign tape, which in the accursed West cannot be spliced. From this episode the following conclusion can be drawn: if it is impossible, but you want to very much, then it is possible after all.

I was extremely young when I got involved with what is called Soviet literature. I started at *Iunost' (Youth)* magazine. I was then a young engineer, and I came there to work as the supervisor of the editorial office. This was the most blessed time for the journal: it was extremely popular, and it was liberal. *Novyi mir (The New World)* and *Iunost'* magazine — these were the two lamps in our lives, and I had landed at one of them. I found myself under the supervision of the managing editor of the journal, Comrade Zheleznov, whose assistant I became.

One day I came into the room in which Comrade Zheleznov did his editing — that is, where he censored things. The piece he was working on, as I remember vividly, was a story by that notorious (as Maurice Friedberg calls him) Vasilii Aksyonov, at that time also a young, gifted beginning author. I believe the story was called "Oranges from Morocco," or it might have been some earlier story. I saw Zheleznov take his pen, read through the text, read through it again, and then cross out some lines. I looked at what he had crossed out, and saw that he had crossed out precisely that for the sake of which this damned story of Aksyonov's had been written. He knew that precisely these particular lines should not appear. He had them shot by a firing squad. I was still young and very stupid then, and I said: "What are you doing, Leopold Abramovich? Why, this is fascism," I said, which was completely outrageous.

I do not want you to think that I was so brave or perhaps such a dissident. This was just an impulsive outburst that I allowed myself. In Russia, you know, they say, "a word is not a sparrow — it flies away, you go to jail."[3] In any case, I had said it. He looked at me. He was not alone in the room; Vishniakov, the assistant editor, was sitting there, I recall, and two old gentlemen, both very decent and quite respectable. They heard that word I had uttered and they stared at me in such a way that I understood that I was through, that it was all over for me, because I had dared to say such a thing.

Zheleznov said to me, "Please leave us, and come back in ten minutes." These were the most difficult minutes of my life. I knew that I was finished. Had I been in his place, I would have forgiven no one such an act. "How dare that snotty kid tell me that this is fascism," I would have said. "I do the censoring, I do the editing, and he says such a thing to me!" Ten minutes later I returned, and he said to me, "We have conferred and decided not to turn you in because you are, politically, completely immature, and you will never become a writer because you lack political maturity." Then for the first time, no longer as a reader but as a participant, I understood how terrifying this was.

Still, many years later I started work at *Literaturnaia gazeta*, on the last page. I tell you honestly that I was very lucky. No one ever required any censorship duties of me personally. On the contrary, they allowed me, speaking in our jargon, "to slip things through" (*podsovyvat'*); to let daring material slip through. I was permitted four attempts at slipping things through. If on the fourth try the material did not get through my editors, who were my superiors, then this material was never again to appear on the editor's desk.

I had a certain folder, a "No" file. It was large and in it I put material that did not make it through all the editorial censors. These were all current and future Soviet satires and Soviet humor, because I had worked specifically on that area. They were the best of their kind: they never saw — and never will see — the light of day. When I emigrated, I wanted to steal that file and bring it with me because I thought that if I could just publish it here, everything would immediately come to a halt in Soviet Russia and life there would become democratic and beautiful. Unfortunately, someone guessed my thought and stole the file I had planned to steal, and hid it from me, understanding that I could make off with it.

How did such material get through despite controls? Our column was a very popular page in the newspaper, page 16, and the newspaper was read, so to speak, the Jewish way — from right to left — because we allowed such daring things that now I can hardly even imagine it. Not long ago I went to the Library of Congress and got the back issues of the *Literaturka* for those years that I was an editor. My hair stood on end. I thought, how did I dare, how did I dare to suggest it all for publication? What was I doing?

Even now that I am here, I can still feel that same fear. In fact, though, all of this did get printed; it all sailed through. How could this happen? Aleksandr Borisovich Chakovskii, editor of *Literaturnaia gazeta*, and his assistants, Sorokomskii and a few others, knew that the popularity of the newspaper depended on page 16. They knew that the newspaper's popularity depended on a few other sections that dealt with social problems that we discussed in very serious and interesting ways — although, of course, this was more talk than action. It was for these reasons that they did not prevent us from presenting certain pieces. And we did, obviously, what *Novyi mir* did, what everyone did who thought that his mission was to print and not to suppress; to discover talent and not to bury it; to assist truth and not to mutilate it.

We would give a story to the senior editor-in-chief or to his deputy in charge of that particular issue of the paper. He would read it and say: "Certainly not! What, have you gone crazy? Certainly not!" We knew that it was powerful stuff. Then we would slip him something else, really strong stuff that already verged on the anti-Soviet. He would say, "Out of the question, this is impossible. Give me something a little simpler." Then we would give him what from our point of view was altogether anti-Soviet material. The editor would think a bit and then say, "Well, OK, bring me the first one." Taking all three pieces together, the first was completely inoffensive, but we knew that it was good material, and that it could get through.

On the other hand, we worked in the period of Aesopian language. Aesopian language — this is when you think one thing, say another, and act in an entirely different way. The reader read and recognized all the nuances, all the hidden meanings, all the allusions, and related very well to us on that level. I love the genre of aphorisms, phrases. Consider, for example, the following sentence, inoffensive, perhaps, for those who think in English but not so inoffensive for people who think in Russian: "It was a silent, St. Bartholomew's night."[4] Why do Russian-thinking people laugh? Because this is an excellent, precise description of Soviet reality — a silent but Bartholomean night.

As for the editor, who conceived of things inversely,[5] he was not able to imagine that this was against the Soviet regime. However, let us assume that he felt the danger in this sentence and needed justification for the sentence for the next higher level of command, perhaps for the Central Committee of the Communist Party. Again and again they taught me at *Literaturnaia gazeta* that we had six readers in all. (These were not those who read us "from below," but those who read us "from above.") Six are responsible for *Literaturnaia gazeta*. "If one of them does not like what we have printed, then where will you be," they asked me. "You will be out on your butt, and with no right to comparable employment. What good is that?"

In a sentence such as "It was a silent, St. Bartholomew's night" there is ostensibly nothing anti-Soviet — really and truly there is not — but in any event the editor asked me, "Where was this night of yours?" (Now we are playing the game, you see, Schweik and the corporal.)[6] I said, "What do you mean,'where'? In France!" "But why is it silent?" "Well, because it's a silent, Bartholomean, so to speak, well, night." "And how does this relate to our life?" I had been waiting for just this question and here I took the offensive: "What? Do you mean to say that our life is a silent, St. Bartholomew's night?" He said, "That . . . that . . . is what I wanted to ask *you!*"

This seems very funny, but in fact it is not quite as funny as it now sounds because every sentence that we printed in *Literaturnaia gazeta*, every word, went through ten departments. Above me, a member of the newspaper staff, were ten more people, and indeed all of these people were the author's superiors.

What does the censor actually do? Valery Golovskoy was quite right in maintaining that the censorship functions of the censorship organization proper are, of course, limited. Editors, associates, staff members of all kinds make up the censorship and carry out censorship functions. I was fortunate in that they did not bother us too much, but they did bother others.

From what point of view is the material considered? Let us take an author; say, Professor Friedberg of Mar'ina Roshcha[7] (we shall transport him there for purposes of discussion). Let us assume he has written an article entitled "Russian Classics in Soviet Jackets." This manuscript appears on the desk of a literary editor, to whose office he has brought it. This first staff member cleans up the material in accordance with his own censorship instincts. This is a kind of intuition, like a talent. He knows that there is something in this sentence: there definitely seems to be something in there, and just to be on the safe side, let's get rid of it. So he does get rid of it, and of another sentence, and of a third. Then he passes the manuscript on to the department supervisor.

The department supervisor knows that the manuscript has already been cleaned up. First, it is no longer entitled "Russian Classics in Soviet Jackets" but, rather, "Russian Classics in Dust Jackets." Has anything important happened? Yes: one changed word, and the meaning is completely different, as you can see. The department supervisor takes a look: is a second interpretation possible here? Is there a hidden meaning at the base of this article? Are there criticisms between the lines? If it seems that way to him, he crosses out those lines.

Then the article — or the book, the story, the screenplay, or the play — moves on to the desk of the assistant managing editor. In this case I am talking about *Literaturnaia gazeta*, but I think the same rule applies everywhere. This person takes a look: is there an allusion here to generational conflict? Is there an allusion to current ethnic problems? Is there a hidden allusion to economic shortcomings? Why an allusion? Because Friedberg, living in Mar'ina Roshcha, is nobody's fool. He is not going to write in so many words that we have shortages. He will hint. He is, after all, an editor in his own right. He is also a "self-censor," living in Mar'ina Roshcha. It is for this reason that one must look for allusions, gentlemen, for allusions.

Then this purified material, already cleaned up, makes its way to the fourth censor, the managing editor, who looks at it, let us say, from the following angle. (We could substitute the functions of each of these people for those of the next, but I have distributed them in this way so as to make clear the direction in which censorship works.) Is there a predominance here of negative attitudes toward Soviet reality? Where is the optimistic view of things? Are there undesirable generalizations here? "Generalizations" — this is the most awful word. Do not generalize. This is the chief principle of Soviet censorship. Maybe Suslov, from Mar'ina Roshcha, is a drunk, but there can be no alcoholism in the Soviet Union. The word "alcoholism," as a social phenomenon, is tabu. It cannot be made public. It is to be found in that same "Talmud" mentioned by previous speakers: in the censor's handbook, where the names of "untouchable" topics are inscribed. One may not "touch" either birth rate or mortality. One may not "touch" alcoholism. One may not touch thousands of problems, many thousands . . .

Next the material ends up with the deputy editor-in-chief, although it has by now been completely cleaned up. The deputy editor-in-chief looks at it from the following standpoint. Are there any allusions here to vacillation of the general Party line? Is there some criticism of a Party bureaucrat of the higher echelon? Is there hidden support for dissident thought? Does the critical part of the article echo the criticism one hears expressed over Western radio stations broadcasting to the Soviet Union? If yesterday, over the Voice of America, for example, Victor Adol'fovich uttered a certain sentence that seemed to him very innocent, and tomorrow that same phrase turns up by chance in *Literaturnaia gazeta*, then it will appear as though "they criticize us, and we support them." Are there many Jewish names among the authors and protagonists of the articles? This is a very important area of censorship. If it seems to the assistant editor-in-chief that there are too many Jewish names, he demands publication of the material under a pseudonym. All my Jewish authors wrote under pseudonyms: all the Shteinboks became Gorins, all the Shteins became Arkanovs, all the Levines became Aleksandrovs, and so on. After all, what can they do? They happen to be writers, and good ones. Of course it would be better if they did not write altogether, but since they do, the problem must be dealt with. Still, their names cannot be mentioned.

Next the article is read by the first deputy of the editor-in-chief — there is such a rung on the ladder. He checks to see that the previous editors have not missed anything. If it seems to him that something was overlooked, he places a check mark on the spot and sends it to the next censor, who is called a "working member of the editorial board" and who, with great satisfaction, crosses out the sentence marked with the check mark. The reason is simple. Why get involved? After all, he is not crazy!

Then the article is directed to the member of the editorial staff known as the "fresh point of view" (*svezhaia golova*), who reads through it attentively on the chance that some sedition has remained; and only then does the unfortunate article arrive at Glavlit, at the actual censor. There it is examined closely to make sure that no names, terms, or ideas have leaked through that have been forbidden for publication according to the black list compiled, of course, in the bowels of the censorship.

Once upon a time Naum Korzhavin came to see us. Korzhavin was a poet, and sometimes he would forget that one must not sign any documents other than poems. If you want to write your poems, go ahead. That is your privilege. Poets should write poetry. But Korzhavin actually had the nerve to sign a letter, which had also been signed by almost all decent people at the time. It was, if memory serves, in defense of the dissident Golonskov, or perhaps it was Ginzburg, another dissident, or someone else he did not know at all but whom he defended simply out of humanitarian considerations, as any decent person should. As soon as Korzhavin had signed this letter, his own name showed up on the black list. This meant that no one anywhere within the territory of the Soviet Union would see the name of Korzhavin again for as long as his name remained on the censors' list.

I knew that Naum Korzhavin was living in abject poverty and had to earn a little money, and so, playing dumb, I called him and said, "Give me a few verses of something funny, humorous, or, to put it crudely, satirical, and I'll print it on page 16 of *Literaturnaia gazeta* and pay you a ruble and forty kopeks a line." He sent me the poem, which I delivered to the deputy editor-in-chief without reading it because I was sure it was good poetry. It was not even important that it was not satirical (I wrote on it "ironic poetry," and they looked for its other, hidden meanings). The deputy editor-in-chief looked at page 16 and said to me, "This you may print, and this you may print, but that you may not." "Why?" I asked. "He is, after all, a poet. He is a member of the Soviet Writers Union." "No," the deputy replied, "you may not print it." "Oh, come on," I urged. "The man wrote a poem especially for us. How can we refuse it?" "Will you lay off!" the editor demanded angrily. He opened the desk drawer and took out a list. "You see, his name is right here. He is 'a signer' of petitions [*podpisant*]." (This is a new word, that only appeared recently.) Of course, the poem did not go through because not even the deputy editor-in-chief had the right to circumvent the list.

Back to the review process: finally, after passing through all the levels described above, the material hits the desk of the editor-in-chief, who deals a final blow to any shadows of ideas that may have seeped through in one way or another and penetrated the newspaper. If the editor-in-chief has questions, whom will he phone? The Central Committee,[8] using the telephone called the *vertushka*, a special direct line on which they speak with each other. Thus there is no need for written communications or recommendations to the Central Committee. All one has to say is "I don't recommend it." That is how I heard it phrased; or "Well, all right then . . . ," or "We don't recommend it." They hang up and it is all over: the issue is dead, because if it has been put this way on the *vertushka*, there are no words that will help you. This is the ultimate level of censorship and there is no appeal.

Even this would not be half as bad, however, were it not for the most important type of censorship, about which our writers spoke earlier in this conference: self-censorship. Voinovich was right when he said that maybe now we do not need censorship because of the way we have learned to live. A writer knows perfectly well what to write and how to write. Each of us has a kind of little engine, a splendid little machine inside of him that knows precisely what may be written and what may not.

Speaking for myself, I knew how to write my stories while I was in Russia. For some reason, though, every word would come out sounding anti-Soviet. I did not know how to write so that it would get through. Some people have this knack, but I did not. Everything I wrote, including "and" and "of," looked anti-Soviet. If I wrote the letter "A," it immediately became anti-Soviet: I do not know why. So I decided to emigrate — because of censorship and self-censorship. I left because over there I would not have been able to write, while here I can and I do. I write here and am not afraid, and I get published. I have lost the little self-censorship device I had in my head. (Maybe it will appear again, since I am working in a government institution, but so far it has not.)

Self-censorship is what has made Russia a state without a society. Of course, the same could be said of East Germany and of Czechoslovakia, and formerly it could have been said of Poland. Why is this no longer so? Because in Poland a society has come into being. The Solidarity trade union *is* society. In Russia there is no society and no public opinion. There is a Soviet story: A sick person comes to the doctor and says, "Doctor, what should I do? I say one thing, think another, and act on a third entirely." The doctor looks at him and says, "We do not treat Marxism." Writers are not the only ones who suffer from this sickness (saying one thing, thinking another, and acting on a third). This is how everyone today in Russia thinks, with the exception of those who do not think like the others and who do not act in the approved way. We all know very well what totalitarian society does with those people, and it is very frightening.

That is why writers leave or are exiled from Russia. Earlier in this conference we heard from the pride of our literature. These writers — Aksyonov, Voinovich, Siniavsky, as well as Vladimov and Kopelev — would be an adornment for any national literature. These are people who knew what censorship was and could not live with it because it was killing us, killing Russia. Let us wish Russia a full and speedy recovery.

Notes

1   Nickname of *Literaturnaia gazeta*.
2   The State Committee on Television and Radio Broadcasting of the USSR Council of Ministers.

3   Russian proverb: A word is not a sparrow; once it flies away, you won't catch it.

4   *Varfolomeevskaia noch'*: A brief but savage onslaught of terror; from St. Bartholomew's Massacre, 16th-century France.

5   See Andrei Siniavsky's foregoing discussion of inverse reasoning.

6   From Jaroslav Hašek's satirical novel *The Good Soldier Schweik*, where the hero's favorite ploy is playing dumb.

7   A northern Moscow neighborhood.

8   Of the Soviet Communist Party (TsK KPSS).

9
Censorship at the Editorial Desk

Boris Zaks

Of all those who have spoken, and those who have yet to speak, I am the most senior in age. I still remember those legendary days of the past when the Soviet Union possessed not one but two censorship authorities. One of these was called Glavlit. This name, mysterious in origin, has survived to this day, like a relic, in the semiofficial lexicon. Glavlit was subordinate to the People's Commissariat of Education [Narkompros]. The other censorship authority was called PolitControl [Politkontrol'] and was under the direct authority of the punitive organs – that is, the secret police.[1] I am not in a position to say precisely how they divided their responsibilities, but at some point they merged, and Glavlit contributed its name to the new joint entity, while PolitControl gave its substance. So one could say, jokingly, that mama is the People's Commissariat of Education and papa is the secret police. This genetic tie with the punitive organs can be discerned to this day in the activities of Glavlit.

In the course of this conference I have noticed a certain tendency to view censorship as boundless. In essence this is entirely correct because, one could say, the one-party system in the Soviet Union is in itself a preclusion of all other parties, and a preclusive function is in turn a censoring function. I shall not go into detail in this area, attempting rather to confine my remarks to direct censorship — that is, to Glavlit, and, even more particularly, to the activities of Glavlit in those years when Tvardovskii edited *Novyi mir*.

The fact is that censorship is an enterprise whose austere activities are directed not toward the outside, abroad, but inward. Its task is not so much to protect secrets from Western imperialists as to defend the ideological virginity of the Soviet reader, the Soviet people. It seems to me that among Glavlit's activities in the period I am about to discuss there were, strange as it may seem, quite a few elements that could be called comical, grotesque.

After all, the humorist and the satirist do not invent their work. The roots of such works — satirical or comical — always lie in reality, and so it is with censorship, with Glavlit.

Imagine — there is an enormous institution, occupying an entire floor in the building in which the Ministry of the Electronics Industry is located, on Kitaiskii proezd, #7. As in Tynianov's famous story, "Lieutenant Kizhe," "its identity is secret; it has no corporeal existence."[2] For example, according to censorship directives, editors do not have the right to advise the author of the censors' comments. They act as if censorship did not exist.

We were told many times, "You will not reveal our comments to the authors." We, of course, disobeyed, and they would then come back to us and ask, "Why did you tell the author that these were Glavlit's comments?" We would answer, "*We* had no such criticisms: what should we have said?" "You should have said that these were your criticisms, the editors' criticisms." In fact, however, if the opportunity presented itself, we would say to authors: "Of course *we* would never make such inane criticisms."

I remember only a single instance in which Glavlit suddenly said to us, "Let the author come to us. We will speak with him." That was an isolated instance, and had to do with the publication of Kataev's story, "The Holy Well" [*"Sviatoi kolodets"*].[3] It must be said that Kataev made an entirely disgraceful showing. The censors had demanded that a great many passages be rewritten. We had agreed that they would drop their demands on roughly half of these, so that he should have had to discuss only those points on which we had not agreed, but he conceded everything that we had already won. This is an exceptional case, however. As a rule, Glavlit hides from the author. That is ridiculous enough, but there is more. I discern elements of the comic and the grotesque in the following as well.

For 10 years Glavlit read and approved each issue of *Novyi mir*. The Glavlit apparatus worked toward changing the direction of this journal. Nothing came of it; the enormous machine worked in vain. It turned out that the journal was produced under censorship but appeared, in effect, in uncensored form. What I have said should not be understood as evidence that Glavlit's methods were insufficiently harsh but only as evidence of its incompetence in the face of Tvardovskii's intelligent and single-minded tactics. In my opinion this is also quite absurd because, after all, they have regular meetings at which they analyze the results of their activities, discussing items that slipped by, and such matters. As far as *Novyi mir* is concerned, they were always forced to acknowledge that they were powerless.

Now I will consider at some length questions that appear quite self-evident to former Soviet writers and journalists but, I think, may not be altogether clear to an American audience. The procedure is as follows. The censors do not read the original manuscript. The editors send the manuscript to the printing shop; there it is set in type, and the galleys are sent to the censors. The censor expresses his observations; then the sheets are corrected and sent back to the censor, who makes sure that all of his observations have been considered and applies a stamp authorizing the printing of the manuscript. This still is not all, however. The issue goes to press, and when the first, signature issues are produced, they are sent back to Glavlit. Then another stamp is affixed, approving the issue for distribution. So you see what a many-staged system it is and how many sieves a manuscript must pass through.

The most important stage is when the censor begins the preliminary reading. This is a rank-and-file censor assigned to a given journal; he himself decides almost nothing. If some kind of cannon of a type not included on the approved list is mentioned in the work, he crosses it out. Or a certain factory may be described as producing a certain product, but one is not allowed to mention that, so the reference is marked for excision. If, however, something more serious is discussed, he will turn to his superior, to the assistant department head, or to the department head himself. If even *he* dares not decide the question, the matter will be passed on even higher, to the assistant head of all of Glavlit, or, in very exceptional cases, even to the director himself. I dealt with almost all of them daily on nearly every issue of *Novyi mir*, but not once was I in the august presence of the head of Glavlit and never even saw him. I do not know why — maybe because I am Jewish, or perhaps for some other reason.

Matters are even worse with military censorship. Publishing anything relating to the army was extraordinarily difficult. Tremendous excisions were made in the text. Why was this so? After all, when all is said and done, what military secrets could there be in a story about a war that was over long ago? The answer is that there are certain rules and regulations about writing that relate to such matters. Certain things may be criticized, others may not. I will cite a very early example. A film script was once printed — not in *Novyi mir*, and much earlier than the period I am discussing — of a documentary, *The Battle of Stalingrad*. Stalin read the script, made some corrections, and approved it. From that time on, a copy of this script lay on every censor's desk, and no matter what was written about Stalingrad, the censors checked to see whether or not it was presented the same way as in that script. It became the standard for how one must write about Stalingrad.

I want to emphasize that the entire nonideological sphere of Glavlit was molded into a stable, well-defined bureaucratic shape; this in turn was reflected in the manual on forbidden information that Glavlit publishes every few years. There everything is formulated very clearly and precisely. Matters are altogether different in the ideological sphere. In this case the Glavlit manual contains directives, like those that Suslov enumerated, but in an exceedingly general form; not as specific as, for instance, in tsarist times. It is precisely this lack of specific instructions that leaves Glavlit at an impasse when it deals with literary works. In these cases Glavlit is sometimes surprisingly powerless and unable to decide on a course of action.

All kinds of people work at Glavlit — some embittered, some mild, some intelligent, some dull — but they all share a common trait: a low level of cultivation and intellectual mediocrity. Frequently they are incapable even of formulating what it is they want from an author. Tvardovskii expressed himself on censorship in various ways: sometimes seriously, sometimes mockingly, and sometimes in a kind of paradoxical manner. For example, he once said, "What has happened? Before the revolution there was always a tradition that censors were professors at Moscow University. And who are they now?" Or he would say, "Give me a censor with a red pencil." I said, "Why, don't you have enough?" He answered, "No — let him use his pencil and go to hell! But he evidently can't even use a pencil!" (These comments applied to literary works and not to various blast furnaces, artillery, airplanes, and so forth.)

Solzhenitsyn gives the following example in his book, *The Oak and the Calf*, writing about Tvardovskii's discussion with Khrushchev concerning the need to abolish completely the censorship of literary works: "And Nikita heard him out quietly, as if he himself held similar views — or so it appeared to Tvardovskii. . . . Judging by his retelling of the conversation to the editorial staff, one can assume that he somehow projected his own views onto the silent Khrushchev." I must take exception to this because I know for certain that Khrushchev was not silent, and I will now repeat what he said. "Yes," he said. "There was a time when all foreign correspondents had to present their work to the press office of the Ministry of Foreign Affairs. We repealed this ordinance. And what happened? They began to tell fewer lies." That Khrushchev did not lift a finger to actually abolish censorship is another matter. Be that as it may, however, he did not keep silent, and Tvardovskii did not project anything onto him.

It is true that censorship functions are not always performed by censors, but this is one of the peculiarities of Soviet conditions. For example, I can tell you the history of a novella by Alexander Bek entitled *A New Assignment* (*Novoe naznachenie*). Originally it was called *Sshibka* (*Collision*). Tvardovskii had changed the title not out of substantive or semantic considerations but only because the original title did not sound right: in the first place, *Ssh*; and in the second, because it would look like a misprint. That is, someone would say that they had meant to print *Oshibka* (*The Mistake*), but the letter *o* had been distorted and looked like the letter *c* (Russian *s*). So he said, "No, no, we can't leave it this way. Not a single Russian will be able to pronounce it."

In this short novel the traits of what Djilas called "the new class"[4] were very vividly and convincingly depicted. Therefore it was necessary to shut the gates before this novel, not to release it. From Glavlit it was sent for consideration to the Central Committee apparatus, and there they came up with the following trick. The real-life model for the main protagonist could be guessed easily enough: it was one Taivasian, Minister of Metallurgical Industry. So they got hold of his wife — or, rather, his widow. She took offense on behalf of her late husband, who had been depicted inaccurately in the novel, and in the Central Committee apparatus they said, "Of course we would be happy to approve the novel, but we cannot offend her."

What did poor, unfortunate Bek — who, unquestionably, had been driven into a corner — do? He invented another character, introduced still another character into the novel, painted all in roseate hues — simply an angel in human form — and gave him the actual name of Ivan Fedorovich Taivasian. And he said, "Here you have Taivasian, and the other one has absolutely no relation to Taivasian." It did not help, however, and the novel appeared only outside the country. Bek was in the hospital dying of cancer. When he had literally only a few days left to live, the secretary of the Moscow organization of the Writers' Union, the notorious Il'in, came to the hospital and brought Bek a foreign edition of the novel. He showed it to him, let him hold it in his hands, and then took it back to the safe at the Writers Union. Be that as it may, I would like to note parenthetically that this was a humane act because, after all, even if only just before death, he did get to see his book.

It was said jokingly about Bek that here was a man who outsmarted himself, but he thought that he could outsmart others. He went to the authorities empowered to issue directives and said, "I do not understand how it is that my unpublished work is being circulated. Somehow copies are being made. I have no control over it. Do you know how it will end? The manuscript will find its way abroad and they will publish it there. What must be done to prevent such an occurrence? We must publish it here." But it did no good.[5]

During this conference there has been much talk about foreign books, or translations of foreign books. One should not think that the publication of foreign books is outside the realm of censorship: this is not true. What we are dealing with here is camouflage, a diversion. The fact is simply that books published by the Foreign Literature Press [Inostrannaia literatura] are not marked with the Glavlit stamp. A stamp is indeed applied in the production process, but unlike other books, it does not appear on the actual volume. This procedure has existed since the day that publishing house began operation. It was headed by a Central Committee employee, Boris Suchkov, and he realized that outside the country it would be thought that these books were not censored. Later he was arrested and exiled. Still later he was released and named director of the Institute of World Literature, but the procedure he introduced continues to this day. I did not think, however, that this stratagem would fool anyone outside the Soviet Union.

I would like to discuss another matter. Very often, to play it safe, the editors of a literary journal will send material first to the Central Committee's department of culture. If they approve, the editors include it in the issue. *Novyi mir* did not do this, except for two instances. The first case had to do with Solzhenitsyn's *One Day in the Life of Ivan Denisovich*, when it became clearly apparent that except for Khrushchev himself, no one could authorize publication. The second case involved Tvardovskii's poem, "Tërkin in the Hereafter" [*Tërkin na tom svete*].[6] It was Khrushchev himself who had banned the first version of the poem, and it was obvious then that no one but he could lift the ban.

To be fair, I want to give credit where credit is due. A writer by the name of Grigorii Svirskii was the first to speak up openly about censorship, loud and clear, at a meeting of Moscow writers in January 1968. He said, for example — I will quote only one of his remarks — "The writer is humiliated, robbed of what is most important: the right to express his innermost thoughts and feelings before the people."

In closing let me relate just one more story. One day I was walking along near the house I lived in at the time, and saw the assistant department head of one of the departments in Glavlit approaching me. We greeted each other. She asked, "And what are you doing these days?" I said, "I have retired." "Oh, then you'll have to write your memoirs." I shrugged and said, "But my memoirs will not be fit to print." You would think I had her there, but she answered, "Well, just don't write about *Novyi mir*!" So everything I have told you today, and everything I may write in the future about *Novyi mir*, was banned in advance in that conversation on the street. I shall end on that note.

Notes

1   OGPU: The Associated State Political Administration of the Council of People's Commissars (1922–1934). — ED.

2   Iurii Tynianov, 1896–1943. This story was published in 1930; it is about a nonexistent officer in the service of Paul I. For an English translation, see Iurii Tynianov, "Second Lieutenant Asfor," in Maurice Friedberg and Robert A. Maguire (eds.), *Russian Short Stories: A Bilingual Collection*, Vol. 2 (New York: Random House, 1965), pp.507–93. The story inspired Prokofiev's suite of the same name.

3   Published in 1966; Valentin Kataev, Soviet novelist and playwright, 1897–1986.

4   Suggesting the "revisionist" ideas of Milovan Djilas, Yugoslav Party and government official under Tito, imprisoned in the 1950s and 1960s for anti-Stalinist and liberal articles and books, such as *The New Class* (1957). — ED.

5   "This excellent novel about bureaucrats and the Communist 'nomenclature' . . . was announced for publication by *Novyi mir* in 1965 but was banned by the censors and never appeared in the Soviet Union. Circulated by Samizdat, it was finally printed in Germany in 1971." Marc Slonim, *Soviet Russian Literature: Writers and Problems 1917–1977*. Second rev. ed. (New York: Oxford University Press, 1977), p. 378. It was finally published in the USSR in 1986. — ED.

6   Anti-Stalinist satire, circulated in Moscow for two years before it was published in West Germany in 1963, then published in *Novyi mir* — see Slonim, *Soviet Russian Literature*, p. 396. — ED.

10

Censorship in the Theater

Alexander Gershkovich

The question of censorship in general, and of censorship in the theater in particular, has at least two aspects: censorship's struggle against art, and art's struggle with censorship. In Russia, and then in the Soviet Union, both had, and have, long and honorable traditions.

The first aspect of the problem — Soviet censorship's struggle against art — has been studied much, although still not exhaustively (every season brings a new "harvest") in foreign, especially English-language, scholarly and popular sources. Serious researchers like Ernest Simmons[1] and Maurice Friedberg,[2] basing their work on rich and hard-to-obtain sources, have written about it in detail. Friedberg's book *A Decade of Euphoria*[3] traces the censors' arbitrary treatment of Western European dramatic productions in the Soviet theater of the post-Stalin era. Mark Zaitsev[4] and Anna Tamarchenko[5] have published articles specifically on Soviet censorship of the theater, including detailed analyses of censorship of Soviet drama in the 1960s and 1970s.

Much less researched is the second aspect of the problem: how art, in particular theater, survives under censorship. How are genuinely meaningful works created, often despite censorship — works that stand out from among the censored pseudo-art? Such problems should be treated seriously and understood in their historical context as the consequence of the particular social conditions under which art has survived, because there was no alternative. Only with this understanding can we attempt a scholarly study of Soviet culture and of the growth of its self-consciousness. Here the researcher is inevitably faced with the question of the artist's self-supervision and self-expression in a socialist society as a means of survival in conditions of censorship.

The history of the Russian theater demonstrates that from its dawn it knew no freedom from censorship. Paradoxical as this may seem to an outsider, the Russian theater, especially during the Soviet period, has grown so accustomed to this misfortune that in all likelihood it could not conceive of life without it. Were one to abolish censorship, little would change for a while because of the ingrained self-censorship. The Soviet satirists Il'f and Petrov came up with an aphorism — it slipped into the papers in the 1930s, at the height of the Stalinist purges — that describes this situation wonderfully. They wrote that if you give sheep freedom of speech, they will bleat all the same. This aphorism has value not only in itself but also in terms of our discussion; it provides an analogy for the artist's self-expression in censored Soviet art.

What Il'f and Petrov called "obedient bleating" is, however, only part of the truth about censored Soviet art. The habit of creating under the constant, vigilant supervision of the "authorities" has produced, particularly in the best examples of Soviet dramatic art, another quality as well: the ability to express in the language of the theater that which is either forbidden or frowned upon in open discourse. And what is especially important for art is the special knack of the audience, at least its more sophisticated part, for interpreting concealed meanings and allusions, and its ability to understand and get to the substance of what the artist wanted to say while circumventing official censorship. As a result of this mutual understanding between actor and spectator — an understanding produced by social conditions during many performances in the Soviet theater by both the classical and the contemporary repertoire – there arises a special atmosphere of trust between the stage and the audience, a kind of secret conversation between the theater and the public. Those who accept the conditions of this game carry on a dialogue, as it were, over the head not only of the censor but also of the highest ideological authorities.

What is at issue here is the special nature of the theatrical spectacle. One actor can perform an author's text one way, another actor another way, today one way, tomorrow an entirely different way, by adding a mimicked comment or a gesture, so that a word takes on a different or even opposite meaning.

Let me cite several very simple instances. Following the example of Stanislavskii, the first to play the role, actors of the Moscow Art Theater school pronounce Satin's famous retort in Gorky's play *The Lower Depths* ("Man—there is a proud ring to that word!") with passion, like a vow of respect for man. This gesture, of course, completely suited the censors of the demagogic Stalinist period. In our time, however, in the early 1970s, an actor in the Moscow workshop theater Sovremennik, Evgenii Evstigneev, revised this convention. Having, in addition to talent, a sense of social awareness, he put an entirely different, ironic meaning into Gorky's words. Unmasking the demagogy of the vagabond leader, he uttered the phrase almost in passing, his head hung low, while lacing up his shoes. Everyone understood what he meant to say by this, including angered guardians of ideological "purity."

An even more instructive incident took place at the Taganka Theater during a production of *The House on the Embankment* by Iurii Trifonov. I was present at the rehearsals. Depicting the atmosphere of Yezhov's reign of terror in 1937, the director introduced a chorus of Young Pioneers who recited pieces on the theme "Oh, how good it is to live in the Soviet land." One of the boys, choking as he spoke, read some praises of People's Commissar Yezhov, the chief of the secret police. Of course, at the dress rehearsal the censor protested: "Why stir up the past?" To save the show, the theater made a concession. The poem was read just up to the name of Yezhov, which rhymed with the preceding line. Then the microphone was turned off and the actor on stage slapped his hand across his mouth — to loud laughter from the entire hall. This proved even more pointed, although formally the censor's demand had been met.

In February 1983 the American Repertory Theater in Cambridge, Massachusetts, performed director Andrei Serban's questionable, and by no means perfect, production of Chekhov's *Three Sisters*, and to packed houses at that (Serban, by the way, is a student of the Russian and Romanian school of theater), and nobody seemed to mind. At that same time performances of the same play in Moscow's best theaters, the Sovremennik and the Taganka Comedy, provoked the severest Party criticism in the newspaper *Moskovskaia pravda*.[6] The Moscow performances enjoyed great success with the public, and tickets were very hard to get, so there was no question of "economic censorship." Indeed, it was precisely this circumstance that doomed these productions. Had the performances been poorly attended, had there been no way to fill the theaters, one doubts that the ideological authorities' wrath would have come down so hard on them. No one would have called them pessimistic, or contrary to the spirit of Chekhov, and no one would have thought of demanding their removal from the repertoire as "ideologically unsatisfactory." Such is the difference between ideological and economic censorship in the free and the unfree world.

The example of the production of Chekhov's *Three Sisters* almost simultaneously in the American Repertory Theater in Cambridge and at the Taganka in Moscow, both of which I saw, offers a rare opportunity to compare the theater in free and totalitarian societies, and to see what different paths they follow while moving, in essence, in the same artistic direction. I shall deliberately put aside here the cognitive aspect of the productions and examine only the *effect* of the two productions. After all, it is precisely in the theatrical form of the production, in its external style and form, that one can make an author's text support one or another idea. The task is made easier by the fact that director Andrei Serban, to his credit, does not conceal his personal admiration for the directing style of his Moscow colleague, Iurii Liubimov, and the indebtedness to Liubimov of his own productions. Following is a large segment of an interview with Andrei Serban, conducted in November 1982, at the opening of *Three Sisters* in Cambridge:

> Now there is a fresh new production at the Taganka Theater in Moscow. It is a *Three Sisters* that cuts totally away from the Chekhovian tradition; the actors are completely removed from the heavy Chekhovian mood. They act very differently. They are not elegant people; they are not refined characters. They are coarse, impulsive. They shout and scream, and feel frustration, but in a different way. They are, in a way, much closer to the way life is now under the communist system. They express the lack of civilization and the spiritual poverty which exists in the Soviet Union today. They have chosen to show the situation of their present lives rather than an imaginary look at how people behaved one hundred years ago. Who knows or cares anyway how people were one hundred years ago? It's just not the Chekhov you expected to see when you bought your ticket.

Therefore the critics for *Pravda* were saying, "Well, this is not Chekhov!" Yes, because it doesn't follow the tradition. Bravo for their courage![7]

Serban's performance, in his own words, was "not just about Russians, but a performance about all of us, about man in general, about questions in his life everywhere today." I can attest to the fact that in his own way, Serban achieved his goal. Judging by the attentive silence in the hall and the applause at the end, the American spectator apparently understood this fact. The cultivated audience of students and professors at Harvard was not disturbed that the performance contained little of the Russia that a spectator even slightly familiar with Russian literature could recognize. To begin with, the external appearance of the production suggested that the action was not necessarily set in Russia. The lifeless, mirror-surfaced marble floor resembled Versailles; there were two slanting rows of Viennese chairs; heavy velvet curtains partitioned the stage lengthwise into two arenas; the granite-gray wall of the horizon recalled an impregnable medieval castle; and all of this, including the huge black piano, produced a sense of a conscious displacement of the time and action of the play. In Serban's performance only one thing pointed to the Chekhovian and Russian theme: the phonograph on the bookcase at the front of the stage on the right. Despite the Chekhovian rule — if there's a gun on stage, it must fire a shot — it sat idle throughout the play.

The actors, especially the men, were dressed in baggy black and gray clothing. They reminded one of some sort of strange, disheveled birds, slipping in different directions over the smooth floor on thin little legs while they flapped their wings in confusion. They spoke Chekhov's lines boldly and heavily, exaggerating them. Because of this Chekhov's captivating humor was lost, as was the concealed meaning on which, in fact, the play rests. Even Doctor Chebutykin's retort, "Balzac was born in Berdichev," which in any Soviet theater is met with laughter, was out of place and got no reaction in the hall: it fell flat! It's true that in the American theater there were few laughs too when, in the fire scene, the same Chebutykin appeared without his pants, and when the Russian peasant Ferapont, serving as a messenger, chirped like a bird and shuffled along in his big felt boots like a man with hemorrhoids. Nor did the audience react when the clever colonel, Vershinin, once played with such brilliance by Stanislavskii, flitted about on the stage like a little monkey, bowed repeatedly, kissed every hand, spoke in a phony voice, behaved mischievously, and unambiguously pursued not only Masha but also her younger sister, as though carrying out his soldierly duty to chase every skirt.

All this played for an entire season in the center of liberal America and produced good returns at the box office, and it did not even occur to anyone to "ban" this slander on Chekhov, this deviation from the Chekhovian-Moscow Art Theater canon, this ideological jumble of misconceived innovation and decrepit theatrical routine. Nobody cared — not the municipality, or the Republican Party, the Democratic Party, or the independent press. It was a matter of taste, a matter of the conscience and imagination of the artist, and of no one else. There was some press coverage — not much, it is true — and, of course, it was favorable.[8]

At this same time in Moscow another performance of *Three Sisters*, produced by director Iurii Liubimov at the Taganka Comedy Theater, was ostracized. What had the Moscow director of the experimental Russian company managed to make of Chekhov's text? What type of production was he able to put together, while circumventing the censor, that could elicit dubious associations among the contemporary public, thus evoking the wrath of the authorities?

When the spectator has been seated in the comfortable chairs of the Taganka Theater's new hall, which ascends in a gently sloping amphitheater, the light slowly begins to dim, and from somewhere on the street outside the sounds of a military brass band are heard. The performance begins. A regiment is departing from a small provincial town somewhere in the remote Russian countryside, and in this Russian backwater life is dying out. Three charming Russian women come to the front of the stage and, seeing off the soldiers, say goodbye to their youth. Their dreams carry them away to Moscow, where, it seems to them, a different, intelligent, interesting life exists.

At this point, from the right, in front of astonished spectators who had no idea of the new hall's structural resources, a broad panel set into the brickwork of the wall has begun to descend slowly. At first a small part of the late afternoon Moscow sky appears, then the heads, shoulders, figures of the soldiers in the band, standing in the square outside. The old military march blares forth from the tubas and trumpets ever louder, more joyously, and with increasing fervor. By now the panel in the wall has been lowered completely, and everyone in the hall is stunned by the indescribable beauty revealed through the opening in the wall. There before the eyes of modern Muscovites, who have come to the theater at the end of a day's exhausting routine, is the real, untheatrical, but all the same fairy tale-like Moscow. The city is bathed in the rays of the setting spring sun. A small church of white stone stands in the distance, on Taganka hill. There are no red banners on that hill and no placards proclaiming unity of the Communist Party and the people — that is, Taganka hill looks just the way it did in the days of Chekhov, Dostoevsky, Gogol, and Pushkin. Because of this Moscow looks so serene and filled with magic when seen from a theater auditorium during these few moments, and one cannot turn one's glance away from it. The feeling for the city that filled Chekhov's three sisters to bursting becomes painfully clear.

This unexpectedly lofty beginning immediately had the spectator thinking about the contemparaneity of Chekhov's drama. The audience began to look forward to new revelations that evening, just as the beautiful image of old Moscow had been a revelation for them. Everyone expected something else of the same sort from the resourceful director, some miracle that might suddenly change something in the fate of Chekhov's heroines and, perhaps, in their (the present spectators') own fate. There was a desire to help Chekhov's sisters realize their dreams to live where they wish and as they wish. They wanted happiness so much, they hid their anguish from others so touchingly, so devoted themselves to youth and gaiety and silly jokes, and they tried so sincerely to make the best of the parting with their friends from the regiment, who were going off somewhere to the sounds of the military march! No, they certainly deserved better than what the pitiless realist Chekhov had in store for them in the play.

But even the all-powerful theater can do nothing for them. It *merely* could let us feel sharply the true cost of hopeless dreams in Russia. Through the special language of the scenes of the play, without words, without commentary, the theater was saying through its performance that life, in spite of everything, is, of course, good, and that Moscow, with the little church on the distant hill, is, of course, beautiful, and that there is no one on Russian soil who would not like to live there, and that, in the end, then, everything in Russia ends inevitably in tears because there is nothing one can do and nothing can be changed.

Then it became clear why the Taganka Theater turned to an old Chekhov play in today's quite un-Chekhovian Moscow, why in the performance the military band made up of contemporary Russian boys from a regiment of military musicians, dressed up that evening in uniforms of the period of Nicholas II, played so loudly, so infectiously, and with such astonishing spirit. Finally, it became apparent why Iurii Liubimov, a theatrical director, revealed to us in the crack in the theater wall not the gray and gloomy Moscow we all knew, where we lived, loved, and worked, but showed us instead a picture of a Moscow that exists today only on advertising posters, and, perhaps, in our inflamed imaginations. That was Moscow washed by the spring rain and the sun, a Moscow with a little gold-domed church on a distant hill.

This story has a typical Soviet ending: the theatrical presentation of Chekhov's gold-domed Moscow, which was in such contrast to today's bright red Moscow, was subjected to severe criticism in the Party press.[9] The Directorate for Artistic Affairs of the Moscow City Executive Committee (its chief, Boris Pokarzhevskii, was himself a former actor) recommended insistently that it be shown less often — no more than once a month — or, even better, that it be dropped altogether from the repertoire.

One can say with confidence that literary and theatrical censorship came into being simultaneously with new Russian literature and theater. They were twin sisters. It happened in the time of Pushkin and Nicholas I. Through Pushkin Russia proclaimed: "Hail the sun and curse the darkness!" and on Tsar Nicholas's brow, in the words of the historian S. M. Solov'ev, it was easy to read, "Stop them, seize them, destroy them!" "A despot by nature," Solov'ev wrote of Nicholas I, "he had an instinctive aversion for any movement, for any expression of individual freedom or independence. Nicholas loved only the soulless movements of the masses of soldiers to commands. He was a terrible leveller. He instinctively hated education as something that raised the people up and endowed them with a capacity to think and form opinions, while he himself was the personification of the command 'No arguments!' "[10]

It is significant that the years of the blossoming of Russian literature — in the years of Griboedov, Pushkin, and Lermontov — were also the years of bloom of official legalized censorship. One was not conceivable without the other. This strange alliance was enshrined in public consciousness as something perfectly natural. Nicholas I's decree of June 25, 1826, on the formation of the special political police, or "gendarmes," with its head, Adjutant General Benckendorff, and his assistant, von Foch, the director of the chancery's Third Section, made provision for the censorship of dramatic works and theater reviews.[11] Benckendorff paid special attention to the latter, to which his resolution attests: "Henceforth, all writing pertaining to the theater must be *shown to me.*"[12] This can hardly be explained by his exceptional weakness for favorite actresses, as certain researchers assume. Instructions that have come down to us from the chief of gendarmes to editors of journals on how to write theater reviews attest to more fundamental goals. "His Majesty," he wrote to Court Minister Volkonskii in 1843, "was pleased to charge me to inform Your Highness that reviews of theatrical works are to confine themselves to praise or *moderate criticism* of the play and of the quality of the acting, and must not relate to history, which the critic, *quite unnecessarily,* joined to the subject, which should not stray from the sphere of the purely theatrical." The chief of gendarmes proposed to take appropriate measures to "keep theatrical criticism within its fitting and proper bounds."[13]

The attempt to separate theatrical criticism from life, to lock it into a tight circle of purely theatrical interests, attests to the special danger that the authorities saw in the theater as an unusually effective form of influence on the minds and attitudes of society. It was another matter that Russian critics managed to get around these artificial barriers. But at what price?

Pushkin, in the first chapter of *Eugene Onegin*, provides a broad, clear view of the theatrical struggle of his time, although encoded entirely in wonderful and melodious verse:

> There Ozerov in national audits
> Reaped ample toll of tears and plaudits
> With young Semyonova to share;
> Corneille's majestic muse was there
> By our Katenin newly rendered;
> There did the mordant Shakhovskoy
> There to Did'lot were laurels tendered,
> There, in the backdrops' shady maze,
> I whiled away my youthful days.[14]

Who today, except for a small group of specialists, can interpret from these lines the dramatic struggle that was in fact under way in the Russian theater of that time? One Soviet scholar, the writer Iurii Tynianov, offered an interpretation of these lines[15] from which it is clear that Pushkin combined in one stanza notions and names that no one of his day could have linked. Mentioning Ozerov and Shakhovskoy in a single breath in the 1820s required greater courage than linking Stanislavskii and Meyerhold in the 1920s. In the 19th century everybody was aware of the mortal hatred between Ozerov and Shakhovskoy, and in Pushkin's days public consensus had it that Shakhovskoy had actually been responsible for the death of his theatrical adversary.

Adding to this picture the hostile artistic camps, Pushkin linked the actress Semënova — a court favorite — with the dramatist and critic Katenin, who was exiled from St. Petersburg in 1822 because he booed her work in the theater and loudly called for the romantic actor Karatygin, her antagonist. Furthermore, it was no mere accident that this kaleidoscope of theatrical passions also included Didelot, the renowned St. Petersburg ballet master, known at that time for his flexible "nonpartisan" position in literary and theatrical polemics.

It happened in Russia that public opinion recognized censorship as a necessary and even useful partner of literature and the arts. The ranks of censors of the reign of Nicholas I included leading writers of prose and verse such as Senkovskii, Aksakov, Viazemskii, Glinka, Tiutchev, Nikitenko, Ochkin, and others. Pushkin, only 25, appealed to the guardians of literature:

> Have no fear, I have no wish, enticed by fancy,
> to defame the censors with risky abuse —
> *What London needs, Moscow is not ready for.*
> I know what sort of writers we have:
> Their thoughts are not constrained by the censor's grip,
> And the pure soul before you is innocent.[16]

This was written by Pushkin, a great poet who prized freedom above all else. What is there to say about the others? The duality of consciousness of the Russian writer with respect to freedom of creation was expressed best of all by the court poet Zhukovskii, to whom Russian literature is greatly indebted for his mediation with the tsar's court. When the *Moscow Telegraph*, a progressive journal, was shut down, Zhukovskii stated his position this way: "I am glad that the *Telegraph* is banned, although I regret that they banned it." Pushkin also approved of the banning of Russia's first democratic journal, for he considered it impertinent to "advocate Jacobin ideas right under the government's nose."[17]

It is interesting in this connection to mention one more not altogether unimportant detail. The editor of the *Telegraph*, Nicholas Polevoi, succeeded in navigating his journal through censorship's underwater reefs only because of his diplomatic skills. Polevoi was among the first to fathom Russia's mechanism of control over literature and the arts. He understood that behind the official censors there were higher governmental interests, which were in turn protected by the secret police. Polevoi established close ties with the police and was thus long protected from harassment by official censors. In 1829, vowing his loyalty to the government, Polevoi appealed to the chief of the Moscow district police (gendarmes), the all-powerful General Volkov, whom Nicholas I valued highly, with a request to place the *Telegraph* under the general's personal patronage. "To achieve the proper benefit for society," wrote Polevoi to Volkov, "before submitting the articles to the usual censors, let me henceforth submit them . . . to a special censorship, delivering them to Your Excellency for consideration." This progressive literary man concluded his letter with this passage:

> In all of this, I trust Your Excellency, will discern a sincere wish to produce, within my abilities, writings that are useful and yet supportive of public order. As a Russian who ardently loves the glory of the monarch, who sees in him not only my sovereign, but a great and brilliant man of our times, I am certain that his enlightened mind knows and values everything, even the smallest means of affecting the nation under his rule, in conformity with his wise plans.[18]

In requesting for himself a *double*, especially thorough censorship, and in his voluntary assumption of a terrible burden, Polevoi, however paradoxical this may seem, essentially freed himself from the struggle with the nagging and petty surveillance of tyrannical regular censorship. One readily discerns in Polevoi's behavior a model for the struggle with state supervision over the arts that was to be waged over a century later by another Moscow editor, Aleksandr Tvardovskii, who, by going over the heads of the censors, enlisted the support of a "higher authority" for the publication of Solzhenitsyn's *One Day in the Life of Ivan Denisovich* and other subversive works of officially censored Soviet literature.[19]

One must note, however, that not everyone in Russian literature could play a double game like this. To serve two gods — art and censorship, freedom and the powers that be — was something that a man of talent could do, although with difficulty, but a genius could not. What Zhukovskii, Faddei Bulgarin, or Nestor Kukol'nik were able to do, Pushkin, Griboedov, and most of all Lermontov and Gogol could not, even had they wanted to. Clearly there were attempts on their part to adapt to the censorship, and these attempts are well known, but each time they ended sadly.

Even Pushkin rejoiced, like a child, that the tsar himself, Nicholas I, had agreed to be his censor and imagined that this would be beneficial to him. In a letter of March 7, 1826, Pushkin vowed to Zhukovskii that in the future he would keep secret — that is, not express — his own views and opinions, and "would not contradict the generally accepted order and requirements." If Pushkin could say that, then how could one speak of freedom of creation in Russian art?

"Who respects us, the truly inspired bards, in a land where value is assessed strictly according to the number of one's decorations and serfs?" Griboedov wrote in a letter to his close friend, S. Begichev, on December 9, 1826. Griboedov, the author of *Woe from Wit*, a brilliant diplomat and state councillor in the service of Nicholas I, despaired of seeing his comedy in print or on the stage. "It is torture to be an ardent dreamer in a land of eternal snows. The cold penetrates your bones, the indifference to people of talent."[20]

Woe from Wit [*Gore ot uma*], completed in 1824, circulated around the country in thousands of manuscript copies. Everyone in Russia at all interested in literature knew it by heart, but it was published first in German, in Revel,[21] in 1831. Not until two years later was it published in Russia, with major excisions, and staged for the first time only many years after the author's death. Pushkin, too, did not see a single one of his plays on stage: *Boris Godunov* was first produced in 1880, the *Little Tragedies* even later. Lermontov did not live to see his plays published. Neither *The Spaniards* nor *Masquerade* met the censors' requirements. Miraculously, Gogol's *Inspector General* made it to the stage, despite the censors, owing to the goodwill of Nicholas I, who, with handouts of money and other maneuvers, attempted to take the talented satirist in hand. Nicholas was more successful with Gogol than he had been with Pushkin.

It is telling, however, that when Gogol died in 1852, the police directorate — which (through either ignorance or scorn) in official documents referred to the writer as Gogel — did all it could to draw as little attention as possible to his demise. Sensing that the government saw in Gogol a dangerous critic of Russian conditions, feeling no sadness at the author's death, and perhaps even glad to be relieved of the worry about any new comedies he may write, Zakrevskii, the governor general of Moscow, ordered that nothing be written about Gogol "other than with special care and strictness."[22] The young Ivan Turgenev, shaken by Gogol's death, wrote an obituary in which he called him "a great man, in whom we take pride as one of our glories." The censorship committee, headed by Musin-Pushkin, did not let that through, considering it "inappropriate to write about Gogol in such extravagant terms." When, despite the St. Petersburg censor, Turgenev had his article published in Moscow, Nicholas I personally ordered that the obstinate author be placed under arrest for a month "and sent home to reside under surveillance."[23] The censorship celebrated its Pyrrhic victory! From this it was only a short step to a situation in which ignorant, dim-witted officials could be found sitting in the censorship office permitting themselves comments on poets' manuscripts like the following:

Author: "To catch the heavenly smile on your lips . . ."
Censor: "A woman is unworthy of having her smile called heavenly."
Author: "You understood the desires of my soul."
Censor: "Forbidden! One may not discuss the soul."
Author: "One tender glance of yours is worth more to me than the attention of the whole universe."
Censor: "Forbidden! There are higher authorities in the universe that must be dearer to us than a woman's glance."[24]

And so on.

The above unavoidably leads to the question: "In view of such intolerable conditions of censorship, how was the great Russian literature and art of the 19th century, in its best years, created? Can it be that censorship is a good thing, like wolves in the forest, eliminating the sick and the weak, and forcing the strong to train their muscles, reactions, and skills in the struggle to survive? Perhaps that is how it should be, if we put life in human society on a par with life among wild beasts. In the civilized world there are also such things as reason, religion, education, ideals, a sense of beauty. All this cannot be so easily cast aside without descending to an inhuman level. And this is understood by those who create art, and by those who stand in their way.

Russian literature is strong precisely because it has managed to survive and bear fruit under incredibly difficult climatic conditions. It can be compared not with an oak but with a supple, white-trunked birch of the northern forests. It has bent branches and leaves quivering with every gust of harsh wind, but it has not broken. It has stretched up toward the sun, toward the light, toward the lofty heavens — even though they are gray as a soldier's uniform.

Pushkin, upon completing *Boris Godunov*, clapped his hands in delight and shouted, "Well done, Pushkin, well done, you son of a bitch!" He wanted very much to write a loyal "comedy," to earn the forgiveness of the tsar, who had exiled him to Mikhailovskoe for infringing on the censorship's rules. However, after reading the finished *Boris Godunov* aloud to himself, he saw that poetic inspiration had prevailed, and he wrote to Prince Peter Viazemskii in November 1825: "Zhukovskii says that the tsar will forgive me for the tragedy — hardly, my friend. Although it was written in good faith, there was no way that I could hide my ears completely under an idiot's cap. They stick out!"[25] Pushkin fought for five years for the publication of his *Boris*, on which, he felt, depended the fundamental reform of the entire system of Russian drama, but Benckendorff was unyielding. Cunningly, Nicholas I recommended to Pushkin that he rework the "comedy" into a novel "in the spirit of Walter Scott." In Russian this meant less politics and "lofty matter" and more simple entertainment.

Nicholas I's attention could not stop an anonymous reviewer, who submitted his opinion to the police directorate, from making an "observation" (the reviewer, as was later revealed, was the notorious Faddei Bulgarin): "The spirit of the whole work is monarchical, for nowhere have there been introduced dreams about freedom, as in other of this author's works, and only one place is objectionable in a political sense: the people cling to the imposter precisely because they consider him the scion of an ancient royal line."[26] The discussion was, for the most part, about the final rejoinder in *Boris Godunov*, which, in Pushkin's clean copy submitted to the censors, sounded not at all the way we know it in the definitive text. Near the end of the act, the people shouted a greeting to the new tsar — "Long live Tsar Dmitrii Ivanovich!" — forgetting that several scenes earlier they had shouted the same thing to another tsar — Godunov, Dmitrii's antagonist. Pushkin seemed to be saying with this that the people's faith in their tsars was fickle and transient. Nicholas was not such a fool as to miss the meaning of the poet's allusion, and he turned very stubborn.

Exhausted by struggle with the censors, Pushkin finally entrusted the matter of the publication of *Boris Godunov* to the court poet Zhukovskii, giving him carte blanche, and then left St. Petersburg. Zhukovskii adroitly took up the matter, and *Boris Godunov* was published by late 1830. It bore no indication of the censors' authorization, as it usually appeared, but the vague formula "with the permission of the government."[27] Of the major changes in the printed text, compared with the author's original, there was one that was striking, one whose origin is still unknown. In place of the people's final rejoinder, the greeting to the new tsar, was printed in boldface, "The people keep silent."

Whose correction was this? Pushkin's? Zhukovskii's? Nicholas's? Would it be accurate to suppose that it belonged to all three? I have expressed my ideas on this in a separate article. Something else is more important for our discussion here: How did Pushkin react to such an unexpected ending to his play, an ending — no matter how brilliant the idea may have been — that changed the tragedy's entire meaning?

Pushkin pretended that nothing had happened. He even seemed content with the turn of events and from Moscow wrote Benckendorff a letter that was clearly intended for Nicholas I. This letter is worth reproducing in its entirety, all the more because Soviet sources, for understandable reasons, do not like to cite it:

> My Dear Sir Aleksandr Khristoforovich!
>
> It was with a feeling of profound gratitude that I received the gracious judgement of His Majesty the Emperor regarding my historical play. Written during the reign of the previous tsar, *Boris Godunov* owes its appearance not only to personal patronage, which His Majesty bestowed upon me, *but to the freedom boldly given by the monarch to Russian writers* at a time and under circumstances when any other government would have tried to inhibit and shackle the printing of books.
>
> Permit me sincerely to thank Your Excellency, as well, as someone of the greatest good will and as a man who has always displayed such indulgent concern for me.
>
> With deepest respect and complete devotion—*I am*, Sir, the humble servant of Your Excellency.
>
> Aleksandr Pushkin
> Moscow, January 18,
> 1831[28]

Everything in this letter — both the exaggerated flattery of Nicholas as the greatest champion of freedom of speech and of the press, and the solemn Church Slavonic locution "I am" in the expression of devotion and respect for the brutal chief of gendarmes (it does not figure at all in the lexicon of Pushkin's language) — pointed again and again to the poet's mockery of the high-ranking censors whom he managed to get by. At the same time, however, this surprising letter also demonstrated that even Pushkin accepted the rules of the game; that the singer of freedom believed in the necessity and inevitability of censorship in Russia, of the powers of the state over the artist. He believed in it and he excelled at evading it. Later another great poet, Nikolai Nekrasov, formulated this destiny of Russian art in a famous couplet. He gave this advice on censorship to his literary colleagues: "Move the action to Pisa / And save the whole puffy novel."

From a recognition of the necessity for the various governmental forms of censorship, it was only one step to the reflex of self-censorship by the artist and to the voluntary implanting of censorship in one's own artistic environment. From here one more step led to spying denunciations of all sorts, as a kind of civic valor. The Soviet system developed and made wide use of this innate defect in Russian literature. It could not have been otherwise.

After the intoxicating victory of the October Revolution and the first years of the "hangover," Russian literature and the arts discovered with bitter consternation that they were falling into even greater dependence on the state, on the censors, than they had in the 19th century, and even more so than in the first decade of the 20th century, when autocracy was shaken. Not only was the censors' mark of Cain not done away with but, quite to the contrary, was gradually perfected by the Leninist state. It strove, in Vasilii Grossman's apt observation, to "turn prominent cultural figures into lackeys from the state's servants' quarters."[29]

Russian theater of the Soviet period (this formulation seems to me more accurately to express its essence than the concept "Soviet theater") has for more than 60 years — during the lives of two generations — lived and worked under conditions of most rigid censorship, incomparably more severe than that in theaters of Europe and America. It is, in my view, not only these conditions that should be studied; not only the tragic way in which the Russian theater gradually lost its former strength, when the Moscow of Stanislavskii and Meyerhold served as a theatrical Mecca; not only the way in which its world-famous masters — Meyerhold, Tairov, Mikhoels, Dikii, Okhlopkov, Akimov, and then, too, Vysotskii — were put out of action; how they, hanging their heads or holding them high in proud defiance, left their native theaters. Most of all, perhaps, such studies are necessary to teach posterity how and why this theater remained alive and managed to preserve its magical power over the heart. After all, it is not by chance that with every change of power in the Kremlin the ideological priests first of all get down to tightening the theatrical "screws," as happened in the first months after the arrival of Andropov, who started his reign, like Nicholas I in his time, by forbidding the production of Pushkin's *Boris Godunov*.

The circle of obstinate masters of the Russian stage who search for self-expression in art despite the censors, and who resist the vigilant surveillance of the state, is now small. There are perhaps one or two innovative directors in Leningrad, three or four in Moscow, and about a dozen out in the provinces, where there are more than 600 theaters. There are another hundred or so of truly creative actors out of the 30,000-strong army of Soviet players. However, those Western critics who have given the Russian theater up for dead before its time, thinking that under Soviet censorship there is no room for nonconformist art nor can there be any, are deeply mistaken; and they are wrong to believe there are no grounds to expect new discoveries from the Russian theater.

The life, work, and posthumous surge in fame of Vladimir Vysotskii, whose funeral on July 28, 1980, turned into a spontaneous national referendum for an earthy, independent Russian theater, inspired new faith.[30] The millions of followers of Vysotskii's art all over the country and at all levels — from top to bottom, especially among the 20-year-olds, including the shaved-headed air assault troops longing for their homeland in alien

Afghanistan (their folklore has recently been published) — confirm that this art is full of life. The circle of artists who variously defined their independence from the censors is narrow now. It is important, however, not because of its numbers but because of the silent support of its audience and of fellow artists. This circle, moreover, has the ability to contract and then expand at the necessary moment, pumping vital, warm blood into the numbed veins of the Russian theater.

Strange as it may seem at first glance, in this pulsation of the theater, terrorized by the censors, in its adaptability to Soviet conditions of existence, the theater reveals not only its weakness but its strength. Of major import have been the Russian theater's centuries of experience of simultaneous conflict and accommodation with the censors, discussed above. "If even Pushkin endured censorship, made peace with it as an unavoidable evil, what then can we do?" This is more or less how many Soviet stage artists think.

It is well known that theater is not only an aural art but also a visual one. It expresses itself not only in words but also in images, and therefore has greater latitude in commenting about its time, even under totalitarian regimes, than the printed word. Monitoring it successfully is more difficult and troublesome, for the art of the actor lives for one fleeting instant, for one unrepeatable moment, while he is on stage and then it disappears from the stage with him. Soviet theatrical censorship was faced with a difficult task. How could complete control be organized? You cannot plant "your man" in the audience at every performance — something which, by the way, is not ruled out and has precedents in the Russian theater. Griboedov has these lines about the theater: "Here, in the dark, scoundrels are lurking, lying in wait for a word and ready to bring destruction with their denunciations." Soviet ideological censorship perfected this system through its own methods and made theatrical control complete and infallible. After organizing an entire network of "selection" boards, "art" councils, and public "viewings," it cunningly created a situation in which the directors, actors, and theater critics themselves became the censors for one another: you for me, and I for you. In the Soviet Union a practice of total theatrical surveillance was worked out, one that has been in effect legally for many years.

How does this cunning system work and who really stands behind it? Let us examine, for example, the case of Professor B. Rostotskii. Besides his main work in the State Institute of Dramatic Art, where he lectured on the history of Soviet theater, he was for many years the section chief for socialist countries at the USSR Ministry of Culture's Art History Institute. Professor Rostotskii was also a permanent member of the editorial board of the journal *Teatr* — the main publication of the aforementioned ministry and of the Soviet Writers Union — and a member of many other boards and editorial boards. Listing them all would be a superhuman task. In addition to his many positions, the professor was also well known throughout Moscow in one other capacity. Everyone knew that this quite intelligent, rosy-cheeked, and nimble little man, who was always fashionably dressed, had close ties to the censorship authorities and served as sort of an intermediary between actors and directors and the officials in the other governmental institutions. His supreme credo was that the basis for the success of the Soviet theater was the "wise leadership of the Communist Party."[31] So as not to be bothered by unnecessary uncertainties — it's always more convenient to have your own "familiar" spy — all the theaters and theatrical editors preferred to invite Rostotskii to participate in their work. It is possible that this special function of his was in fact his main mission in life. Such was B. Rostotskii, overseeing order in the Soviet theater. And he was not alone. Others like him are everywhere, in any city, in any college and research center, on any newspaper, in any theater, in every institution.

Theatrical censorship differs from other kinds in that it is not performed by invisible people without names or faces who sit somewhere in basements or in attics, or the devil knows where else behind closed doors. It is accomplished by entirely real people who are well known — often even respected — in the theater world, people who consider themselves specialists not only in theatrical matters but also in psychology, in theater politics, and in diplomacy. What is most surprising is that often they are in fact precisely that.

An excellent portrayal of the workings of this special Soviet system of control over artistic creativity was given by Aleksandr Galich, when he recounted how his play, *Sailor's Silence* [*Matrosskaia tishina*], was banned from production at the Sovremennik theater workshop in 1956 after Party and art community representatives attended one of its dress rehearsals. Consider the following:

In the auditorium of the Palace of Culture the largest group — about ten people — was a group of administrators from the Art Theater, and some minor officials from the Directorate of Culture. . . . Heading the group, in a well-tailored suit, was the important-looking Aleksandr Vasil'evich Solodovnikov. Not a stupid man, but decidedly petty, he . . . served and waited on the powers that be with such diligence that, by going too far, he would every so often commit some sort of blunder, and then he would disappear for a while . . . only to surface again as director of the Art Theater, or the Bolshoi, the Malyi, the Committee for Artistic Affairs, the Ministry of Culture. . . . Off to the side, completely apart from everyone else, head thrown back and attentively examining something on the ceiling, sat Georgii Aleksandrovich Tovstonogov, artistic director of Leningrad's Gorkii Drama Theater. It was decidedly incomprehensible how and why he had come to this dress rehearsal, although he would be the one to utter the fatal sentence that Solodovnikov would make use of. . . . A genuinely gifted person, Tovstonogov had achieved a leading position in the theater world because of his talent, energy, and even a certain amount of courage. But it is one thing to make it to the top, and it is quite another to stay there.

(At this point I will skip a large section and cite the concluding part of the performance's discussion, in which the participation in World War II of boys with Jewish names was recounted. That was the real reason the performance was banned.) Galich continued:

> We returned to the hall and took our seats. Tovstonogov, who, as before, sat off to the side, suddenly turned around and, across several empty rows that separated us, said to me in a low but distinct voice, so that his words were clearly heard by everyone, "No, those kids can't bring it off! For the time being this play is beyond them! Get it?!"

> Solodovnikov looked at Tovstonogov attentively, his eyes slightly screwed up. On his impassive, commanding face there was some semblance of thought. The phrase had been found! Unintentionally, Tovstonogov had uttered the mercifully elusive formula. Nothing will have to be explained. Nothing will have to be banned. In the end, it's not a bad thing that, as part of their training, the drama school students worked a little bit on a script that is unacceptable. But now we must look for an appropriate, life-affirming drama. Thank you, comrades! Thanks for the work, comrades! Onward and upward, comrades! Solodovnikov blurts out all this behind the scenes, after the end of the performance. Then he shakes my hand, shakes Efremov's hand, smiles once again, gratefully, to everyone who took part in the performance, and quickly, without allowing any questions, leaves. And that's the end of it![32]

The legitimate question arises, what is behind all this absurdity? Is it possible that Solodovnikov, who took part in his time in the persecution of Meyerhold, and who today is still prosperous and successful, and who gives himself up to lyrical reminiscences ("We Were Young Then" — see his piece in the book, *Teatral'nye stranitsy* [*Theatre Pages*], Moscow, 1979), as well as Tovstonogov, the universally recognized master of the stage and diplomacy, did all of this on their own initiative?

The late Galich performed a great service for Soviet art when he revealed the real reason his performance had been banned. He continued his story: The next day he was invited to the Central Committee on Staraia Ploshchad', where, in the office of Comrade Sokolova, who was in charge of the ideological department, he was given a frank explanation for the banning of the performance. Comrade Sokolova said, "'What do you want, Comrade

Galich — a play running in the heart of Moscow, in one of the capital's new theaters, in which it is recounted how the Jews won the war?! The Jews of all people! The Jewish question, Aleksandr Arka-die-vich' — she pronounced my patronymic unusually carefully, syllable by syllable[33] — 'is a very complicated question! Take for example, Comrade Galich, the cinema.' She paused and, lowering her voice, said almost in a whisper, 'It's all Jews in there! Shouldn't we correct this situation?' "[34] So, in the person of this senior official of the Central Committee of the Communist Party of the Soviet Union, the Soviet playwright Galich saw with his own eyes his principal censor.

Of course, the Jewish question is far from being the only one to be eliminated by Soviet theatrical censorship. The history of prohibitions of theatrical performances for a variety of reasons began during the first days of the Soviet regime. One of its first victims, strangely enough, was the founder of socialist realism, Maxim Gorkii. As Iu. Annenkov attested in *Diary of My Meetings* [*Dnevnik moikh vstrech*], Gorkii's satirical comedy about the vulgarity and boorishness of the nouveau riche who had come to power was banned in Petrograd in 1919 and disappeared without a trace. From that time, and up to the day when, in December 1982, in Moscow, Iurii Liubimov's production of Pushkin's tragedy *Boris Godunov* was, it was rumored, banned from public view, and Viktor Rozov's *Nest of the Woodgrouse* [*Gnezdo glukharia*] was removed from the repertoire, the martyrology of banned performances in the Soviet theater is endless.

In the Taganka Theater alone, the theater with which I am most familiar, productions of Boris Mozhaev's well-known story, *From the Life of Fedor Kuz'kin* [*Iz zhizni Fedora Kuz'kina*], and Bulgakov's *Master and Margarita*, were banned in 1970 as "ideologically harmful." True, after certain cuts were made the latter was soon authorized for performance, but a short time later it was subjected to fierce criticism in *Pravda* (May 29, 1977). This, by the way, is also one of the refined methods of public execution. When it is necessary not simply to ban a performance but to publicly discipline a particular theater, to compromise it in the public's eyes, and to inspire fear in other theaters, the authorities resort to press campaigns, which are usually followed by administrative measures. So, for example, on January 8, 1938, two weeks after the publication in *Pravda* on December 17, 1937, of P. Kerzhentsev's article "An Alien Theater" ["Chuzhoi teatr"], an order was published on the abolition of the Meyerhold Theater as an enterprise alien to Soviet art. One need not guess who was behind this decision. On January 17 of the same year, Zhdanov, at the first session of the Supreme Soviet, delivered a speech in which he declared bluntly that the Meyerhold Theater "was attempting to ruin the plays of the classical repertoire with its affectations and stunts," and was a "harmful enterprise, squandering state funds."

The Stalin and Zhdanov methods of reprisal against Soviet theaters continue today. Though adjusted to fit new times, though less crude and more flexible, they are essentially immutable. Directors are no longer thrown into prison, as Meyerhold, Dikii, and others were in their time. In their struggle with recalcitrant theaters, the authorities now resort to other methods. They fight them with silence and with isolation. From the moment the biting article "Black Magic Performances at the Taganka," by the critic N. Potapov, appeared in *Pravda*, the press was forbidden not only to write about the Taganka Theater but even to refer to it. The thick volumes of the valuable Soviet indexes *Letopis' gazetnykh statei* (Chronicle of newspaper articles) and *Letopis' zhurnal'nykh statei* (Chronicle of journal articles) for 1978–1982 attest to the fact that for five years there was not a single article on the Taganka anywhere in the Russian-language Soviet press — as though it did not exist. People were going to the Taganka, struggling to get tickets, talking about it and arguing about it, but no one wrote about the Taganka. That is to say, nothing was printed about it.

Here is something from my personal experience. My last book, *Ocherki teatral'noi zhizni Vengrii* (*Sketches of Hungarian Theater Life*), was published in Moscow in 1979. The editors, in cooperation with the censors, removed entire pages about Liubimov's work in Budapest on *Crime and Punishment*. This was before his production of the work in Moscow. An article on the same subject in the journal *Theater* was swiftly suppressed. (The same can be said about the silence regarding the experimental Southwest Theater [*Na Iugo-zapade*], popular with the Moscow intelligentsia, the Russian Drama Theater in Riga, Iu. Sherling's Jewish musical and dramatic ensemble, and so on.)

In Soviet censorship practice, the creation of an artistic vacuum around unwelcome developments in the theater and in art in general is a well-tested means of doing battle with dissident thought. Efim Etkind described this well in an article entitled, "Soviet Taboos" (*Sintaksis*, Paris, no. 9, 1981). The point of this policy is to force on the Soviet people a corrupt and, at the same time, ridiculous train of thought: what we do not want to see does not exist; what we do not want to mention loses its reality.

During the post-Stalin years, Soviet theater has continued to suffer from this ostrichlike behavior. For many years it was deprived of its best national playwrights, such as Bulgakov, whose work was suppressed for 25 years after his death and who even today is allowed on the stage only reluctantly (with the exception of *The Days of the Turbins*, a favorite of Stalin's); the gifted Nikolai Erdman, who never saw his *The Suicide* [*Samoubiitsa*] on stage; Isaac Babel and his *Sunset*; Iurii Olesha and his plays; Aleksandr Galich and his *Sailor's Silence*; and Solzhenitsyn and his plays. Aleksandr Vampilov made it to the stage after considerable delay, following his tragic death (but without *Duck*

Hunting [*Utinaia okhota*], which for a long time was allowed in only one theater in Riga). The arrival on the stage of Iurii Trifonov, one of the most talented urban writers of the last 20 years, was artificially delayed. His *The Exchange* [*Obmen*] and *House on the Embankment* [*Dom na naberezhnoi*] remained the property of the audience only on the small Taganka stage. Even recognized playwrights like Viktor Rozov, for example, must wait many years for the publication of their cherished plays. Rozov's *The Nest of the Woodgrouse* was printed in the late 1970s, and in 1983 we discovered that it had already been removed from the repertoire as "ideologically inconsistent."

Controls over foreign drama, including plays from Eastern Europe, are even harsher. In the late 1950s and early 1960s, the plays of the Czech dramatist Pavel Kohout (*Such as Love, The Third Sister*) and an antifascist play by his countryman Milan Kundera (*The Turn of the Key*) made the rounds of the Moscow theaters. These writers were described as innovative artists, as the best playwrights of socialist Czechoslovakia, but their participation in the Prague Spring movement made the mention of their names taboo in the Soviet press. Their plays were quickly removed from the repertoire despite their success with the public.

Ideological supervision deprives the Soviet theater of opportunities to assimilate successfully the rich Western European and American theatrical experience and progressive theatrical thought. In his detailed monograph, *A Decade of Euphoria: Western Literature in Post-Stalin Russia, 1954–1964*, Maurice Friedberg showed how Friedrich Dürrenmatt struggled to make his way to the Soviet stage even in the most favorable period of Khrushchev's "thaw," and how the Soviet theater fought for productions of Arthur Miller's *View from the Bridge* and *Incident at Vichy*. To this list of plays from around the world we can add Peter Weiss' *The Investigation* [*Die Ermittlung*], which only one theater in the country, the Taganka, managed to save from the censors — because of the forbidden "Jewish theme" — and then for just two seasons. A great many plays that have shaped world theater in the second half of the 20th century were never produced in Soviet theaters, thus depriving audiences of important spiritual nourishment. Rolf Hochhuth's *The Deputy*, which raised the question of the responsibility for the deaths of millions of Jews in the fascist torture chambers; the brilliant satires of Mrozek; the absurdist theater of Ionesco and Becket; right up to the world-famous *Waiting for Godot*, the author of which has not waited long enough to see it appear on the Soviet stage — all of this passed the Soviet theater by, which inevitably detracted from the theater's aesthetic resources.

To reveal the true processes taking place in the Soviet theater today, to expose the conditions in which it operates, means to show its moral opposition to falsehood, to aid in the recovery and revival of the great

Russian humanist art. Time itself often makes corrections and additions to our feeble attempts to reflect its uniqueness and complexity. That happened in this case as well: When my paper for this conference had already been completed, I received some new, extremely important information touching directly on my subject of the relationship between Soviet censorship and the theater. In the *London Times* of September 5, 1983, there appeared an interview with the well-known Soviet director and artistic head of the Taganka Theater, Iurii Liubimov. Liubimov had come to England with his wife and young son to produce a performance of *Crime and Punishment* at one of the London theaters. The performance was a great success.

In his interview with a *London Times* correspondent, Liubimov stated that his creative fate and the fate of his theater in Moscow were hanging by a thread. The situation was extremely tense. In recent years the authorities had banned three of his productions: *Alive* [*Zhivoi*], Mozhaev's *Kuz'kin*, a play dedicated to the memory of Vladimir Vysotskii, and Pushkin's *Boris Godunov*. Finding himself in an intolerable situation, Liubimov continued, he had complained, threatening to resign, and had written to Iurii Andropov about his intention to give up theater. "And so, what was Andropov's reaction?" the English journalist asked. Liubimov shrugged his shoulders and answered, "Apparently, my statement is still somewhere on his desk."[35]

Hanging over the Taganka Theater, as many times before in its 20-year history, was the threat of closing. This time the threat was palpable. The final straw for the theater and its director had been the banning of their production of *Boris Godunov* in December 1982. This last circumstance requires me to tell in more detail how it happened, and, in so doing, to conclude for the time being the discussion of a subject that may resume in a new and unexpected way.

In early December 1982 Moscow's Taganka Theater held a dress rehearsal of Pushkin's tragedy *Boris Godunov*. An official commission in charge of artistic affairs that viewed the performance was horrified at the production and refused permission for it to be shown to the public. The news that the new leaders in the Kremlin had banned Pushkin quickly made the rounds in snowy Moscow, immediately made its way abroad, and gave rise to gossip that was by no means of a merely artistic nature. What had happened? What had the leaders found to quarrel with in a great work of the Russian classics — one studied in all Soviet university courses — in its production by Liubimov's theater?

In the history of Russian drama, theatrical lances have long been broken over *Boris Godunov*, and heads have rolled for the attempt, casting routine aside, to penetrate the depths of Pushkin's idea and to follow his lead in the transformation of "obsolete theatrical forms." The play's troubled history had already begun during the lifetime of the poet, who never even saw his favorite creation on stage. *Boris Godunov* was first produced in 1870, 33 years after Pushkin's death, on the stage of the Mariinskii Theater in St. Petersburg, but without particular success. After that, productions at other theaters also failed, including even V. I. Nemirovich-Danchenko's 1907 production at the Art Theater.

Serious attempts to solve the mystery of Pushkin's drama were made in the Soviet period by Vsevolod Meyerhold. Twice — in 1925–1926 and especially in his last creative season, in 1936–1937 — Meyerhold began work on the play with characteristic enthusiasm, but circumstances prevented its completion. In 1937, after Meyerhold had announced his grandiose idea for a political "people's" drama, Sergei Prokofiev had written the music for it, and V. Shestakov had created the scenery, Meyerhold's theater came under brutal attack in the Soviet press and was soon shut down. Meyerhold was forbidden to work and was, soon thereafter, arrested and killed. Detailed notes on his rehearsals were preserved, however, and there are recollections of his contemporaries about his last passionate undertaking. Here is one of his observations about *Boris Godunov* at a meeting of his theater company on September 30, 1937, when the rehearsals had been all but stopped: "The theater," said the master, "has such an expressive language that it can through its words, gesture, and perspective show a situation in such a light that it will be perceived as entirely different by the contemporary spectator."[36]

Iurii Liubimov, the head and creator of the Taganka Theater, approached *Boris Godunov* at a critical juncture in his career, after 20 years of work with his own theater company, which had won world renown. Liubimov had long dreamed of producing Pushkin's play but did not begin serious rehearsals until the spring of 1982, on a new stage, in the modern angular red brick building joined to the unpresentable gray walls of the old one. (I mention in passing that Meyerhold had prepared his *Boris Godunov* in 1937 also with the idea of opening the season with it at a new Meyerhold Theater, TIM, which was being built, according to his plan, at the place where the Tchaikovsky Concert Hall stands today. Truly, one's native walls do not forgive betrayal!)

The rehearsals at the Taganka Theater began with the training of the chorus. Under the guidance of Dmitrii Pokrovskii, the well-known collector of folk songs, who was specially invited to the theater, in Liubimov's performance the chorus virtually became the play's main character. As we have now learned, the chorus never left the stage during the action, and lived its own special life, which was only indirectly connected to the tsarist scenes. It served as a motley national backdrop against which the intrigues were woven and the struggle proceeded on the proscenium for the power of the Muscovite state in the Time of Troubles. The chorus was dressed in costumes from various periods — from Russian women's national sarafans to long hippie skirts, leather jackets, and jeans in the crowd scenes. This mixed chorus, consciously disrupting historical reality, created a surprisingly colorful and dynamic picture of the ordinary people united through the various periods by the richness of the Russian folk songs. The free and mischievous, lyrical and doleful singing, traditional dances, laments and wailing, performed at the highest level of musical folklore by this unusual chorus, carried the entire performance from scene to scene, as though on the waves of a national sea, binding with its singing the montage of freely constructed *mise en scènes* and determining their emotional mood.

Of course, we still do not know everything about this banned performance, but various sources — first of all, witnesses who were present at two closed daytime viewings — suggest the outline of an unusually grand and impressive theatrical presentation. In its boldness it surpasses everything we know of former stage interpretations of *Godunov* in the Russian and Soviet theater. Here is a recent letter from Moscow, from one theatergoer, with a brief description of the performance:

Of the events worth describing in this letter the first I'll name is my trip to the Taganka Theater to a public rehearsal (as Liubimov himself presented it) of Pushkin's *Boris Godunov*. Of course, I was very fortunate to receive this . . . kindness (oh, and grateful!).

I don't remember that a performance ever made a similar impression on me. Everything seems to follow Pushkin, who sounds surprisingly timely, especially in the crowd scenes, which accompany all of the other scenes. The individual roles are in general not as strong as the mass scenes, which are performed on the whole with singing (old Russian songs, learned brilliantly and with very impressive lyrics). There are not so very many "Liubimov" devices. But, for example, in the scene by the fountain, a rusty old bucket appears that is used more than once in other scenes, and from which the "fountain" spurts forth in two streams (Marina — Alla Demidova, and the False Dmitrii-Zolotukhin). But this comic device is not the main thing, although it "cancels out" a certain pathos. There are costumes of all kinds — right up to the leather jacket and boots on V. Shuiskii (he has a small wedge-shaped beard!) and the quilted Tartar robe (of dark gray) on Boris (Gubenko looks great!). The backdrop is a brick wall with bricked-up windows that are open only at the very bottom, and the people enter through them.

I don't think that the fate of this production was happy. But God help it. It would be a shame if such work goes to waste.

So *Boris Godunov* at the Taganka is banned for the time being. Its fate is unknown. Let me try to reconstruct an image of the performance from what is known today.

Pushkin's *Boris Godunov* in Iurii Liubimov's 1982 production was a performance without a central hero, a performance whose main character was the people, who did not keep silent but who had lost hope in its rulers — a people who had become dazed and who unburdened its heart only in song. Liubimov, who does not produce a single work without a central metaphor — the floating curtain in *Hamlet*, the military truck in *The Dawns Here Are Quiet* [*A zori zdes' tikhie*], and the swinging pendulum in *Master and Margarita* that always froze during hard times — on this occasion found a theatrical, visual course in the "meaningful" costuming of Pushkin's characters. Although we find this tendency in other productions of his consistently, as a device, Liubimov used it for the first time in *Boris Godunov*.

I have already mentioned the pointedly extrahistorical costuming of the chorus. This resulted in a whole set of theatrical and costume metaphors. Grishka Otrep'ev — the actor V. Zolotukhin — was dressed like a sailor boy, while the main intriguer, the smooth-tongued and experienced courtier, Boyar Shuiskii (I still have not established the name of the actor in this role), stood out from all the other characters in the tragedy because of his long unbuttoned leather coat. Perhaps a leather jacket means nothing to someone from the West, but to a Russian spectator it says a great deal. If, moreover, one adds that the actor playing Shuiskii had a "little wedge-shaped beard" and a swift manner of walking that blew open the flaps of his leather coat, then one need not say more. It evoked the period of "Iron Felix."[37]

The greatest surprise was Tsar Boris himself — the actor Gubenko. He carried on the whole performance in his quilted Tartar robe, which was completely in keeping with the barbarousness of the tsar's rule, and also true to historical record, according to which Godunov had Mongol blood. The main thing came later, however. The action moves to its bloody resolution. Tsar Boris dies, his scions are poisoned, and the new tsar, Dmitrii Ivanovich, is proclaimed; but the people, according to Pushkin's famous stage direction, have already lost faith and are silent. At this point in the performance, right before the end of the act, Liubimov puts his last, most important stroke on the work. It seems as if he put on the whole play for this moment. This has happened many times in art. I know another successful Soviet director who admitted to me that he had put on *King Lear* for the sake of just one phrase: "There is no one guilty in the world!"[38] For Liubimov, such a counterpoint, linking various periods and simultaneously heard melodies into a single whole, is the play's final rejoinder, addressed to the people by the courtier Mosal'skii: "Why are you silent? Shout 'Long live Tsar Dmitrii Ivanovich!' "

Russian literature, as has been noted, is a literature of questions: "What Is to Be Done?" "Who Is to Blame?" "Who Can Live Happy and Free in Russia?" and even "How Ivan Ivanovich Quarrelled with Ivan Nikiforovich."[39] Our contemporary Liubimov found in Pushkin, in *Boris Godunov*, one more "accursed" question of Russian life. By an irony of fate, he made this discovery at the most "inappropriate" time for himself.

From accounts of those who saw this performance, which immediately became history without ever being shown in public, one can get an idea of the two versions of its final scene. Although they do not vary a great deal from one another, in diverging in perspective in the *mise en scènes*, in some essential way they change the tone of the entire performance.

According to the first version, in the finale the actor Gubenko, who played Godunov in the Tartar robe, appears from the wings. Now he is dressed in his usual street clothes and looks like an ordinary Muscovite. He carries some red carnations in his hand (someone even counted them — there were six). Gubenko walks up to the audience, the lights come on, and the actor, standing face to face with the spectators at the very edge of the stage, asks them the "accursed" question: "Why are you silent?" His voice sounds a bit tired, colorless, and almost too familiar. He turns without reproach to his partners in misfortune, without particular hope of hearing an answer, and is far from rousing them to any sort of action. Instead of "you" he just as calmly and simply could have said "we," without changing the intonation. In fact, the significance of the final rejoinder, and its impact, was precisely in this possible concealed meaning.

Specialists have noted that in this version of the finale Liubimov abridged Pushkin, having eliminated the second half of courtier Mosal'skii's rejoinder: "Shout 'Long live Tsar Dmitrii Ivanovich!'" It turned out that the production questioned not this particular case but the people's silence in general.

In another version, Gubenko, in the same contemporary costume, comes out of the hall and goes to the stage, as though from the audience, appealing on its behalf to the chorus on the stage, and in his voice there is a different, mocking and condemnatory tone: "Why are you silent? The tsar is dead — long live the tsar!" From one single *mise en scène*, as we see, the tone of the finale is changed immediately and the entire performance takes on a different perspective — a bit rhetorical, a bit remote, as if viewed from the present.

Both versions of the finale are equal in force and artistic expression, but they reflect the director's well-known vacillations on how to put the emotional finish on the performance: with a tired note of hopelessness (*"beznadëgi,"* as the late Vysotskii would have said) or with the author's irony toward the silent crowd. In the end, Liubimov had the right to try both versions — after all, the occasion was only a theatrical rehearsal, even if a dress rehearsal.

All the same, what was hidden behind the different readings of the finale? Which version was closer to Pushkin? The answer to this question would lead us to other, fundamental problems of the Russian dramatic theater, and that is another topic.

Notes

1 Ernest J. Simmons, "The Origins of Literary Control," *Survey*, no. 36 (April-June 1961): 78–84; ibid., no. 37 (July-September 1961): 60–67.

2 Maurice Friedberg, "Soviet Books, Censors, and Readers," in *Literature and Revolution in Soviet Russia, 1917–1962* (London: Oxford University Press, 1963), pp. 198–210.

3 Maurice Friedberg, *A Decade of Euphoria: Western Literature in Post-Stalin Russia, 1954–1964* (Bloomington: Indiana University Press, 1977).

4 Mark Zaitsev, "Soviet Theater Censorship," *The Drama Review* 19, no. 2 (June 1975): 119-28.

5 Anna Tamarchenko, "Theatre Censorship," *Index on Censorship* 9, no. 4 (August 1980): 23–28.

6 Richard Owen, "Theatre Crackdown. Curtains for Moscow's Cult of the Anti-Hero," *London Times*, (February 28, 1983), p. 5.

7 Andrei Serban, "Three Sisters," *The A.R.T. News* (Cambridge: Loeb Drama Center) 3, no. 1 (November 1982): 1–4.

8 See, for example, Jack Kroll, "A Pair of 'Three Sisters,' " *Newsweek*, January 10, 1983, p. 70.

9 Ned Temko, "Soviet Press Cracks Down on Theaters," *The Christian Science Monitor*, (February 11, 1983). p. 3.

10 From Mikhail Lemke, *Nikolaevskie zhandarmy i literatura 1826–1855 gg. (Po podlinnym delam tret'ego otdeleniia sobstv. E. I. Velichestva kantseliarii)* (St. Petersburg, 1909), pp. 1–2.

11 See Sidney Monas, *The Third Section: Police and Society in Russia under Nicholas I* (Cambridge: Harvard University Press, 1961). — ED.

12 Lemke, *Nikolaevskie zhandarmy*, p. 46.

13 Ibid., p. 141.

14 A. S. Pushkin, *Polnoe sobranie sochinenii v 10 tomakh*, vol. 5 (Leningrad, 1978), p. 14. Translation from Walter Arndt's translation, *Eugene Onegin: A Novel in Verse* (New York: E. P. Dutton, 1981), p. 12, chap. 1, stanza 18.

15 Iu. N. Tynianov, *Pushkin i ego sovremenniki* (Moscow: Nauka, 1969), pp. 357–58.

16 Lemke, *Nikolaevskie zhandarmy*, p. 31, emphasis added by author.

17 Ibid., p. 32.

18 Ibid., p. 49.

19 See Zaks's article in the present collection and also Zhores Medvedev's book *Desiat' let posle "Odnogo dnia Ivana Dnisovicha"* (London: Macmillan, 1973).

20 A. S. Griboedov, *Sochineniia* (Leningrad: Khudozhestvennaia literatura, 1940), p. 534.

21 Present-day Tallin, capital of Estonia. — ED.

22 Lemke, *Nikolaevskie zhandarmy*, p. 204.

23 Ibid., p. 208.

24 Ibid., p. 226.
25 Pushkin, *Polnoe sobranie*, vol. 10, p. 146.
26 Lemke, *Nikolaevskie zhandarmy*, p. 608.
27 See the first edition of *Boris Godunov* (St. Petersburg, 1831 — for example, in the Kilgour Collection of Russian Literature, 1750–1920, at Harvard University's Houghton Library, Kilgour no. 884).
28 Pushkin, *Polnoe sobranie*, vol. 10, p. 260.
29 Vasilii Grossman, *Vse techet*, 2d ed. (Frankfurt/Main: Possev, 1974), p. 180; also for more detail see E. Etkind's article "zhizn' i sud'ba" on Grossman's novel.
30 See Alexander Gershkovich's article "Posledniaia rol' Vladimira Vysotskogo" in *Obozrenie* (the analytical journal of *Russkaia mysl'*), no. 2 (December 1982): 37–39.
31 See his main work: B. I. Rostotskii, *K istorii bor'by za ideinost' i realizm sovetskogo teatra* (Moscow: Izdatel'stvo Adademii Nauk SSSR, 1950), p. 112.
32 Aleksandr Galich, *General'naia repetitsiia* (Possev, 1974), pp. 19–20, 124.
33 Arkadi is a Russian name allegedly favored by Jews. — ED.
34 Galich, *General'naia repetitsiia*, pp. 169–70.
35 "The Crosses Yuri Lyubimov Bears," *London Times*, September 5, 1983, p. 13.
36 V. E. Meyerhold, *Stat'i, pis'ma rechi. Chast' vtoraia* (Moscow: Iskusstvo, 1968), p. 571.
37 Feliks Dzerzhinsky, head of the Soviet Secret Police during the early postrevolutionary years. — ED.
38 Quoted by Gershkovich as "Net v mire vinovatykh"; in the Pasternak translation, "Vinovnykh net, pover', vinovnykh net." This appears to be a translation of Act IV, scene 6, line 168: "None does offend, none, I say none"; see *The Riverside Shakespeare*, ed. by G. Blakemore Evans (Boston: Houghton Mifflin, 1974), p. 1287. — ED.
39 Titles of works, respectively, by Chernyshevsky (and Lenin!), Herzen, Nekrasov, and Gogol (actually, "How Ivan Ivanovich Quarrelled . . ."). — ED.

The Mass Media: Discussion

Ilya Rudyak (Chicago, Illinois) opened the discussion with a comment on censorship on the stage and screen. Speaking of life in Odessa before World War II, he recalled the irreverent attitude characteristic of that city; there were many parodies, for instance, of official Soviet slogans. He reminded listeners that we tend to forget that Joseph Stalin himself was the most important censor. People used to believe that he read 500 pages a day. When Rudyak was a schoolboy, people would point this out to him, saying "Look here: Joseph Vissarionovich Stalin reads 500 pages a day, so why don't you follow his example?" (He remembered a story, perhaps a true one, that when Stalin read the manuscript of a book by Konstantin Simonov entitled *With You and Without You*, he wrote on the margin "publish two copies, one for him and one for her.")

In Odessa Rudyak made films and staged plays. Speaking as a practitioner rather than a theoretician, he offered a few stories about himself and his friends to provide some concrete examples. He began by describing the film studios in Odessa, situated right at the seashore, on the former French Boulevard (renamed Proletarian Boulevard). Next door to the studio a beautiful 12-story building was constructed in a two-year period (that is, with a speed unheard of in the Soviet building industry). The building was inhabited by communist functionaries — military, trade union, and Young Communist big shots — and the witty inhabitants of Odessa immediately gave that building a Turgenev-like name: "A Nest of Gentlefolk on the Proletarian Boulevard."

What was most interesting, he recalled, was that a real-life censor whom they all knew in person actually lived in that building. An entire floor was taken up by the secretary for Ideological Problems of the Provincial Committee of the Communist Party. This little man, with a huge head and a short neck, lived literally two steps from the film studio. He would come to inspect every film and also to examine new scripts and new films. Each time he appeared at the studio people would whisper to each other exactly in the same manner as they do when the soundtrack is being recorded.

Whenever the secretary-censor would come to the film studio, there was much excitement. The director trembled in his shoes, the Party organizer would try to flatter the visitor, the imposing lady in charge of the trade union would prepare a fancy meal. Of course it was the director of the film then being made who was most excited. After all, it would be his job, after the secretary-censor made his suggestions, to shoot some new footage, to change certain scenes, to add and to subtract, to introduce changes in the dialogue, to find more beautiful backdrops against which the actors would be filmed, and, above all, to change the end of the film in a way that would make it more uplifting, more optimistic, and more imposing. It is true, Rudyak noted, that some directors always did the job correctly in the first place, but there were others who had to remake their films. He recalled one young man whose very first film was approved. He was so overcome with emotion that he said to Rudyak, "Listen, he (the censor) actually shook my hand!" (The director probably did not wash that hand for three days afterward, Rudyak speculated.) That is how happy he was that his first film sailed through the first obstacle course of the censorship.

Still, Rudyak cautioned, one should remember that even *before* reaching that institution, it was necessary to deal with the editor-in-chief, the ordinary editor, the director, the Party organizer, and the local section of the Union of Cinematographers of the Ukrainian Republic. He commented that everyone at this conference had been speaking about the way things are done all over the Soviet Union, on a national scale. In his view the local republic scale is even more complex because one has to do everything *twice*. First one has to clear everything with the Cinematographers Union of the Ukrainian Republic, the State Film of the Ukrainian Republic, and the Central Committee of the Ukrainian Republic's Communist Party; only after that can one deal with the State Film of the USSR, the USSR Union of Cinematographers, and the Central Committee of the Communist Party of the Soviet Union. Each one of these bodies will, of course, suggest some corrections and some additions, make some criticism, and so forth.

Rudyak maintained that the poor film director has no alternative but to carry out all the demands and accept all the suggestions if he really wants to continue making films. In other words, he will have to do it for the sake of his prestigious profession and of the team shooting the film. (In fact, Rudyak added, he will have to do it if he simply wants to obtain the cooperative apartment he has been waiting for all these years.)

Rudyak recalled a film entitled *Venushkin's Adventures*, a happy musical comedy for children. The Glavlit censors read the script and approved it. Shooting was completed, there were some screenings, and a special copy of the film was sent to Moscow. Everything was fine, but suddenly they discovered that the filmmakers had failed to notice something of importance. It turned out that the boy in the film was named Arkasha, a nickname for Arkadii. People in Moscow said that this name is not really Russian; much worse, the name in question is used frequently by Jews. For that reason Venushkin's first name had to be changed.

Anyone who knows anything about the movie business knows what it means to change even one single sentence in a film that is already completed. The man in charge of the soundtrack probably turned gray because changing the name — and the names Arkadii and Arkasha were used a thousand times in the course of the film — meant, in fact, changing the entire soundtrack of the film. This, in turn, meant that actors had to be brought back from Moscow because the actors in the film were Muscovites. It also meant getting the authorities to somehow agree to have the studio used at night and getting a new allotment of tape to re-record the soundtrack — and all of this had to be done with a straight face.

Someone had tried to prove to the Moscow bureaucrats that the well-known children's writer Arkadii Gaidar was not Jewish in spite of his first name and that the author of the script named his character Arkadii in honor of his favorite writer. Somebody else remembered Arkadii Kirsanov, the protagonist of Turgenev's *Fathers and Sons*, who was also Russian and a nobleman at that, but it did not do any good.

On another occasion, Rudyak recalled, there were problems with the film version of Mikhail Lermontov's *A Hero of Our Time*. Someone influential decided that Lermontov's central character, Pechorin, did not "look" the way these influential people thought he *should* look. No matter that Pechorin is a fictional character and no one knows how he really looked. The film was never completed.

In conclusion, Rudyak remarked that someone at this conference had called Glavlit, the censorship organization, the father of the arts in the USSR. In his view, Ideology is the mother; with such parents, he hoped we would all become orphans!

Golovskoy continued the discussion, expressing his pleasure that some differences of opinion had emerged at the conference, as the purpose was not to exchange compliments but to try to arrive at some objective truths. He raised a number of objections concerning Zaks's presentation. Zaks said there were two censorship authorities; that the OGPU censorship was called PolitControl. In Golovskoy's view this is wrong. The Glavlit censors were called Politcontrollers, and the entire censorship apparatus was called PolitControl because in the 1920s the word "censorship" itself was considered bourgeois, tsarist, and so they preferred to call it PolitControl. Golovskoy agreed with Zaks that there was a department within the structure of the GPU that handled literary matters, but he claimed that it did not work directly in censorship; it had a variety of functions, but different ones. As for the connection with the KGB, the GPU, Golovskoy maintained that it unquestionably does exist and continues to exist. One of the deputy heads of Glavlit is always a KGB general. Glavlit receives a great many documents from the KGB on the basis of which it formulates instructions, which are then sent directly to the censors.

Golovskoy also disagreed with the general thrust of Zaks's story. He acknowledged that Zaks was referring to an exceptional situation, an exceptional period, but claimed that for that reason many of his specific examples do not square with the work of journals, newspapers, and publishing houses. Even *Novyi mir* now works differently, Golovskoy said. For instance, the process for presenting materials to the censors is shorter, not as complicated as it was at that time (although he was willing to believe that Zaks had described it accurately as he knew it). He added that, of course, all questions concerning *Novyi mir* were decided not by rank-and-file censors but by the likes of Romanov and the Central Committee secretary at the level of the propaganda department; and it was precisely for this reason that the publication of *Novyi mir* was so often delayed.

Golovskoy found Zaks's account of his meetings with censors at different levels to be extraordinarily interesting. What was involved in these meetings, he wondered? What demands were made by these people at the different levels of censorship — the department head, the deputy chief censor, and so on? He noted that within the censorship there are groups that correspond to different disciplines, so that Zaks would deal with the group responsible for fiction and not the group with which Leonid Finkelstein dealt. He agreed with Finkelstein that the censors are not fools or idiots; they are all people with higher educations. This is not the intellectual elite, he conceded, but these are very often educated, informed, intelligent people. He charged that from Zaks's story it follows that the censors are all bad and the editors of *Novyi mir* are all good. In Golovskoy's opinion, even under the stupendous, exceptional conditions that existed at *Novyi mir*, the editors were simply editors, no better and no worse than usual. Solzhenitsyn and other authors have written about Tvardovskii's personal tastes, as well as those of his tastes that were not merely personal, and about how he cut some things that he, as a communist, felt should not go through or knew could not get through. For this reason the editorial staff, including Zaks, also made cuts, also told the authors that a particular passage could not get through. Golovskoy sees that as a noble goal — the desire to help the material through to ultimate publication — but pointed out that nevertheless we should not forget the existence of the editorial apparatus, of that editorial control preceding the censor's.

Finally, Golovskoy disagreed with Zaks regarding translated foreign publications. During his nine years at the Iskusstvo Publishing House he edited many books on motion pictures — his assigned area — translated from foreign languages. The last persons who signed off on these at the publishing house were the head of the editorial staff and the editor-in-chief but not the censor.

Journals may have been handled a little differently because they included translations as well as domestic works. *Novyi mir*, for instance, printed translations, as did *Inostrannaia literatura (Foreign Literature)*, which does bear the censor's stamp. It is all completely in the open. Why is the stamp not removed, then, in *Inostrannaia literatura*, a journal with a circulation of 600,000? This is because censorship exists there as well, Golovskoy maintained. Why is there censorship? Because they publish commentaries and articles, and all of these are subject to normal, ordinary censorship.

The same is true of a book published by Progress Publishing House, Golovskoy noted; he published fairly frequently there as a translator from Polish, appearing in print rather as an author does. He added that at Progress a book is required to have a foreword, and the more shocking or dangerous the book, the more preeminent the person writing the foreword must be. This is called protective coating. Immediately the editor starts thinking, "Whom can I get to write the foreword?" This is very important; an author equivalent to a marshal or a general will shield the seditious content. If one looks at many translated books, he observed, one will see that some of them contain both a foreword and an afterword. These are the most dangerous books; that is, they must be covered from both ends. ("Yes, of course, the content — but we have advised the readers, we have explained it to the readers.") The third element in the protective coating is commentary, done by the editor, the editor-in-chief, or a special personage invited for this purpose. Golovskoy emphasized that all of these supplementary materials are written in Russian and undergo censorship because, unlike the translated foreign book itself, these materials could reveal Soviet state or military secrets.

He added that the censor's mark does not appear on all current books published by the Russian Language Publishing House (Russkii iazyk), which are aimed for the most part at foreign audiences. Recently, for example, he saw a book published by Voenizdat, publishers of military literature, called the *Military Translation Manual* [*Uchebnik voennogo perevoda*]. There was no censor's mark in this particular book, although other Voenizdat books do have them, because the manual would not reveal military secrets. He observed that literary classics are now being published without censorship; and the second and third printings of some Soviet writers — for example, the second printing of Astaf'ev's *Kingfish* — bear no censor's mark, although the first printing certainly had one.

Finkelstein observed that the editor of the *Manchester Guardian* once said that facts are sacred and comment is free. For the sake of facts, then, he wanted to make some corrections. He did not disagree with the opinions expressed by Golovskoy and Zaks, or with facts presented by Suslov, but he did find several obvious mistakes in Golovskoy's remarks. First, Golovskoy said that the censor does not bear responsibility for the ideological content of the censored material. This is not true, Finkelstein maintained. His assertion is based on personal experience with a much less important magazine than *Novyi mir*: at the editorial offices of *Znanie sila*, where he worked, an article by Varshavskii was passed by the censor. It was a discussion of the impact of popular science writing upon the development of science, a sort of speculative article. The entire press run was bumped because of ideological objections to the article's contents. Of course the censor bears responsibility for ideology, Finkelstein asserted: if not he, then who?

Finkelstein also took issue with Golovskoy's assertion that censorship is decentralized, stating that specialized branches were created to help the central censorship cope with specialized questions, such as military matters. Golovskoy, who worked for an art publication, might never have seen the military censorship's large rubber stamp that reads as follows:

> So storony voennoi tsenzury General'nogo shtaba Vooruzhennykh Sil SSSR ne imeetsia vozrazhenii protiv publikatsii prilozhennogo materiala na (propusk) stranitsakh. Nashi zamechaniia na stranitsakh (propusk). Ostal'naia chast' . . . reshenie o publikatsii vsego materiala dolzhno byt' priniato organami Glavlita. (No objection on the part of the military censorship of the Headquarters of the USSR Armed Forces to publication of attached material, on pages such-and-such. Comments may be found on pages such-and-such. Decision on publication of remainder of material to be made by Glavlit authorities.)

The military censorship was absolutely subordinate — if not administratively, then ideologically; it was just a special branch.

Finkelstein's experience differed from Zaks's, however, in that Finkelstein found the military censorship rather easy and even pleasant to deal with. Indeed, the level of the censors was much higher there: they were all senior officers and forthcoming; one could talk to them. He mentioned a startling instance in which a censor, a colonel, actually facilitated the publication of a very interesting book. A ruse was employed by the author, and the military censor certainly played the game. Regarding the ideological guidance of the secret police over films and such, Finkelstein mentioned his friend of years ago, a KGB colonel named Sergei Diakonov, who worked in the same institute as he did; Diakonov was well known to people who worked in cinema. His office was even in Mosfilm, which he supervised on behalf of the KGB, and not even a tiny mouse could pass beyond him as far as film shooting was concerned.

Based on his own experience of working in television, Finkelstein stressed the importance of control over live TV. Far from being merely a subjective perception, control in this area is absolutely fundamental and real. He recalled that when the cosmonauts Nikolaev and Popovich landed, he interviewed them on TV. During the interview itself the conversation flowed, but three hours earlier he, Nikolaev, Popovich, Tamara Stepova (the manager of the TV science department), and Mikhail Galaktionovich Kroshkin, the chief interplanetary censor, had sat in a little room preparing for the broadcast.

Finkelstein would say: "OK, I'll ask this question," and Kroshkin would say no, so Finkelstein would respond: "OK, I'll ask that question," and Kroshkin would approve. Then someone would ask: "Comrades, who is going to be responsible?" and Nikolaev would say: "I will." "OK," someone would ask, "what would you say next?" "I would say this," someone would respond, and Kroshkin would say no, and so on. This sifting process continued for three hours, Finkelstein recalled. Then the pop card, the foldout, was prepared, and on the face of the folder in the left corner was this formidable inscription: *Razreshaetsia peredat' v efir. Predsedatel' gosudarstvennogo komiteta* ("May be broadcast. Signed by Chairman, State Committee"). In the lower left-hand corner there was a number. So much for live broadcasting, Finkelstein concluded.

Regarding the absence of censorship numbers on books, Finkelstein asserted that all books, including translations, are censored. One can open any work of fiction published between about 1960 and 1964 and find no censorship number because that was a happy period, when not only Boris Suchkov but others were convinced that censorship should conceal its existence. Those books were certainly censored, however; Finkelstein had no doubt about that.

With regard to the uncensored second edition referred to earlier in the discussion, Finkelstein mentioned the famous story about Arkadii Belinkov's book *Yurii Tynianov*, into which he inserted something that had not been in the first edition. This does not mean that the second edition was not censored, however; Finkelstein maintained that it was indeed censored. The censor was simply deceived: he was told that there were no textual changes, and he failed to check. Finkelstein reminded his audience that if one presents a censor with something as a cited source published in the Soviet Union more than three years before, the censor requires the *nomer razresheniia*, the authorization number. They may not have had computers, he remarked, but somehow they immediately established that the number was genuine.

He recalled that Lunacharskii, the one-time commissar of education, had approved some articles that had been forbidden by Glavlit; more recently Mikhail Andreevich Suslov, the Politbureau's Chief of Ideology, did the same thing. Finkelstein knew of at least one instance — in the magazine *Semia i shkola* (*Family and School*) — in which an article was stopped by the censor but subsequently permitted by such intervention. The deputy editor-in-chief, who used to be Suslov's friend, telephoned him and Suslov passed the article.

Finkelstein addressed his last remark to Zaks's assertion that the first public protest against censorship was made by Svirskii in 1968. In Finkelstein's view, it depends on what is considered "public": Svirskii spoke at a closed meeting, and his comments were not published anywhere. Finkelstein gave precedence to Solzhenitsyn, who in his famous letter to the Writers Union in 1967 wrote that "censorship intends to continue, with the longevity of Methusela, right into the 21st century."

Zaks responded to Golovskoy's comments about his presentation, re-marking that he was an old man and therefore still remembered when there were two censorship authorities in the Soviet Union: Glavlit and PolitControl. To emphasize his point he told a story about his experience in the 1930s, when he worked in the city of Arkhangel'sk on a young people's magazine. There was a man — stout, with his stomach protruding over his belt, an insignia in the buttonhole of his lapel — a functionary of the local secret police. The rhomboid in his lapel was equivalent to the rank of general today. It happened that this man had a weakness for writing verse (to this day Zaks remembers some of it). For this reason he used to visit the editorial office of the newspaper instead of having them bring the newspaper pages to him, and he would personally take from his pocket the stamp that read "Printing authorized by PolitControl" and press it on the newspaper pages. This helped him get his poetry published in that newspaper. PolitControl did indeed exist side by side with Glavlit at that time; Glavlit was subordinate to the People's Commissariat of Education [Narkompros], and PolitControl was subordinate to OGPU, the secret police.

Documents do not always tell the true story, Zaks observed. For example, it might seem from paper sources that military censorship was created relatively recently, when in fact it was already in existence before World War II. Documents suggested to Golovskoy a certain organization chart, a splitting up of the censorship department, a separation of ideological control from the rest of its functions. In reality, Zaks insisted, the censorship structure dates from the first days of the Soviet regime. It may have taken on a more distinct shape formally, but the essence remains the same. On the occasion of *Novyi mir*'s jubilee, when they published their 500th issue, they published some documents relating to the history of the journal. Included was correspondence of Lunacharskii, Skvortsov-Stepanov, Polonskii, and others who made up the editorial staff in those years, the mid-1920s. Zaks noted that the same distinct types of ideological control were evident then that one might think had split off only recently.

In response to Golovskoy's statement that no translations are subject to censorship, Zaks suggested looking at the publisher's imprint on any book published, for instance, by the State Literature Press [Goslitizdat]: there one will see Glavlit's number. He noted that books published by the Foreign Literature Press [Inostrannaia literatura] do not include information about the number of copies printed (at least before 1973, when the USSR signed the Copyright Convention). The size of the press run is, as a rule, indicated on all Soviet books; the absence of such information in this case does not mean that only one copy was printed, so why should one assume that the absence of a censorship mark means that no censorship took place?

Glad observed that we may speak about the tremendous losses of Russian culture but that when we begin to make a total evaluation of modern Russian culture, we find ourselves in a cruel dilemma: Do we say that there is nothing left? Friedberg responded that anyone holding to this view ought to consider Russian culture in the year 1952, when, he noted, there were many more reasons to state that Russian culture was a thing of the past, that it was finished. The theater was in a shambles, cinema was ruined, poetry was a disgrace, and novels were at best ridiculous. It took a total of four years for all of this to start coming to life, he observed; and this in spite of the fact that the people who brought it back to life were for the most part those who had been further damaged by attending Stalinist schools. Nevertheless, they were able to overcome these handicaps, and Russian culture was revived.

In Friedberg's opinion, the losses sustained by Russian culture as a result of emigration were all the more serious and painful because these were self-inflicted wounds. They were not at all inevitable; there was no reason for this process to take place. He sees it as the result of cruel and ultimately stupid and counterproductive policies on the part of the Soviet cultural establishment. In his view it would be giving the Soviet cultural establishment too much credit, however, to suggest that it is capable of destroying the culture of a nation as resilient and as mighty as Russia.

Igor Belousovitch (U.S. Department of State) commented on earlier discussion of the process by which manuscripts are examined and everything is eliminated that violates the formal rules of censorship or that sounds suspicious in the slightest degree. In spite of this very methodical and careful procedure, he observed, occasionally one finds in the Soviet press the appearance of some things that represent anomalies, a seeming violation of this careful procedure. He raised what he sees as a very important and interesting question — how do these anomalies occur? — and suggested that there are really only two possibilities: Either the system of censorship somehow miscarried, in which case someone got into serious trouble; or the material appeared deliberately, in full consciousness of what was involved and of the true meaning of the material in question.

He had in mind an example, a small satirical piece that appeared in *Avrora*, a literary magazine, late in 1982. This was a piece that any Soviet reader, and perhaps even a naive American, could read in no other way than as a mockery of Brezhnev. He also mentioned another similar piece that appeared more recently, in *Pravda*, an anthropological article describing a primitive tribe somewhere in Guinea, the name of which sounded suspiciously similar to the Ibansk in Zinoviev's book *The Yawning Heights*. The chief of this tribe sounded suspiciously like a parody of Brezhnev. Belousovitch wondered how material like that is introduced, noting that it would appear to be through a process in which somewhere along the line someone very influential creates the possibility for its publication.

Friedberg cautioned that we should not fall into the habit, so common in Soviet criticism and journalism, of assuming that nothing is accidental: *Ne sluchaino, a vpolne zakonomerno* — it is not an accident, but rather a logical sequence of events. He contended that there are indeed many accidents arising from sloppiness or inattentiveness: all sorts of people do not do their job thoroughly enough, and things slip by. He contended that a great many people (including himself) read the works just mentioned, but without our suspicious minds they might not notice anything. And even if they did notice, they might just shrug their shoulders and say, "Big deal, so we find out that Leonid Il'ich is a damned fool: is that news?" — and the matter is forgotten.

Belousovitch conceded the possibility that something might appear through accident, stupidity, or miscarriage; that the system somehow does not function. In other cases, however, he felt that these things are too pointed, too obvious; and within the context of political circumstances, it seems doubtful that it is altogether accidental.

Ermolaev commented on the treatment of nationalities in literature — Jews, for example. He noted that in Sholokhov's *The Quiet Don* or other works of the 1920s and early 1930s, the characters would have used a derogatory term for Jews. In the mid-1930s that appellation disappeared, at least in some cases. As far as *The Quiet Don* is concerned, in the 1953 edition — the worst Stalinist edition — all of those derogatory terms about Jews were deleted in all four volumes. Friedberg noted that something else had been deleted in the edition of 1953: the long speech by Anna Pogudko, the positive Jewish character, the woman machine-gunner in the novel, in which she explains that she does not fit the old Jewish stereotype but is instead a valiant soldier of the revolution.

Ermolaev added that in the first two volumes of the 1956 edition the word *evrei*, Jew, was retained, while in the last two volumes the word *evrei* was changed back inexplicably to *zhid*, "kike." He noted that in the last two volumes almost everything was restored, perhaps because of intensified de-Stalinization. As far as he knows, the word *zhid* is no longer used in the speech of characters in recent Soviet works. Friedberg observed that in the case of *The Quiet Don*, however, this particular textual change may be linked to the restoration to the text of slang that was previously deleted and then restored. These words did not appear in the Stalinist edition, and vulgarities had been deleted as well. They were restored in the post-Stalin text, and the word *zhid* was viewed as one of those folksy, somewhat vulgar expressions that belong in the text at this level of discourse.

Ermolaev conceded this possibility and mentioned the word *khokhol*, a derogatory term for Ukrainians also used in *The Quiet Don*. *Khokhol* was apparently not considered derogatory, at least not particularly in the context of this book. Kriukov used the word in his works, but in 1933 all *khokhols* were deleted from the author's writings, and they are now called Ukrainians. In the first postwar edition the German named Stockman was changed to a Latvian, and a Latvian he remains today. Ermolaev also mentioned changes in Libedinskii's work *The Week*: the commander of the military district had the good old Russian name Vlasov, but since 1955 he has had the name Gordeev.[1] In the same work there is a party official, described as small and swarthy and with a Jewish name. In 1955 that character disappeared, and his role in the story was absorbed by a broad-shouldered Russian whose name had appeared before.

Mariia Rozanova (Paris, France) began her comment by apologizing in advance to those who might find her remarks disagreeable. When she was small, she recalled, she was very mischievous; after a typical episode at home her mother would reproach her, saying, "*Nemka* (the little German girl) taught you to act this way. You pick up the worst things in the street!" This would really hurt Rozanova's feelings because she knew perfectly well that she had not learned it from the *nemka*, but that she herself could teach any *nemka* whatever mischief there was to learn.

She told this story, Rozanova said, because participants in this conference have spent two days discussing the "terrible Soviet censorship," how it oppresses here and suppresses there; they have argued about where it oppresses the most and talked about the horrors of Soviet censorship. It distressed her very much that the only paper about the *sources* of Soviet censorship was not a Russian presentation but, rather, was presented by an American woman. An American scholar has begun to think about where this terrible and very unpleasant phenomenon — Soviet censorship — has come from.

In Rozanova's view, the attitude of Soviet émigrés can be stated simply: this bad boy or that bad girl, which we call the Soviet system, is to blame for everything. Now that the third emigration is already ten years old, Rozanova thinks it is time to undertake the task of studying the system a bit more seriously. The present emigration should be examined like a drop of blood, a sample drawn for an analysis of this ailing organism called the Soviet Union. This drop of blood is composed of the best minds and most illustrious people: Aksyonov, Siniavsky, and others. She accused the third emigration of creating within its new society its own censorship, its own idols, its own cult of personality. The only thing the émigrés have not been able to do, she observed — and this failure is due only to the fact that the countries that gave them refuge have not so far allowed it — is to build their own Lubianka prison.

As an example, Rozanova pointed to the fact that the emigration already has its own émigré samizdat. Quite a few articles now circulate in manuscript; émigrés send them to each other because they could not be published in any of the official émigré journals. (She added that she defines "official émigré journals" as those published at the expense of the American taxpayers.) A kind of "struggle for a place at the trough" takes place around those journals, she noted; each one attracts specific groups from the new emigration. There are subjects that may not be raised, that are banned from discussion; words that are tabu — there is a distinct lexicon.

Friedberg asked Rozanova for an example. She responded that people can talk and write as much as they want to about Soviet anti-Semitism, but they are not permitted to discuss in the pages of this press the anti-Semitism that clearly does exist among the dissidents. They may discuss and describe as much as they like how bad Kochetov[2] is, and how poorly written his novels are, but not a single official émigré newspaper will print an article discussing the true literary merits of "our paragons." A literary analysis of Maksimov's[3] last novel could not be published: Rozanova declared herself ready to bet a case of vodka on that, fully convinced that she would win.

She asserted that the emigration has created its own censorship: it is building for itself the same old world. She recounted her own and Siniavsky's experience when they and a small group of new émigrés decided to publish their own newspaper, one that would be completely free of censorship and in which you could print anything you like. Suddenly they found themselves using the same words they had used in the Soviet Union. When it came to placing an announcement about this newly created infant in the official émigré press, they found themselves asking, "Will we be able to get this announcement through or not?" They tried for a month and a half, and one day Siniavsky observed that it was easier to get an article printed in *Novyi mir* than to place this ad in the émigré newspaper.

Glad asked Rozanova in which newspaper the ad appeared; in Paris, in *Russkaia mysl'* (*Russian Thought*), she replied, and repeated that debates had continued for a month and a half about whether to publish a paid advertisement for the newly formed newspaper *Tribuna*. She reminded her audience that this newspaper had been founded by quite respectable people, each of whom had spent as many years in the camps as the next. As for bans on certain words, she cited an example from the second issue of *Tribuna*, in which they printed an appeal by Poles concerning the Constitution of May 3. The émigré Russian press refused to print the appeal because it included a statement that 192 years ago, Russian intervention suffocated Poland: this is the sort of thing that may not be discussed.

Rozanova gave another example: a Jewish writer named David Markish wrote a short novel about a soldier who served in Central Asia. A critic by the name of Natal'ia Rubinstein wrote a brief article about the novel and offered it to the journal *Grani*, also an offical émigré journal. Rubinstein dared call this novel by David Markish a "colonial novel." Subsequently she met with one of the editors of *Grani*. In the course of the conversation she was told that Russia never had any colonies, that we never tried to conquer the Caucasus; we only, as it were, liberated it and shared our culture with it. Therefore, they told her, the article would not be published unless she removed all references to this subject.

Rozanova concluded her comments by conceding that it was very good and very appropriate to gather together and discuss the horrors of Soviet censorship. However, in her opinion the time has come to take this third emigration and examine it under the microscope; American scholars would learn a great deal from such an examination.

Glad noted that if one wants to study the roots of Russian censorship, one should look at the very effective censorship of pagan culture by the Orthodox Church lasting for perhaps seven centuries. Friedberg added that of all the writings of Chekhov, an author he loves, his favorite lines are not from *The Cherry Orchard* or from any short story; they are, rather, a chance remark of Anton Pavlovich Chekhov himself, who said in a private letter, *"kaplia po kaple vyzhimaiu iz sebia raba"* — "I am squeezing out the slave in me, drop by drop." Rabbinic commentators of the Bible, he noted, usually point out that the 40 years of wandering in the desert by Moses and the Israelites were prompted by this same consideration. It was feared that the people who grew up to be slaves in Egypt could not undergo a complete change into free men, even when they entered the Promised Land. Friedberg observed that in his view, Rozanova is a bit too pessimistic in some of her prognoses; he had in mind five or six publications, other than her own *Sintaksis*, where one may publish an objective evaluation of Maksimov's literary merit, including less than laudatory ones. There are, for example, the American scholarly journals such as *Slavic Review*, *Russian Review*, and

Russian Language Journal (which publishes articles in Russian), as well as journals printed in Israel and Canada.

Friedberg believes that the taboos that exist were not addressed at this conference because these taboos *need not* exist. He noted that there is absolutely no problem in stating the most preposterous things in print in the *New York Times* if you are willing to publish them as a paid advertisement, and cited the example of an open letter to President Reagan, published in the *New York Times*, from a civic-minded Soviet clergyman known as Patriarch Pimen in which Pimen accused Reagan of inadequate Christian charity and of un-Christian behavior. (Friedberg added that he was less than certain that the letter was Pimen's own idea, or, for that matter, that he wrote its text or paid for its publication.)

In America, Friedberg continued, as a result of the technological revolution in printing the line between informal publication and the regular press is gradually fading. You can simply type whatever you like on a typewriter, and near any American university you will find a dozen establishments with names like Quick Copy or Ready Copy, and for three or five cents a page they will print whatever you want; they will even bind it. You can make 100 copies, or 300, or one or two thousand if you wish, and you can then mail them at the post office at a discount rate for printed matter. Fortunately, there is no Glavlit here, he observed.

Given this situation, Friedberg fails to understand why people complain that *Russkaia mysl'* or *Novoe russkoe slovo* does not print their ads. He added that for a certain fee you can obtain from any American publisher or specialized journal devoted to Slavic studies a list of subscribers interested in the subject so that you can send a copy of the advertisement for this book to each subscriber. Many American writers begin precisely this way, not for political reasons but simply because they are beginning writers unknown to the public. A first novel may get a good review from one influential critic, along with two bad reviews, and the next time it will be much easier for the author to find a publisher.

In Friedberg's opinion, the misfortune is that émigrés in the West continue — intentionally or unintentionally — perhaps out of inertia, to live, as it were, Soviet lives. They limit their friendships to other émigrés. They publish advertisements only in other émigré publications. Why not publish such an advertisement in a different journal, not necessarily a Russian-language journal, that is read by people interested in the subject? You can publish an announcement in Russian in an English-language newspaper: If you pay for it, you can use the same free press as any American. That is why the question of censorship *within the emigration* lies outside the proper scope of this conference.

Censorship also existed in the first Russian emigration, before World War II, Friedberg added, reminding the audience that Vladimir Nabokov's novel *The Gift* was subject to censorship because it derided the illustrious radical critic Chernyshevskii. Again, as Chekhov said, you will have to wring out the slave in yourself, "painfully, drop by drop."

Before closing the conference, Friedberg asked participants to discuss what appears to them to be the future of Soviet culture and intellectual life, and whether they think it is possible to hope for the disappearance of censorship in the near future. In what directions will cultural and intellectual life develop in the Soviet Union? These remarks form a kind of epilogue to the book.

Aksyonov commented first, recalling a remark made by someone at the conference that Russian literature had suffered many losses because of the emigration of writers. In his view, however, the emigration of writers cannot be considered a loss for Russian culture. Despite the fact that he and others are here, off their native soil, they are still working for Russia, for Russian culture; indeed, perhaps the writers who are here are working more effectively for Russian culture than are those who remain in Russia. He suggested that emigration, this obvious crisis of contemporary Soviet culture, perhaps should be considered a loss for *Soviet* rather than for *Russian* culture. He speculated that writers might gain some advantages from their expulsion and that they might bring some benefits to the cultures of the countries in which they have found shelter.

Glad asked Aksyonov whether he would be happy if 50 years from now people were to know as much about him as the third emigration knows about the first wave. That is what he had in mind, Aksyonov responded, and recalled that in the early 1950s Soviet youth knew nothing about Russian culture abroad: the gap was fantastically deep and broad. Then all of a sudden he and his contemporaries began to discover more and more names, more and more books; it was really a new world for them, and these books enriched them enormously. It is said, he added, that the fruits of emigration never benefit the next generation, and in this case it is true that a generation was skipped. The first wave wrote in the 1920s, and the "grandchildren" in the 1950s benefited from their writing. Emigration is a time capsule, Glad observed. Yes, agreed Aksyonov, or a time bomb!

Voinovich commented next, observing that Friedberg's question was not formulated quite precisely enough. Whether Russian or Soviet censorship continues to exist does not really answer the question; it all depends on what form it takes. If we are talking about its present form, then there will be absolutely no developments in the near future because, in his view, censorship is everything — the entire Soviet system is censorship.

As Voinovich sees it, this is the situation in literature: Young talent cannot break through at all because corruption exists there that simply cannot be dealt with by an individual alone. For a writer to get ahead in literature he must have relatives, acquaintances, someone he can offer a bribe to, and so forth. Such a person can hardly become a good writer, and nothing can be expected of him; but a talented person without connections simply will not break into the literary establishment.

Voinovich characterized the situation in the Soviet Union as uniquely abominable. Even taking into account all of Soviet history — and things do change periodically — there seems to be a special situation now in which one cannot expect any changes for the better. Tomorrow some Soviet leader might declare: "We have gone too far, we have ruined literature. Let all the flowers bloom. We will relax censorship. Censorship will deal only with this, that, and the other thing." Voinovich stressed that in this scenario censorship would continue to exist but would be less harsh; literature, of course, would improve very quickly as a result of the change.

Voinovich observed that in the 1960s, when he, Aksyonov, and many other people of their generation entered the literary establishment, they succeeded only because Party control had, for a short time, been somewhat weakened. Perhaps this was not evident to others, but it was to these young writers. They entered the official literary establishment, they even developed in it somehow, and went so far as to end up here. Had his generation never entered it, however, had there never been such a period, perhaps he and Aksyonov would now be somewhere else and people here would not even know their names.

Friedberg asked Voinovich if he allowed for the possibility that in the USSR at this time there may be an Akhmatova, a Tsvetaeva, a Bulgakov, a Pasternak, who writes but does not publish. Voinovich replied that the situation is especially difficult now for young beginning writers. A poet may develop without being published, but it would be very hard for a prose writer. Someone at the conference had asked him, "What does a writer need, after all, beyond pen and paper?" In Voinovich's opinion, a writer needs more: he also needs a publisher and a reader, because only then can he develop. He conceded that it is not impossible to manage without those things — for example, Solzhenitsyn developed outside the channels of official publication — but maintained that this path is not for every gifted writer.

Siniavsky spoke next, confessing that with regard to the possibility of sociopolitical liberalization in the Soviet Union he is a pessimist, and a very somber pessimist at that. He has no hope at all that censorship will disappear in a few years. On the contrary, it may even become harsher. There are periodic fluctuations, but without censorship the system could not exist.

Siniavsky is an optimist, however, with regard to another subject: prospects for Russian culture. The experience of his entire life had suggested that following Stalin's death nothing would be left at all. It was not merely that the wonderful orchard of Russian literature had been cut down. It was far worse: even the stumps had been uprooted, and then everything that was left had been burned. But then, completely unexpected, little green shoots suddenly began to appear on this scorched earth. At the beginning these did not necessarily have to be great people, brilliant writers, of the stature of Pasternak. Such phenomena take shape over decades; they can be in the making even for epochs. These timid shoots did appear, and Siniavsky thinks they will continue to appear in the future.

He predicts that censorship will continue to exist, will continue to undo the writers, and that they will continue to circumvent censorship. If they do not succeed using official channels, they will resort to circulating their work in samizdat or having it published abroad, as is now the practice. A precedent has been established. The practice will continue, however harsh the censorship, even if it is harsher than now. That would be terrible, of course, but be that as it may, Russian culture, in Siniavsky's view, can no longer be destroyed.

In his comment Yarim-Agaev repeated two things he considers fundamental. First, he feels it is essential to distinguish categorically between Soviet and prerevolutionary censorship. While in no way idealizing tsarist Russia in this respect, he stressed again that there is a qualitative difference between these two systems. One should not, in his opinion, devote so much time to looking for Soviet censorship's roots. Rather, one should examine the discrete, separate system. There are two parameters that fundamentally distinguish Soviet censorship. First is the fact that the executive powers have complete authority over the legislative powers, and this in a broad sense means unlimited freedom of action for the censor. Second is the absence of private property, which is a direct form of censorship because if people had the opportunity to own printing presses, film studios, and the like, then the question of censorship would be much more abstract than it is at the moment.

Second, in his view censorship consists of three stages, all extremely important. The first stage is control of the creative process. Do people have an opportunity to create? This may be harder to discern in literature, but in areas such as film, theater, or science it is immediately apparent. The second stage is control over the publication of the results of such creative activity. We tend to devote all our attention to this stage of the problem, although the first stage is very important as well. The third stage is punishment of the person who somehow, in some way, managed to publish the results of his creative work. Yarim-Agaev noted that there are two alternatives. One is to change censorship itself. We know, however, that in the course of recent years a completely different approach to the problem has arisen: to ignore censorship. At this time this approach has proved to be, in his opinion, the most fruitful; that is, the majority of writers, arriving ultimately at a point where further compromise with the Soviet censors was impossible, simply began to publish their work abroad.

A very important factor is technological progress: in Yarim-Agaev's opinion, a crucial event for the entire structure of the Soviet Union and Soviet censorship was the appearance in the Soviet Union of shortwave radios and of radio stations broadcasting to the Soviet Union, a breakthrough that occurred as a result of purely technical developments. He is an optimist only in this regard, and hopes that the development of various technical devices will seriously erode this system. He has in mind portable photocopying machines, small movie cameras and tape recorders, computers. Perhaps we underestimate the degree to which these technical devices will be able simply to brush aside and block the activities of some of the censorship institutions in the Soviet Union. In his opinion, however, if there is any reason to be optimistic somewhere or about something, then it would be precisely with regard to this aspect of the problem and not with regard to the prospects for changes within the Soviet system.

Concerning his specific topic, science, Yarim-Agaev's sincere opinion is that secrecy, which is the basic form of censorship in science, will intensify, as will the tendency of Soviet science to classify as secret an ever greater number of laboratories. This, in part, bespeaks the militarization of Soviet science, and it has already had serious political consequences. He is rather pessimistic concerning the prospects for change in the opposite direction on the initiative of the Soviet leadership.

Zaks, agreeing with previous speakers, observed that in his view there is no basis for optimism regarding the evolution of censorship, inasmuch as there is no basis for thinking of any kind of progressive or liberal development. When asked by Friedberg to comment on the evolution of literature in conditions of censorship, he replied that so long as we see censorship intensifying in all its forms, in all its phases, and on all levels, it is impossible to count on anything positive at all in Soviet literature. Only one path remains: publishing abroad.

What Yarim-Agaev said concerning technical devices strikes Zaks as extraordinarily important. In earlier times, when the reproduction of printed materials was accomplished with duplicating machines, by law these had to be kept in a separate room that was sealed each day with sealing wax; someone had to be specially assigned to this room, under whose control the copies were made, so that not one copy could drift off somewhere on the side. Now, when a considerable number of photocopying machines have appeared in establishments in the Soviet Union — however far behind it may have fallen technically — it has become impossible to guard them as the ancient duplicating machines were guarded. Access to these copiers has become easier; indeed, it has even happened that in the absence of personal copy machines, many underground samizdat manuscripts have been reproduced on institutional copy machines. In Zaks's view, technology is not simply a question of mechanics but, rather, a truly substantive factor.

Friedberg recalled the words of Evgenii Zamiatin written 60-odd years ago in his collection *Litsa* (*Faces*),[4] containing the prediction that under these very conditions of suppression by censorship, Russian literature would have only one future: its past. It seems, Friedberg observed, that he was too pessimistic.

Linda Lubrano was asked next to comment on what she believes, in conditions of continued censorship, is likely to be the evolution of science in the USSR in the coming decade or so. How will censorship affect the development of science? She responded that although she agrees with Yarim-Agaev that there has been an impact on the quality of Soviet science as a consequence of censorship in scientific institutions and in scientific publications, she has found that over the years Soviet scientists, as is true of scientists in other countries, have been very resilient and resourceful in finding ways to circumvent the censorship in the absence of financial and material support for the conduct of science and the limitations on equipment and supplies for the conduct of research.

If one wants to stop creativity and productivity in the sciences, she noted, all one has to do is withhold the resources for the conduct of that research. If one does not withhold the resources — and the Soviet authorities have been forthcoming in certain areas of science where they want the research done; they provide the resources and allow for creativity — then the government has to deal with the reality of some substantive results from having performed the research, including unauthorized publication abroad of articles based on the research results. It seems to her that the economic support systems and the technical difficulties of performing research far outweigh, in their negative impact, the impact of censorship on the long-term development of Soviet science.

Golovskoy speculated that new forms of censorship might appear — by radar, perhaps, or by use of chemicals, or some such specialized censorship. There may also be more streamlined ideological controls and an improved bureaucratic system. Fortunately, however, the Soviet system is not that efficient, and alternatives do exist. It may be Stalinism, with its almost complete suppression of art and spiritual life, or it may be a delicate balancing act.

There are occasionally some opportunities in art, in each instance for different and complicated reasons. Something may slip through in literature, or even in film, although in the case of film — indeed, in everything connected with technology — the situation is much more complex.

He added that in film, unfortunately, there can be no "underground or foreign production." Filmmakers find themselves in a much more difficult position. Nevertheless we can name a few artists who, for whatever reason, are given the opportunity to express themselves. There is Tarkovskii, for example, who is now tolerated as an export commodity.[5] They gave him permission to make *The Mirror* [*Zerkalo*] and *Stalker*. The authorities even support this, and one could name many such examples. In the long run, he concluded, he is an optimist: he thinks that Russian culture will not die. It will outlive the Bolsheviks.

Finkelstein spoke next, remarking that he subscribed fully to Golovskoy's view. However, he added, the damage done to Russian culture by censorship is enormous, catastrophic, immeasurable. Of course literature does exist, very good writers emerge now and then, and they create interesting works, but in poetry, in prose, in theater, in each area it is like the foot of a Chinese girl. We recall that in China it was customary to put wooden clogs on the foot of a newborn baby girl so that when she grew her feet would remain small, deformed, distorted. Yet the girl did walk — the feet were good for walking despite everything — but of course they were terribly deformed. The fact is that in Russia, with its censorship system, there are now perhaps 100 good writers; there probably would have been 3,000 good writers without that system.

Ours is a very interesting period for historians, Finkelstein continued. Some of the best literary works of our time have been inspired, if that is the proper word, by its events and institutions, however tragic. If there were no Gulag, there would probably be no Solzhenitsyn. It would be far better not to have the Gulag, not to have 20 million dead, and — pardon the sacrilege — not to have a writer of Solzhenitsyn's stature. We cannot say that what is going on in the Soviet Union facilitates in any way the development of art or literature in Russia; it only distorts and bars it. The fact that Russian culture still lives, the fact that from 1953 to 1956 there was suddenly an outburst of good writers, is a startling and encouraging fact. Of course Russian culture will outlive the Bolsheviks, but the horror is enormous and the damage is uncountable because we do not know how many good writers have already been nipped in the bud.

Rudyak observed that he too is an optimist; he too believes in the endurance of traditions. He mentioned the example of Odessa: the spirit of that city nourished such authors as Babel, Paustovskii, Kataev, Il'f and Petrov, and Bagritskii. In his view the spirit of Odessa, and of all Russia, will always exist and will always be influential. Major writers will appear. Still, in his view, Russia's faith in the printed word must gradually fade. Right now in Russia they love what is uncensored but believe in what is printed. "Manuscripts do not burn," as we know. It is possible, Rudyak speculated, that even now some very important works may appear. After all, despite all the suppression, a few things have appeared: Platonov's[6] work did not perish, although its author did; a book of Pasternak's was published, with a foreword by Siniavsky,[7] as was Andrei Bely's *Petersburg*. One or two interesting films have also appeared. We do not need to be quite so pessimistic, he concluded.

Gershkovich commented that when asked to look into the future, even if only the near future, he has the historian's urge to glance back and take a look at the past. He observed that it is here in America, strange as it may seem, that he has enriched his knowledge of Russian culture extraordinarily and has come to believe in its abilities. He feels fortunate to have found his way to Boston, where he has the opportunity to work in the library at Harvard; there he has seen things he could not see sitting in Moscow working in the Lenin Library, such as the manuscript of *Woe from Wit*[8] and the first edition of *Boris Godunov*,[9] which they have in several versions.

Gershkovich realizes now that there was no period in the modern history of Russian drama and theater, beginning with Pushkin's time, when the theater existed without censorship in one or another form, and not necessarily minor. Looking at the Soviet period, one finds much the same thing. Consider what happened under Stalin, in the years of Yezhov's terror; consider Meyerhold, who worked until 1937 and produced his best plays at the price of his life — a high price indeed. Remember the speech he made at the directors' conference in 1939, two days before his arrest, after which no one ever saw him again: certainly this was the act of a courageous person who believed in Russian humanist art.

In our time there is Liubimov,[10] and who knew of him before April 1964? He was known widely as a leading man, a matinee idol, the young Cossack in the film *Don Cossacks*, but that was all — although it was also known that during the war he was master of ceremonies for the secret police ensemble of song and dance. People knew Liubimov as a successful actor, in no way a nonconformist. He even won the Stalin prize in 1952. Then suddenly, out of the blue, he became an artist with a clear-cut creed, firm in his convictions, knowing how to stand up for himself. This too is our Russian culture, Gershkovich observed.

What can we do, he asked, to perpetuate Russian culture, to help those who have remained there? In his view this is in part the task of Russian criticism here and of Russian writers outside the Soviet Union. Another of their tasks is to help those Russian writers and artists who have emigrated to "find themselves." Despite everything, he sees even greater opportunities for the Russian theater than for literature to prove itself under the totalitarian regime and under conditions of censorship. Drama may be dead, or almost dead, but the classics remain and can carry very modern messages. It was for good reason that Khrushchev, at a meeting with the creative intelligentsia in 1962, said "Staging Griboedov is a rotten idea." (This was on the occasion of Tovstonogov's production of *Woe from Wit* in Leningrad.) The classics will remain; and through *Woe from Wit*, through *Boris Godunov*, as we have already seen, through *The Inspector General*, Russian theater will continue to speak. It will live as long as the Russian people live.

Choldin observed that the long-standing and deep Russian interest in foreign publications seems to continue unabated today and undoubtedly will continue in the future. The only foreign publications to which most Soviet readers have access are Soviet-made translations, however; and judging from the results of her preliminary study reported at this conference, as well as investigations by Friedberg and other colleagues, there is reason to be concerned about the accuracy of these translations.

She suggested that those in the West might be able to influence the process from their side. Interviews with authors and publishers indicate that many appear to be unaware of the kinds of changes that are being made; they simply do not seem to know what happens to their books once the rights have been sold and the translation process is under way. Could we not make this situation better known in the West? After all, since 1973 the Soviets have had to negotiate translation rights to Western publications. Why not insist that translations of Western works reflect accurately the intentions of their authors?

Friedberg concluded the discussion by observing that through a number of coincidences, the timing of this conference turns out to be exceptionally propitious, coinciding with the end of the Brezhnev era — one of the longest eras in the history of the Soviet Union. By now the Soviet Union's Stalinist period, if one adds to it the Leninist period as well, is already shorter than the period of Soviet history since the death of Stalin in 1953. At the same time, when this conference was organized no one was aware that except for very occasional additional departures such as the much-awaited arrival in the West of Georgii Vladimov from Moscow, emigration from the USSR would, for all intents and purposes, come to a halt.

What we have here, then, barring the unexpected — and unfortunately we have no reason to anticipate a change in the immediate future — is a fairly static population of émigré Russian intelligentsia, including the literary intelligentsia. Thus the timing of this gathering, bringing together people who have firsthand experience dealing with Soviet censorship, has unexpectedly turned out to be singularly felicitous.

Notes

1   Andrei A. Vlasov, a renegade Soviet general, collaborated with the Nazis. He was executed in 1946.

2   Vsevolod Kochetov (1912–1973), a Stalinist novelist.

3   Vladimir Maksimov, dissident Soviet writer now living in France, founder-editor of *Kontinent*, a Russian-language literary journal. Mariia Rozanova is editor of *Sintaksis*, another Russian journal published in Paris.

4   Published by Izdatel'stvo imeni Chekhova, New York, 1955.

5   Then living and working in the West.

6   Andrei Platonov (1899–1951), whose banned work was published abroad in the 1970s. Some of his writings are still proscribed in the USSR.

7   Boris Pasternak, *Stikhotvoreniia i poemy*, 2d ed. (Moscow: Sovetskii Pisatel', 1965).

8   Alexander Griboedov's classic comedy in verse, begun in 1822.

9   Pushkin's early play, 1825.

10   Iurii Liubimov, known for innovative productions at Moscow's Taganka theater, now in exile in the West.

Annotated Bibliography

Introduction

This is a selected bibliography, intended to update and supplement the excellent bibliography in Martin Dewhirst and Robert Farrell's invaluable work, *The Soviet Censorship* (see entry below). Readers interested in updating this bibliography are advised to consult annual volumes of *The American Bibliography of Soviet and East European Studies* and *The European Bibliography of Soviet, East European and Slavonic Studies*, and current issues of *Abstracts of Soviet and East European Emigré Literature*. Most issues of the journal *Index on Censorship* (see entry below) contain relevant material.

In the entries that follow names are spelled as they appear in the pieces cited. Annotations are provided where the title fails to suggest the content.

How the System Works

Betaky, V. P. "Poets, Translators, and the Soviet Censor." *Soviet Analyst* 4 (4 September 1975): 5–7.

Bitov, Oleg. "The Man from the Ministry of Truth." *The Sunday Telegraph*, 5 February 1984, pp. 8–9.
  Bitov, a senior editor of the Soviet newspaper *Literaturnaia gazeta*, defected and settled in Britain. (He later returned to the Soviet Union.) See also Duff Hart-Davis, "Writer Given Asylum" and "Escape from a Nightmare," *The Sunday Telegraph*, 29 January 1984, pp. 1 and 17; and "Trudnoe reshenie Olega Bitova" (Oleg Bitov's difficult decision), an interview with Bitov conducted by Leonid Vladimirov and published in *Novoe russkoe slovo*, 26 March 1984, p. 3.

Bitov, Oleg. "How We Lived in Andropov's Closed World." *The Sunday Telegraph*, 9 February 1984, pp. 8–9.

Bitov, Oleg. "Dear Konstantin Ustinovich . . ." *The Sunday Telegraph*, 1 February 1984, p. 8.

Bol'shaia sovetskaia entsiklopediia, 3d ed., s.v. "Tsenzura" (Censorship), by B. M. Lazarev and B. Iu. Ivanov. Moscow: Sovetskaia entsiklopediia, 1978.

The Cambridge Encyclopedia of Russia and the Soviet Union, s.v. "Censorship," by M. D. 1982.

"Censorship." In *Handbook of Russian Literature*, ed. Victor Terras, 74–75. New Haven: Yale University Press, 1985.

Choldin, Marianna Tax. *Censorship in the Slavic World*. Catalogue of an exhibition in the New York Public Library, June 1–October 15, 1984. New York: The New York Public Library, 1984.

Czarna ksiega cenzury PRL. Vols. 1–2. London: "ANEKS," 1977.
  A two-volume compilation of rules and regulations for censors smuggled out of Poland and published in London. English edition: *The Black Book of Polish Censorship*. Translated and

edited by Jane Leftwich Curry. New York: Vintage Books, 1984. There is a Soviet counterpart of Poland's "Black Book," known as the "Index," or, even more ironically, "The Talmud," but it has not made its way to the West.

Dewhirst, Martin, and Farrell, Robert, eds. *The Soviet Censorship*. Metuchen, NJ: Scarecrow Press, 1973.

Etkind, Efim. "Sovetskie tabu" (Soviet taboos). *Sintaksis* 9 (1981): 3–20.
  Discusses prohibitions by means of which the Soviet government maintains ideological control over literature.

Golovskoy, Valery. "Sushchestvuet li tsenzura v Sovetskom Soiuze?" *Kontinent* 42 (1984): 147-73.
  In English: *Is There Censorship in the Soviet Union? Methodological Problems of Studying Soviet Censorship*. Washington, DC: Kennan Institute for Advanced Russian Studies, 1985. Occasional Papers, no. 201.

Haraszti, Miklos. *The Velvet Prison: Artists under State Socialism*. Translated by Katalin and Stephen Landesmann with Steve Wasserman. New York: Basic Books, 1987.

Index on Censorship. Vol. 1, Spring 1972. London: Writers & Scholars International.

Jakobson, Michael. "Literary Censorship in the USSR." In *USSR Facts & Figures Annual*. Vol. 5. Gulf Breeze, FL: Academic International Press, 1981.
  In Russian: Iakobson, Mikhail. "Tsenzura khudozhestvennoi literatury v SSSR." *Strelets*, May 1984, pp. 42–47.

Khazanov, Boris. "Kontrol' nad slovom v SSSR" (Control of the word in the USSR). In *Proceedings of the Fourth International Sakharov Hearing*, Lisbon, October 1983, ed. Semyon Reznik, 107–21. London: Overseas Publications Interchange Ltd., 1985.

Kurman, George. "Literary Censorship in General and in Soviet Estonia." *Journal of Baltic Studies* 8 (Spring 1977): 3–15.

Lifshitz-Losev, Lev. "Books as Vodka." *New York Review of Books*, 31 May 1979, pp. 29–33.

Losseff, Lev. *On the Beneficence of Censorship: Aesopian Language in Modern Russian Literature*. Arbeiten und Texte zur Slavistik, 31. Munich: Verlag Otto Sagner in Kommission, 1984.

Lubrano, Linda L. "Soviet Science Specialists." In *Social Scientists and Policymaking in the USSR*, ed. Richard B. Remnek, 59–85. New York: Praeger, 1977.

Miller, John H. "The Top Soviet Censorship Team? — A Note." *Soviet Studies* 29 (October 1977): 590–98.

Nekrich, A. "Rewriting History." *Index on Censorship* 9 (1980): 4–7.
  This is a special Soviet issue of *Index on Censorship*; several other relevant articles are included in this bibliography.

Parrott, Bruce. *Information Transfer in Soviet Science and Engineering. A Study of Documentary Channels*. Prepared for the Defense Advanced Research Projects Agency (R-2667-ARPA). Santa Monica, CA: Rand Corporation, November 1981.

Parrott, Bruce. *Politics and Technology in the Soviet Union*. Cambridge: MIT Press, 1983.

Popovsky, Mark. *Manipulated Science: The Crisis of Science and Scientists in the Soviet Union Today*. Translated from the Russian by Paul S. Falla. New York: Doubleday, 1979.

Popovsky, Mark. "Science in Blinkers." *Index on Censorship* 9 (1980): 14–18.

Proffer, Carl R. *The Widows of Russia and Other Writings*. Ann Arbor: Ardis, 1987.
  See in particular chapters entitled "In the Shadow of the Monolith," "A Disabled Literature: Are There Any Writers Left in the Soviet Union?" and "Russian Writing and Border Guards: Twenty-five Years of the New Isolationism."

Reznik, Semen. "Tsenzura i samotsenzura v SSSR" (Censorship and self-censorship in the USSR). In *Proceedings of the Fourth International Sakharov Hearing*, Lisbon, October 1983, ed. Semyon Reznik, 159–73. London: Overseas Publications Interchange Ltd., 1985.

Shneerson, M. "Razreshennaia pravda" (Permitted truth). *Kontinent* 28 (1981): 361–80.

Suslov, Ilya. "Esse o tsenzure" (Essay on censorship). *Vremia i my* 56 (1980): 195–210.

Venclova, Tomas. "USSR: Stages of Censorship." *Index* 7 (July-August 1978): 61–62.

Venclova, Tomas. "The Game of the Soviet Censor." *New York Review of Books*, 31 March 1983, pp. 33–35.

Vladimirov, Leonid. *Soviet Media and Their Message.* Chicago: American Bar Association, Standing Committee on Education about Communism, 1977.

Voinovich, Vladimir. "O literature razreshennoi i napisannoi bez razresheniia" (On permitted literature and literature written without permission). *Kontinent* 37 (1983): 439–45.

Voinovich, Vladimir. "Sidelights on Censorship." *Survey* 28 (Autumn 1984): 221–26.

Voinovich, Vladimir. "Tri vida tsenzury v SSSR" (Three kinds of censorship in the USSR). In *Proceedings of the Fourth International Sakharov Hearing*, Lisbon, October 1983, ed. Semyon Reznik, 137–43. London: Overseas Publications Interchange Ltd., 1985.

    In this and the preceding article Voinovich discusses the process of censorship. See also his *Antisovetskii sovetskii soiuz* (Ann Arbor: Ardis, 1985); in English, *The Anti-Soviet Soviet Union*, translated from the Russian by Richard Lourie (San Diego: Harcourt Brace Jovanovich, 1986).

Wishnevsky, Julia. *Information on the Operations of Glavlit Section No. 2.* (RL 494/76). New York, Munich: Radio Liberty Research, 8 December 1976.

    Glavlit is the nickname for the Central Administration for the Protection of State Secrets in the Press, the chief organ of censorship in the Soviet Union.

Wishnevsky, Julia. *The Sixtieth Anniversary of Glavlit.* (RL 213/82). New York, Munich: Radio Liberty Research Bulletin, 26 May 1982.

Yarim-Agaev, Yuri. "Persecution of Scientists and How Western Scientists Can Support Their Colleagues in the East." *Index on Censorship* 10 (October 1981): 27–29.

Culture and Politics

Alt, Noamy. "Is There a Cultural Thaw?" *Index on Censorship* 15 (September 1986): 11–13.

Brown, Edward James. *Russian Literature since the Revolution.* Rev. and enl. ed. Cambridge: Harvard University Press, 1982.

Bush, Keith. *Books in the Soviet Second Economy.* Occasional Paper, no. 116. Washington, DC: Kennan Institute for Advanced Russian Studies, 1980.

Condee, Nancy P., and Vladimir Padunov. "The Outposts of Official Art: Recharting Soviet Cultural History." *Framework* 34 (1987): 59–106.

Condee, Nancy P., and Vladimir Padunov. *Soviet Cultural Politics and Cultural Production.* IREX Occasional Papers. Princeton: International Research and Exchanges Board, December 1987.

Dewhirst, Martin. "Soviet Russian Literature and Literary Policy." In *The Soviet Union since the Fall of Khrushchev*, ed. Archie Brown and Michael Kaser, 181–95. London: Macmillan, 1975.

Fox, Cindy J. "The Politics of Culture in the USSR: Art and the Soviet Government." *Fletcher Forum* 1 (Spring 1977): 204–25.

Frankland, Mark. "Gloomy Signal from the Party Congress." *Index on Censorship* 15 (June 1986): 12–14.

Friedberg, Maurice. "Soviet Letters under Brezhnev." *Problems of Communism* 24 (May/June 1980): 53–64.

Friedberg, Maurice. *Russian Culture in the 1980s.* Significant Issues Series, vol. 7, no. 6.

Washington, DC: Center for Strategic and International Studies, Georgetown University, 1985.

Friedberg, Maurice, ed. *Soviet Society under Gorbachev: Current Trends and the Prospects for Reform*. Armonk, NY: M. E. Sharpe, 1987.

Hingley, Ronald. *Russian Writers and Soviet Society, 1917–1978*. New York: Random House, 1979.

Hollander, Paul. "The Subordination of Literature to Politics: Socialist Realism in a Historical and Comparative Perspective." *Studies in Comparative Communism* 9 (Autumn 1976): 215–25.

Kagarlitsky, Boris. "*Glasnost*, the Soviet Press and Red Greens." *Times Literary Supplement*, 25–31 December 1987, p. 1430.

On the reformist "green" movement in the Soviet press.

Kavolis, Vytautas. "On the Deformations of Intellectual Culture." In *Mind against the Wall: Essays on Lithuanian Culture under Soviet Occupation*, ed. Rimvydas Silbajoris, 34–56. Chicago: Institute of Lithuanian Studies, 1983.

Laird, Sally. "Soviet Literature — What Has Changed?" *Index on Censorship* 16 (July-August 1987): 8–13.

Medvedev, Zhores A. *Desiat' let posle "Odnogo dnia Ivana Denisovicha."* London: Macmillan, 1973.

In English: *Ten Years after Ivan Denisovich*. New York: Knopf, 1973.

Shneidman, N. N. *Soviet Literature in the 1970's: Artistic Diversity and Ideological Conformity*. Toronto: University of Toronto Press, 1979.

Silbajoris, Rimvydas. "Socialist Realism and the Politics of Literature in Occupied Lithuania." In *Mind against the Wall: Essays on Lithuanian Culture under Soviet Occupation*, ed. Rimvydas Silbajoris, 74–106. Chicago: Institute of Lithuanian Studies, 1983.

Solzhenitsyn, Aleksandr Isaevich. *Bodalsia telenok s dubom; ocherki literaturnoi zhizni*. Paris: YMCA Press, 1975.

In English: *The Oak and the Calf: Sketches of Literary Life in the Soviet Union*. Translated from the Russian by Harry Willetts. New York: Harper & Row, 1979.

Publishing, Copyright, the Book Trade

American-Soviet Publishing Relations. Visit to USSR by AAP President, October 1975. New York: Association of American Publishers.

Baumgarten, Jon A. *US-USSR Copyright Relations under the Universal Copyright Convention*. Patent, Copyright, Trademark and Literary Property Practice Handbook Series, no. 3. New York: Practicing Law Institute, 1973.

Boguslavsky, Mark. *The U.S.S.R. and International Copyright Protection*. Translated from the Russian by Yuri Shirokov. Moscow: Progress Publishers, 1979.

Book Publishing in the U.S.S.R. Reports of the Delegations of U.S. Book Publishers Visiting the U.S.S.R. October 21-November 4, 1970; August 20-September 17, 1962. 2d ed., enl. Cambridge: Harvard University Press, 1971.

Choldin, Marianna Tax. "Good Business, Bad Business, No Business: Selling Western Books to the Soviets." In *Books, Libraries and Information in Slavic and East European Studies: Proceedings of the Second International Conference of Slavic Librarians and Information Specialists*, ed. Marianna Tax Choldin, 254–71. New York: Russica, 1986.

"Khristianskoe izdatel'stvo v Sovetskoi Rossii (Une maison d'edition chretienne en URSS)" (A Christian publishing house in Soviet Russia). *Vestnik Russkogo khristianskogo dvizheniia*, no. 115 (1975): 221–26.

Lacy, Dan. "Breaking Faith with the Tsars." *World*, 22 May 1973, p. 15.

Levin, Martin B. "Soviet International Copyright: Dream or Nightmare?" *Journal of the Copyright Society of the U.S.A.* 31 (December 1985): 127–62.

Levitsky, Serge L., and William B. Simons. *Copyright in Russia and the USSR: A Selected Bibliography of Works Published in English, German, French and Russian: 1827–1983.* Internationale Gesellschaft für Urheberrecht e. V., Schriftenreihe, Bd. 61. Vienna: Manzsche Verlags- und Universitäts- Buchhandlung, 1985.

Loeber, Dietrich A. "VAAP: The Soviet Copyright Agency." *University of Illinois Law Forum* 1979: 401–52.

Lottman, Herbert R. "The Soviet Way of Publishing." *Publishers Weekly*, 18 September 1978, pp. 101–31.
    A PW Special Report including several pieces on Soviet publishers and publishing.

Majoros, Ferenc. *Die Rechte ausländischer Urheber in der UdSSR seit dem sowjetischen Beitritt zur Genfer Konvention* (The rights of foreign authors in the USSR since Soviet accession to the Geneva convention). Berichte des Bundesinstituts für ostwissenschaftliche und internationale Studien, 1981: 2. Cologne: Bundesinstitut für ostwissenschaftliche und internationale Studien, 1981.

Owen, Lynette. *A Guide to the Passage of Rights between the United Kingdom and the Soviet Union.* London: The Publishers Association, 1983.

Schwartz, Alan U. "The State of Publishing, Censorship and Copyright in the Soviet Union." *Publishers Weekly*, 15 January 1973, pp. 32–37.

Soviet Book Exports, 1973–82. Prepared by William E. Freeman with Scott Righetti. Research Report R-5-84. Washington, DC: Office of Research, United States Information Agency, March 1984.

Trelford, Donald. "Through the Door Marked Glasnost." *The Bookseller*, 2 October 1987, pp. 1427–28.

Walker, Gregory. *Soviet Book Publishing Policy.* Cambridge: Cambridge University Press, 1978.

Walker, Gregory. "Personnel Policy in the Control of Soviet Book Publishing." In *Books, Libraries and Information in Slavic and East European Studies: Proceedings of the Second International Conference of Slavic Librarians and Information Specialists*, ed. Marianna Tax Choldin, 242–53. New York: Russica, 1986.

Libraries

Kopeikin, A. "Kak popast' v spetskhran." *Russkaia mysl'*, 9 February 1984, p. 6.
    Discussion of restricted-access "special repositories" in Soviet libraries.

Korsch, Boris. "The Role of Readers' Cards in Soviet Libraries." *Journal of Library History* 13 (Summer 1978): 282–97.

Korsch, Boris. *The Permanent Purge of Soviet Libraries.* The Hebrew University of Jerusalem, Soviet and East European Research Centre, Research Paper no. 50. Jerusalem, April 1983.

Korsch, Boris. "The Role of Catalogs in Soviet Libraries." In *Books, Libraries and Information in Slavic and East European Studies: Proceedings of the Second International Conference of Slavic Librarians and Information Specialists*, ed. Marianna Tax Choldin, 210–41. New York: Russica, 1986.

Raymond, Boris. *Krupskaia and Soviet Russian Librarianship, 1917–1939*. Metuchen, NJ: Scarecrow Press, 1979.
    On the role played by Nadezhda Krupskaia, Lenin's wife, in Soviet librarianship.

Rogers, A. R. "Censorship and Libraries in the Soviet Union." *Journal of Library History* 8 (January 1973): 22–29.

Theater

Gershkovich, Aleksandr. "Tsenzura i iskusstvo" (Censorship and art). *SSSR: Vnutrennie protivorechiia* 11 (1984): 37–88.

Gershkovich, Aleksandr. *Teatr na Taganke (1964-1984)* (Taganka: The rebellious Soviet theater). Benson, VT: Chalidze Publications, 1986.
    Under the direction of Iurii Liubimov, then one of the Soviet Union's most interesting and important theaters.

Law, Alma H. "Soviet Theatre Today: The Struggle for Artistic Expression in the 1970's." *The Philological Papers* 25, ser. 79, no. 8–3 (February 1979): 28–37.

Law, Alma H. "Setting the Record Straight." *Newsnotes on Soviet and East European Drama and Theatre* 3 (June 1983): 22–25.

Law, Alma H. *Soviet Theatre in Transition: The Politics of Theatre in the 1980s*. Kennan Institute for Advanced Russian Studies, Occasional Papers, no. 195. Prepared for presentation at the Kennan Institute for Advanced Russian Studies, Washington, DC, 10 December 1984.

Law, Alma H. "The Trouble with Lyubimov." *American Theatre*, April 1985, pp. 4–11.

Lioubimov, Youri. *Le feu sacre; Souvenirs d'une vie de theatre* (The sacred fire: Memoirs of a life in the theater). With the collaboration of Marc Dondey. Paris: Fayard, 1985.

Tamarchenko, Anna. "Theatre Censorship." *Index on Censorship* 9, no. 4 (August 1980): 23–28.

Weiner, Jack. "Lope de Vega's *Fuenteovejuna* under Tsars, Commissars, and the Second Spanish Republic (1931–1939)." *Annali*, Instituto Universitario Orientale, Napoli, Sezione Romanza, 24 (January 1982): 167–223.

Zaitsev, Mark (pseud.). "Soviet Theatre Censorship." *The Drama Review* 19 (June 1975): 119–28.

Music

Braun, Joachim. *Jews in Soviet Music*. Jerusalem: The Hebrew University of Jerusalem, Soviet and East European Research Centre, Research Paper no. 22. June 1977.

Braun, Joachim. "Shostakovich's Song Cycle *From Jewish Folk Poetry*: Aspects of Style and Meaning." In *Russian and Soviet Music: Essays for Boris Schwarz*, ed. Malcolm Hamrick Brown, 259–86. Russian Music Studies no. 11. Ann Arbor, MI: UMI Research Press, 1984.

Brown, Royal S. "The Three Faces of Lady Macbeth." In *Russian and Soviet Music: Essays for Boris Schwarz*, ed. Malcolm Hamrick Brown, 245–52. Russian Music Studies no. 11. Ann Arbor, MI: UMI Research Press, 1984.

Gojowy, Detlef. "Half Time for Nikolai Roslavets (1881–1944): A Non-Love Story with a Post-Romantic Composer." In *Russian and Soviet Music: Essays for Boris Schwarz*, ed. Malcolm Hamrick Brown, 211-20. Russian Music Studies no. 11. Ann Arbor, MI: UMI Research Press, 1984.

Lamont, Rosette C. "Horace's Heirs: Beyond Censorship in the Soviet Songs of the Magnitizdat." *World Literature Today* 53 (1979): 220–27.

Ogen, Don (pseud.). *The Leningrad Branch of the RSFSR Union of Composers* (in Russian). Soviet Institutions Series, Paper no. 2. The Hebrew University of Jerusalem, Soviet and East European Research Centre, September 1975.

Schwarz, Boris. *Music and Musical Life in Soviet Russia*. Enl. ed., 1917–1981. Bloomington: Indiana University Press, 1983.

Shostakovich, Dmitri. *Testimony: The Memoirs of Dmitri Shostakovich*. As related to and edited by Solomon Volkov. Translated from the Russian by Antonina W. Bouis. New York: Harper & Row, 1979.

For discussions of this controversial work, the reader might consult articles and reviews listed in *The American Bibliography of Slavic and East European Studies* (1979 and later volumes).

Singurel, Gregore (Efim Krimmerman). "Tsenzura kontsertnykh programm" (Censorship of concert programs). In *Proceedings of the Fourth International Sakharov Hearing*, Lisbon, October 1983, ed. Semyon Reznik, 145–57. London: Overseas Publications Interchange Ltd., 1985.

Smith, Gerald Stanton. *Songs to Seven Strings: Russian Guitar Poetry and Soviet "Mass Song."* Bloomington: Indiana University Press, 1984.

Sosin, Gene. "Magnitizdat: Uncensored Songs of Dissent." In *Dissent in the USSR*, ed. Rudolf L. Tökes, 276–309. Baltimore: Johns Hopkins University Press, 1975.

Vishevskaya, Galina. *Galina: A Russian Story*. San Diego: Harcourt Brace Jovanovich, 1984.

Volkov, Solomon. "Scissors and Music: Music Censorship in the Soviet Union." *Keynote* 7 (August 1983): 14–18.

Weiner, Jack. "The Destalinization of Dmitrii Shostakovich's 'Song of the Forests,' Op. 81 (1949)." *Rocky Mountain Review* 38 (1984): 214–22.

Cinema

Betz, Kate. "As the Tycoons Die: Class Struggle and Censorship in the Russian Cinema, 1917–1921." In *Art, Society, Revolution*, ed. Nils A. Nilsson, 198–236. Stockholm: Almquist & Wiksell International, 1979.

Chertok, Semen. "Kinotsenzura v SSSR" (Film censorship in the USSR). *Obozrenie*, July 1983, no. 5, pp. 21–23.

See also the version (with the same title) in *Proceedings of the Fourth International Sakharov Hearing*, Lisbon, October 1983, ed. Semyon Reznik, 123–35. London: Overseas

Publications Interchange Ltd., 1985. (The last four pages consist of questions to Chertok and his responses.)

Fisher, William. "Gorbachev's Cinema." *Sight and Sound: International Film Quarterly* 56, no. 4 (Autumn 1977): 238–43.

Golovskoy, Valery. "Amerikanskie fil'my na sovetskikh ekranakh (1957–1980)" (American films on Soviet screens). *SSSR: Vnutrennie protivorechiia* 12 (1985): 180–95.

Golovskoy, Valery. "Kinotsenzura v SSSR: Istoricheskii obzor, struktura, praktika" (Cinema censorship in the USSR: Historical survey, structure, practice). *SSSR: Vnutrennie protivorechiia* 12 (1985): 138–79.

Golovskoy, Val S., with John Rimberg. *Behind the Soviet Screen: The Motion-Picture Industry in the USSR 1972–1982*. Translations by Steven Hill. Ann Arbor: Ardis, 1986.

Kennedy, Harlan. "Soviet Spring." *Film Comment* 23 (June 1987): 34–36.

Rosten, Keith A. "Legal Control of the Soviet Cinema: The Scenario Writer's Contract." *Rutgers Law Journal* 14 (Fall 1982): 115–33.

"Sakharov's Views on Historical Film Printed." *Current Digest of the Soviet Press* 39, no. 46 (1987): 12.

On the screening by Soviet television of Dmitrii Barshchevskii's documentary film *Risk*, which deals candidly with some events in Soviet history.

"Symposium on Socialist Realism: Cinema and the Arts." *Studies in Comparative Communism* 17 (Fall/Winter 1984–85): 157–239.

Albert Leong was guest editor of this special issue, which includes the following articles: Valery Golovskoy, "*Cinema Art*: Portrait of a Journal" (pp. 219–26); Albert Leong, "Socialist Realism: Cinema and the Arts" (pp. 157–62), "Socialist Realism in Tarkovsky's *Andrei Rublev*" (pp. 227–34, discussing the odyssey of a controversial Soviet historical film); Ronald Levaco, "Censorship, Ideology, and Style in Soviet Cinema" (pp. 173–84); Sidney Monas, "Censorship, Film, and Soviet Society: Some Reflections of a Russia-Watcher" (pp. 163–72); Ernst Neizvestny, "Art and Freedom" (translated by Albert Leong, pp. 235–39); Harlow Robinson, "'The Most Contemporary Art': Sergei Prokofiev and Soviet Film" (pp. 203–18); and Richard Taylor, "Soviet Socialist Realism and the Cinema Avant-Garde" (pp. 185–202).

Television, Broadcasting, the Media

Alexeeva, Ludmilla. *US Broadcasting to the Soviet Union*. New York: Helsinki Watch, 1986.

Cunniff, Lois. "Soviet Photojournalism: Three Emigrés Open Their Portfolios." *Columbia Journalism Review* 22 (May-June 1983): 45–50.

Curry, Jane Leftwich, and Joan R. Dassin, ed. *Press Control around the World*. New York: Praeger, 1982.

Dizard, Wilson P., and S. Blake Swensrud. *Gorbachev's Information Revolution: Controlling Glasnost in a New Electronic Era*. Boulder, CO: Westview Press, 1987.

Edwards, Keith. "The Jamming of Western Radio Broadcasts." In *Proceedings of the Fifth International Sakharov Hearing*, London, April 1985, ed. Allan Wynn, 82–88. London: André Deutsch, 1986.

Eniutina, Vera. "Sovetskaia tsenzura" (Soviet censorship). *Novoe russkoe slovo*, 24 January 1982, p. 3.

On the author's years with Radio Moscow.

Heffner, Richard. "Offener Himmel oder Vorzensur? Moskau gegen Satelliten-Fernsehen" (Open sky or prior censorship? Moscow against television via satellite). *Osteuropa* 24 (July 1974): 486–96.

Katz, Zev. *The Communications System in the USSR.* (C/77–10) Cambridge: Research Program on Communications Policy, Center for International Studies, Massachusetts Institute of Technology, May 1977.

Lendvai, Paul. *The Bureaucracy of Truth: How Communist Governments Manage the News.* Boulder, CO: Westview Press, 1981.

Mickiewicz, Ellen Propper. *Media and the Russian Public.* New York: Praeger, 1981.

　　On the mass media and the Soviet Russian public.

Roth, Paul. *SOW-Inform: Nachrichtenwesen und Informationspolitik der Sowjetunion* (SOW-Inform: The news system and information policy of the Soviet Union). Düsseldorf: Droste Verlag, 1980.

Roth, Paul. *Die kommandierte öffentliche Meinung: Sowjetische Medienpolitik* (Directed public opinion: Soviet media policy). Stuttgart: Seewald, 1982.

Satter, David. "Western Correspondents in the USSR and the Flow of Information." In *Proceedings of the Fifth International Sakharov Hearing*, April 1985, ed. Allan Wynn, 125–29. London: André Deutsch, 1986.

Schöpflin, George, ed. *Censorship and Political Communication in Eastern Europe. A Collection of Documents.* London: Frances Pinter (Publishers), in association with Index on Censorship, 1983.

　　Documents relating to Czechoslovakia, Poland, Hungary, German Democratic Republic, Rumania, and Yugoslavia but not the USSR. This reference is included here because the material is relevant to the Soviet Union as well.

Effect of Censorship on Writers

Berman, Filipp. "Razgrom nezavisimogo kluba pisatelei v Moskve" (The rout of the independent writers' club in Moscow). In *Proceedings of the Fourth International Sakharov Hearing*, Lisbon, October 1983, ed. Semyon Reznik, 175–87. London: Overseas Publications Interchange Ltd., 1985.

Ermolaev, Herman. *Mikhail Sholokhov and His Art.* Princeton: Princeton University Press, 1982.

Ermolaev, Herman. "Solzenicyn's Self-Censorship: Two Versions of *V kruge pervom*." *Russian Language Journal* 38 (1984): 177–85.

Ianevich, N. "Institut mirovoi literatury v 1930-e – 1970-e gody" (The institute of world literature 1930–1970). *Pamiat'* 5 (1981–82): 83–162.

　　Contains a wealth of information on political infighting and censorship in the foremost Soviet institute for literary research.

Kern, Gary. "Solzenicyn's Self-Censorship: The Canonical Text of *Odin den' Ivana Denisovica*." *Slavic and East European Journal* 20 (Winter 1976): 421–36.

Lifshitz-Losev, Lev. "What It Means to Be Censored." *New York Review of Books*, 29 June 1978, pp. 43–50.

Mihalap, Leonid Isaakovich. *Leonid Leonov's Revision of "Vor": A Case Study in Soviet Literary Censorship.* Ph.D. diss., University of North Carolina at Chapel Hill, 1973.

Radley, Philippe D. "Censorship as a Creative Stimulus: The Russian Experience." *World Literature Today* 53 (Spring 1979): 201–5.

Siniavsky, Andrei. "My Life as a Writer." *Index on Censorship* 15 (June 1986): 7.

Censorship and Reading

Brine, Jenny. "The Soviet Reader, the Book Shortage and the Public Library." *Solanus* n.s. 2 (1988): 39–57.

Brooks, Jeffrey. *Information and Power: The Soviet Paradigm for Revolutionary Cultural Change, 1921–28.* Final Report to the National Council for Soviet and East European Research, March 1985. (Council Contract no. 628–7)

Brooks, Jeffrey. *When Russia Learned to Read: Literacy and Popular Literature, 1861–1917.* Princeton: Princeton University Press, 1985.
    Provides background for the Soviet period.

Garrard, John, and Amy Corning. "The Soviet Reader: New Data From the Soviet Interview Project." *Solanus* n.s. 2 (1988): 3–38.

Mehnert, Klaus. *Uber die Russen Heute. Was sie lesen, wie sie sind.* Stuttgart: Deutsche Verlags-Anstalt, 1983.
    In English: *The Russians and Their Favorite Books.* Stanford, CA: Hoover Institution Press, 1983.

Pomerantzev, Igor. "The Right to Read." *Partisan Review* 49 (1982): 54–67.

Walker, Gregory. "Readerships in the USSR: Some Evidence from Post-War Studies." *Oxford Slavonic Papers*, n.s. 19 (1986): 158–73.

Postal Censorship

Avzeger, Leopol'd. *Chernyi kabinet: Zapiski tainogo tsenzora MGB* (The black office: Memoirs of a secret censor of the Ministry of State Security). Tel-Aviv: Khoken, 1987.
    See also his earlier article: "Ia vskryval vashi pis'ma . . . Iz vospominanii byvshego tainogo tsenzora MGB" (I opened your letters . . . From the memoirs of a former secret censor of the Ministry of State Security). *Vremia i my* 55 (July-August 1980): 224–53; 56 (September-October 1980): 254–78.

Pavlenkov, Vladlen. *Postal communications between the USA and the USSR and How to Improve Them.* Jersey City, NJ: FC IZDAT, 1983.

Pavlenkov, Vladlen. "Soviet Postal Restrictions." In *Proceedings of the Fifth International Sakharov Hearing*, April 1985, ed. Allan Wynn, 89–91. London: André Deutsch, 1986.

Pochta v SSSR. Informatsionnyi biulleten' organizatsii "Freedom of Communications." 1982- (semiannual).

Also published in English: *Mail to the USSR. Information Bulletin of Freedom of Communications Committee*. (Distributed by Freedom of Communications, 80 Grand Street, Jersey City, NJ 07302, 201/332–7962)

Dissent, Samizdat

Alexeyeva, Ludmilla. *Soviet Dissent: Contemporary Movements for National, Religious, and Human Rights*. Translated by Carol Pearce and John Glad. Middletown, CT: Wesleyan University Press, 1985.

Emerson, Susan Vince. "Writers Who Protest and Protesters Who Write: A Guide to Soviet Dissent Literature." *Collection Building* 4 (1982): 21-33.

An End to Silence. Uncensored Opinion in the Soviet Union: From Roy Medvedev's Underground Magazine Political Diary. Edited and with introductions by Stephen F. Cohen. Translated by George Saunders. New York: Norton, 1982.

Hopkins, Mark. *Russia's Underground Press: The Chronicle of Current Events*. Foreword by Andrei Sakharov. New York: Praeger, 1983.

Kwiatkowski, Alexandra. "Nonconformist Trends in the Soviet Literary Press: *Novy Mir*." In *Education and the Mass Media in the Soviet Union and Eastern Europe*, ed. Bohdan Harasymiw, 65–79. New York: Praeger, 1976.

Langley, John H. "Copyright, Censorship, and Dissidents in the Soviet Union." In *The Soviet Union: The Seventies and Beyond*, ed. Bernard W. Eissenstat, 237–45. Lexington, Mass.: Lexington Books, 1975.

Non-conformity and Dissent in the Ukrainian SSR, 1955–1975. An Annotated Bibliography. Compiled by George Liber and Anna Mostovych. Cambridge: Harvard Ukrainian Research Institute, 1975.

Pospielovsky, Dimitry. "From *Gosizdat* to *Samizdat* and *Tamizdat*." *Canadian Slavonic Papers* 20 (March 1978): 44–62.

On "official" publishing; unapproved material reproduced unofficially within the Soviet Union, and unapproved material published abroad and smuggled back into the Soviet Union.

Reddaway, Peter. "Can the Dissidents Survive?" *Index on Censorship* 9 (1980): 29–34.

Reddaway, Peter. *Soviet Policies on Dissent and Emigration: The Radical Change of Course since 1979*. Washington, DC: Kennan Institute for Advanced Russian Studies, August 28, 1984. Occasional Paper no. 192.

Saunders, George, ed. *Samizdat: Voices of the Soviet Opposition*. New York: Monad Press, 1974; distributed by Pathfinder Press.

Shanor, Donald R. *Behind the Lines: The Private War against Soviet Censorship*. New York: St. Martin's, 1985.

Siniavsky, Andrei. "Samizdat and the Rebirth of Literature." *Index on Censorship* 9 (1980): 8–13.

Sosin, Gene. "Censorship and Dissent." *Studies in Comparative Communism* 19 (Summer 1966): 147–55.

A review article.

Spechler, Dina R. *Permitted Dissent in the USSR: Novyi mir and the Soviet Regime*. New York: Praeger, 1982.

The story of the leading liberal Soviet journal during the Khrushchev thaws of 1956 and 1962.

Volkov, Oleg. "It's Hard to Be Optimistic." *Index on Censorship* 16 (February 1987): 7–8.

An abridged version (translated by Frank Williams) of the Russian original, published in the November 1986 issue of *Strana i Mir* (Munich).

Walters, Philip. "Christian Samizdat." *Index on Censorship* 9 (1980): 46–50.

Woll, Josephine, in collaboration with Vladimir G. Treml. *Soviet Dissident Literature: A Critical Guide*. Boston: G. K. Hall, 1983.

Updates an earlier version, *Soviet Unofficial Literature: Samizdat* (Duke University Center for International Studies, March 1978).

Soviet Treatment of Western Literature

Bregel, Y. "The Bibliography of Barthold's Works and the Soviet Censorship." *Survey* 24 (Summer 1979): 91–107.

Brown, Deming Bronson. *Soviet Attitudes toward American Literature*. Princeton: Princeton University Press, 1962.

Bukowski, Peter. "Der Zensor ist Lektor" (The censor is a publisher's reader). *Die Zeit*, 10 January 1986, Sec. 2, p. 18.

On Soviet censorship of works by Günter Grass.

Cherfas, Teresa. "Waugh and Peace Revisited: Russian Readers, Western Writers." *Encounter* 66 (January 1986): 64–68.

Criticized by Georgii Zlobin in "Replika redaktoram zhurnala 'Enkaunter' " (Rejoinder to the editors of the journal *Encounter*), *Inostrannaia literatura*, June 1986, pp. 185–89.

Choldin, Marianna Tax. *A Fence around the Empire: Russian Censorship of Western Ideas under the Tsars*. Durham, NC: Duke University Press, 1985.

Provides background for censorship of foreign publications in the Soviet period.

Choldin, Marianna Tax. "The New Censorship: Censorship by Translation in the Soviet Union." *Journal of Library History* 21 (Spring 1986): 334–49.

Friedberg, Maurice. *American Literature through the Filter of Recent Soviet Publishing and Criticism*. U.S. Information Agency, Office of Research, Report R-3-76., Washington, DC: 1976

Friedberg, Maurice. "The US in the USSR: American Literature through the Filter of Recent Soviet Publishing and Criticism." *Critical Inquiry* 2 (1976): 519–83.

Friedberg, Maurice. *A Decade of Euphoria: Western Literature in Post-Stalin Russia, 1954–64*. Bloomington: Indiana University Press, 1977.

Friedberg, Maurice. *American Literature through the Filter of Soviet Translation*. Research Report R-34-78, December 22. Washington, DC: International Communications Agency, 1978.

Update of his *Soviet Translations and Translators of Western Literature*. Research Report R-4-78. Washington, DC: International Communications Agency, 1978.

Friedberg, Maurice. *A Helsinki Record: The Availability of Soviet Russian Literature in the United States*. New York: Helsinki Watch, 1980.

In his book *Rubezhi i knigi* (Frontiers and books; Moscow: Sovetskaia Rossiia, 1981) Boris Pankin, a writer, publicist, and Lenin Prize winner, devotes an essay to this report entitled "Udivitel'nyi doklad professora Fridberga" (The astonishing report of Professor Friedberg).

Glade, Henry. "Aspects of Soviet Censorship of West German Belles-Lettres, 1974–1980: An Overview." *Germano-Slavica* 4: 151–57.

Glade, Henry. "Heinrich Böll in the Soviet Union: 1973–1984." *University of Dayton Review* 17 (Summer 1985): 71–75.

Glade, Henry, and Konstantin Bogatyrev. "The Soviet Version of Heinrich Böll's *Gruppenbild mit Dame*: The Translator as Censor." *University of Dayton Review* 12 (Spring 1976): 51–56.

    Bogatyrev was a Soviet dissident poet and translator who died under mysterious circumstances.

Johnson, Margaret S., and Ann C. Vinograde. "Blue Pencil for Böll." *Index* 5 (Summer 1986): 78–82.

Reilly, Alayne P. *America in Contemporary Soviet Literature*. New York: New York University Press, 1971.

"*Science* in Russia Is Full of Holes." *Science* 205 (July 1979): 284.

    See also Carey, William D. "Censorship, Soviet Style." *Science* 219 (25 February 1983): 911. Both short articles deal with (and, in the first case, illustrate graphically) censorship of imported copies of *Science*.

Soviet Criticism of American Literature in the Sixties: An Anthology. Edited and translated by Carl R. Proffer. Ann Arbor: Ardis, 1972.

Tall, Emily. "Who's Afraid of Franz Kafka? . . ." *Slavic Review* 35 (September 1976): 484–503.

Tall, Emily. "James Joyce Returns to the Soviet Union." *James Joyce Quarterly* 17 (Summer 1980): 341–58.

Tall, Emily. "The Joyce Centennary in the Soviet Union: Making Way for *Ulysses*." *James Joyce Quarterly* 21 (Winter 1984): 107–22.

Telesin, Iulius. "Ispravlennyi Xheminguei, ili po kom strigut nozhnitsy." *Vremia i my* 75 (1983): 135–44.

    This article appeared first in English: "For Whom the Scissors Cut: How to Improve Hemingway (Moscow Style)," *Encounter*, June 1976, pp. 81–86.

Venclova, Tomas. "The Reception of World Literature in Contemporary Lithuania." In *Mind against the Wall: Essays on Lithuanian Culture under Soviet Occupation*, ed. Rimvydas Silbajoris, 107–29. Chicago: Institute of Lithuanian Studies, 1983.

Moscow Book Fairs

General

Drew, Joseph S. *A Bow of Burning Gold: American Publishers & the Moscow Book Fair*. Washington, DC: The University of the District of Columbia, December 1983.

Drew, Joseph S. *Through American Eyes: The Moscow Book Fair. A Survey of U.S. Publishers Who Have Attended*. Washington, DC: Political Science, University of the District of Columbia, January 1983.

Freeman, William E. *The Moscow Book Fair*. Research Report R-29–84. Washington, DC: Soviet and East European Branch, Office of Research, United States Information Agency, November 1984.

1977 Fair

"Buchmesse in Moskau: Zwischen skepsis und optimismus" (Book Fair in Moscow: Between skepticism and optimism). *Börsenblatt für den deutschen Buchhandel*, 13 September 1977, pp. 8–11.

Graham, Gordon. "Moscow Book Fair: An Open Door for Those with Patience." *The Bookseller*, 17 September 1977, pp. 2043–45.

Lottman, Herbert R. "Despite Aura of Censorship, First Moscow Book Fair Has Positive Results." *Publishers Weekly*, 3 October 1977, pp. 46–53.

Tarasenko, I. N. "Pervaia Moskovskaia mezhdunarodnaia knizhnaia vystavka-iarmarka" (First Moscow international book exhibit-fair). *Kniga; issledovaniia i materialy. Sbornik* 36 (1978): 187–93.

1979 Fair

"Abschlussbericht von der 2. internationalen Moskauer Buchmesse" (Concluding report from the 2nd international Moscow Book Fair). *Börsenblatt für den deutschen Buchhandel*, 14 September 1979, pp. 1776–78.

Lottman, Herbert R. "Dramatic Moments Vie with Busy Trading in a Paradox Called the Moscow Book Fair." *Publishers Weekly*, 1 October 1979, pp. 26–34.

"Steady Business at Second Moscow Book Fair." *The Bookseller*, 22 September 1979, pp. 1406–12.

"Vtoraia Moskovskaia mezhdunarodnaia knizhnaia vystavka-iarmarka" (Second Moscow international book exhibit-fair). *Kniga; issledovaniia i materialy. Sbornik* 40 (1980): 186–93.

1981 Fair

"Boris Pankin (VAAP): Gedanken zur dritten Moskauer Buchmesse" (Thoughts on the third Moscow Book Fair). *Börsenblatt für den deutschen Buchhandel*, 28 August 1981, pp. 2139–40.

"Igor Kazanski: Gedanken zur dritten Moskauer Buchmesse" (Thoughts on the third Moscow Book Fair). *Börsenblatt für den deutschen Buchhandel*, 28 August 1981, pp. 2140–41.

"Minister B. Stukalin, Gedanken zur dritten Moskauer Buchmesse" (Thoughts on the third Moscow Book Fair). *Börsenblatt für den deutschen Buchhandel*, 28 August 1981, pp. 2138–39.

"Moscow Book Event in Exile Salutes 21 Russian Writers." *Publishers Weekly*, 2 October 1981, p. 40.

"The Third International Book Fair." *The Bookseller*, 26 September 1981, pp. 1147–49.

"Tret'ia Moskovskaia mezhdunarodnaia knizhnaia vystavka-iarmarka" (Third Moscow international book exhibit-fair). *Kniga; issledovaniia i materialy. Sbornik* 44 (1982): 184–91.

"Umfrage zur dritten internationalen Buchmesse in Moskau" (Inquiry into the third international book fair in Moscow). *Börsenblatt für den deutschen Buchhandel*, 22 September 1981, pp. 2406–7.

1983 Fair

"Fourth Moscow Book Fair: Controversy as Usual." *Publishers Weekly*, 23 September 1983, pp. 14–15.

Nurnberg, Andrew. "Letter from Moscow." *The Bookseller*, 17 September 1983, pp. 1240–41.

Tarasenko, I. N. "Chetvertaia Moskovskaia mezhdunarodnaia knizhnaia vystavka-iarmarka" (Fourth Moscow international book exhibit-fair). *Kniga; issledovaniia i materialy. Sbornik* 49 (1984): 201–7.

"Vierte Internationale Moskauer Buchmesse" (Fourth international Moscow Book Fair). *Börsenblatt für den deutschen Buchhandel*, 16 September 1983, p. 1922.

1985 Fair

von der Lahr, Helmut. "Erster Bericht über die fünfte internationale moskauer Buchmesse" (First report on the fifth international Moscow Book Fair). *Börsenblatt für den deutschen Buchhandel*, 20 September 1985, pp. 2370–71.

"Piataia Moskovskaia mezhdunarodnaia knizhnaia vystavka-iarmarka" (Fifth Moscow international book exhibit-fair). *Kniga; issledovaniia i materialy. Sbornik* 51 (1985): 183–88.

"Yanks in Moscow. Three Publishers Reflect on Bringing Books to the Soviet Capital." *Publishers Weekly*, 1 November 1985, pp. 28–31.

1987 Fair

Barringer, Felicity. "Book Fair Samples Glasnost." *New York Times*, 9 September 1987, Sec. 1, p. 1.

Barringer, Felicity. "After Soviet Book Fair: The Main Questions." *New York Times*, 16 September 1987, sec. 3, p. 23.

Bernstein, Robert. "A New Leaf (and Old Ones) at Moscow Book Fair." *New York Times*, 3 October 1987, p. 15.

"Bundesdeutsche Verlage in Moskau wieder stark vertreten" (FRG publishers strongly represented again in Moscow). *Börsenblatt für den deutschen Buchhandel*, 11 September 1987, p. 2333.

Hobbs, Jenny. "Moscow Book Fair – Something Old, Something New, Something Borrowed . . ." *The Bookseller*, 9 October 1987, pp. 1511–13.

Lottman, Herbert R. "Moscow '87: The 'Glasnost' Fair." *Publishers Weekly*, 16 October 1987, pp. 21–39.

See also Lottman's article on the Soviet presence at the 1987 Frankfurt Book Fair, "Frankfurt '87: Riding the Merger Wave" (*Publishers Weekly*, 30 October 1987, pp. 19–23); and an article by Ray Moseley, "Soviets Invade the Frankfurt Book Fair" (*Chicago Tribune*, 14 October 1987, sec. 5, p. 3).

Nurnberg, Andrew. "Moscow after Glasnost." *The Bookseller*, 28 August 1987, pp. 893–94.

Conference Participants

Mikhail Agursky, Hebrew University
Vassily Aksyonov, writer
Muriel Atkin, George Washington University
Dick Baker, *America Illustrated*
Marjorie Mandelstam Balzer, Harvard University
Igor Belousovitch, U.S. Department of State
Diana Bieliauskas, National Academy of Sciences
James H. Billington, Director, The Wilson Center
Igor Birman, Editor, *Russia* magazine
Vera Borkovec, American University
E. Willis Brooks, United States Information Agency
William Buell, Board for International Broadcasting
Judith Buncher, U.S. Department of State
Robert Campbell, Fellow, Kennan Institute
Marianna Tax Choldin, University of Illinois at Urbana-Champaign
Timothy Colton, Fellow, Kennan Institute
Richard E. Combs, U.S. Department of State
Michael Confino, Fellow, Kennan Institute
Walter Connor, Foreign Service Institute
Paul Cook, U.S. Department of State
James Critchlow, Board for International Broadcasting
Richard Dobson, United States Information Agency
Herman Ermolaev, Princeton University
Kaara Ettesvold, National Academy of Sciences
Charles Fairbanks, U.S. Department of State
Murray Feshbach, Georgetown University
Leonid Finkelstein, British Broadcasting Corporation
Ludmila Foster, Voice of America
Viktor Frantsusov, Voice of America
William Freeman, United States Information Agency
Maurice Friedberg, University of Illinois at Urbana-Champaign
Alfred Friendly, Washington, D.C.
John Garrard, University of Virginia
Lydia Gershkovich, Brookline, Massachusetts
Alexander Gershkovich, Harvard University
Prosser Gifford, Deputy Director, The Wilson Center
John Glad, Secretary, Kennan Institute
Roberta Goldblatt, Arlington, Virginia
Valery Golovskoy, University of Michigan
Andre Gyorgy, George Washington University
Lisa Jameson, Voice of America
Juri Jelagin, Chevy Chase, Maryland
Dina Kaminskaya, Arlington, Virginia

Amy Knight, Library of Congress
George Kolt, National Intelligence Council
David Korn, Foreign Service Institute
David Kraus, Library of Congress
Gail Lapidus, Fellow, Kennan Institute
Maya Latynsky, Poland Watch
Marcia Levenson, Kennan Institute
Ilya Levin, Voice of America
Larisa Levitskaya, Washington, D.C.
Dallas Lloyd, U.S. Department of State
Linda Lubrano, American University
David Martin, Arlington, Virginia
Eileen Materson, Center for Strategic and International Studies
Priscilla Johnson McMillan, Harvard University
Vadim Medish, American University
Denis Mickiewicz, Emory University
Ellen Mickiewicz, Emory University
Pam Miller, American Studies Program
Steven Miller, Radio Free Europe/Radio Liberty
Boris Orshansky, Radio Liberty
Olga Orshansky, Radio Liberty
Mark Palmer, U.S. Department of State
Mark Popovsky, New York, New York
Scott Powell, Roosevelt High School
Walter Reich, Fellow, Kennan Institute
T. H. Rigby, Fellow, Kennan Institute
Francis Ronalds, Voice of America
Priscilla Roosevelt, Washington, D.C.
Mariia Rozanova, *Sintaksis* (Paris)
Blair Ruble, National Council for Soviet and East European Research
Ilya Rudyak, theatre and film director
Stephen Sestanovich, U.S. Department of State
Julia Sih, Visiting Grantee, Kennan Institute
Konstantin Simis, Arlington, Virginia
Andrei Siniavsky, writer
Sonya Sluzar, *Problems of Communism*
Gene Sosin, Radio Liberty
Chris Squire, Voice of America
Richard Stites, Georgetown University
Rosemary Stuart, Kennan Institute
Ilya Suslov, United States Information Agency
Albert Todd, Flushing, New York
Vladimir Toumanoff, National Council for Soviet and East European Research
Laura Thurston, *America Illustrated*
Vladimir Nikolaevich Voinovich, writer
Solomon Volkov, music critic and writer
Rex Wade, Visiting Grantee, Kennan Institute
Eric Willenz, U.S. Department of State
Josephine Woll, Howard University

John Wright, Foreign Broadcast Information Service
Mark Wyatt, Central Intelligence Agency, retired
Heln Yakobson, George Washington University
Yuri Yarim-Agaev, physicist
Boris Germanovich Zaks, former editor, *Novyi mir*

Index

Abuladze, T., 132
Actors, 166–7, 187–94
Aesopian language, 101, 149. *See also*
  Allusions
Agursky, M., 57–8, 76–7, 105–6
Aitmatov, C., 3, 86–7, 94
Aksyonov, V., 55–6, 61, 81–7, 102–3, 105–8,
  110–12, 113n.8, 131, 147, 153, 202,
  205–6
Alekseeva, L., 3
Ali, M., 62
Allusions, 78, 88, 149–51, 164, 175–6, 187
Andropov, Y., 102, 108, 177, 184
Anti-Semitism, 95–6
  of émigrés, 202
Aragon, L., 66
Arrogance of Power, The, 33, 35–7, 40–1,
  43–8
Art, struggle of with censorship, 163
Astaf'ev, V., 3, 8, 11
Audience:
  of émigré writers, 110–11
  theater, 164, 166, 168, 186
Authors:
  foreign, effects of censorship on, 21–2
  U.S., censored, 24–7

Babel, I., 99, 182
Babi Yar, 19, 65
Baldwin, J., 27

Banned material, 161n.5
  films, 130–2
  theater (drama), 167, 181, 186–7
Basov, V., 131
Bek, A., 158–9
Belinkov, A., 78, 197
Bellow, S., 24, 58
Belousovitch, I., 199–200
Bely, A., 211
Benkendorff, General, 169–70, 175–6
Billington, J. H., 56
Birman, I., 65, 101–2
Bliakhin, P., 118, 121
Bogin, M., 131
Bolsheviks, 16, 20
Bondarev, I., 11
Books, translated, 195, 197
Boris Godunov, 77, 95, 174–5, 177, 184–8
Brezhnev, L., 3, 5–6, 34, 49n.12, 95, 108,
  202, 212
Broadcasts (radio, television), effects of
  censorship on, 22
Brodsky, J., 99
Bulgakov, M., 91, 181–2
Bunin, I., 21, 111
Bykov, R., 3, 10
Bykov, V., 10

Capote, T., 26
Censors, 93, 101, 194

attitudes of, 107–8
characteristics of, 62–3
compared to writers, 101
defined, 32
fate of, 63
of films, 117, 119, 124, 130, 191–3, 196
functions of, 17–19, 26–7, 32, 149–52
number of, 65
rivalry of, with Soviet organizations, 119
Stalin as, 191
training of, 62–5
work of, 157
Censorship:
    activities of, 155–7, 182
    and aesthetics, 89–90
    authorities of, 193, 196, 198
    of behavior, 105
    benefits of, 94, 99–100, 106–7, 174
    circumventing, 164
    as compromise, 61
    contemporary, 126–7, 205, 208
    as creative process, 107–8
    and criticism, 102–3
    defined, 32
    dysfunctional aspects of, 65–6
    effects of, 21, 56–7; on art, 20; future,
        75–6; technology and, 208–9; on
        writers, 160
    of émigrés, 108–10
    at editorial desk, 155–60
    and favorable moments, 102
    film, 117–43; advantage of, 130; current,
        126–7; functions of, 121–6; goals of,
        122; history of, 117–21, 126, 141,
        141n.7; local, 124; structure of,
        121–6
    and foreign authors, 21–8
    of foreign literature, 61, 183
    future of, 75–6, 206–7, 209
    goals of, 91, 106, 122
    history of, 1–12, 15–21, 25, 29, 75, 78, 81,
        99, 113n.8, 155, 169–80, 193, 200,
        203, 207
    ideological, 19, 65
    influence of, on cultural changes, 75
    internal, 16, 56
    in journalism, 147–53
    legalized, 169
    in literature, 81–100
    meaning of, 94
    military, 64, 157
    mistakes arising from 98–9
    as negative, 101, 108
    perversion of, 88

    as political institution, 57
    and politics, 89
    postal, 62, 64–5
    process of, 18–19, 23–4, 71–2, 150–2
    regulations of, 58
    responsibilities of, 196
    and rewriting, 32
    Russian, 29–33, 113n.8; vs. Soviet, 75–8,
        207
    in science, 71–7
    secrecy and, 72–4, 76
    sources of, 201, 203
    Soviet, 1–12, 15–17, 29–33, 62, 66–7, 89,
        169; courts and, 73–4; of films,
        117–21, 126–41, 141n.7; history of,
        15–17, 19, 21; vs. Russian, 75–80, 207
    and Soviet culture, 1–12
    of Soviet works, 66–7
    stages of, 19–20, 207–8
    struggle of against art, 163
    and subtext, 77
    as symbol of culture, 1
    and talent, 104
    in television, 145–6
    of textbooks, 62
    in theater, 163–89; of foreign drama, 183
    and translations, 26, 29–48
    types of, 24
    and U.S. writers, 58
    in West, 109, 112, 113n.8
    and Western political writing, 29–48
Central Repertory Committee, 118–22,
    134–5
    functions of, 123–6, 141n.7
    structure of, 122–6
    tasks of, 122–3
Chakovskii, A. B., 103, 148
Chekhov, A., 165–8, 203, 206
    Three Sisters, 165–8
    Uncle Vanya, 4–5
Chernenko, K. U., 5–6
Chief Directorate for the Protection of State
    Secrets in the Press. *See* Glavlit
Choldin, M. T., 24, 29–48, 212
Chukhrai, G., 131–2
Chuprynin, S. Ia., 104
Cinema. *See* Films
Communism:
    censorship of references to, 26
    image of in translations, 40–2
Communist party, and artists, 6–7
Conscience, writer's, 6
Corporations, and USSR, analogy between,
    76–7

Courts, Soviet, and censorship, 73–4
Culture:
  Russian: future of, 205–7, 211–12; losses
    of, 199, 205, 210; vs. Soviet, 205
  Soviet, 2–4, 207; censorship and, 1–12;
    flux in, 11–12; history of, 1–6; "Indian
    summer of," 2–3, 11; of the mid-'80s,
    1–12; vs. Russian, 205; thaw in? 1–12

Dead Souls, 111
Demichev, P., 2, 6
Department for Film Repertory Control,
  126–9, 138
De-Stalinization, 102
Diakonov, S., 196
Directors:
  film, 120–7
  theater, 177, 182
Djilas, M., 102–3, 159, 160n.4
Dos Passos, J., 25
Dostoevsky, F., 8–9
Doyle, C., 87
Drama, foreign, 183. *See also* Playwrights;
  Theater
Durrenmatt, F., 183

Editorial desk, censorship at, 155
Editors, and censorship, 171–2
Efgrafovich, P., 7–8
Efremov, O., 102
Efros, A., 2
Ehrenburg, I., 66
Elagin, Y., 58, 61
Emigration, 199, 202, 205
  as problem, 109
  of writers, 81–2
Emigrés, 211–12
  anti-Semitism of, 202
  attitudes of, 3–4, 201–2, 204
  audience of, 110–11
  as authors, 108–12
  as censors, 202, 204
  and censorship, 108–10, 202, 204
  censorship of, 24, 108–9
  films of, 131–2
  journals of, 203
  literature of, 2–3, 81–2
  publication of, 109–10
  as readers, 109
  as unpersons, 60
  and USSR readers, 111
  views of censorship of, 3–4
Erdman, N., 182
Ermolaev, H., 111, 200–1

Eroticism, 103–4
Etkind, E., 182
Eugene Onegin, 170
Euphemisms, 97–8
Evolution of Diplomatic Method, The, 34–9,
  41, 44–6
Evstigneev, E., 164
Evtushenko, E., 2, 9. *See also* Yevtushenko, E.
Excisions, 54, 59–60, 95, 157, 173
  in translations, 27, 31, 34, 39, 43

Fast, H., 25
Fedorova, V., 131
Fellini, F., 85
Film Committee. *See* Goskino USSR
Film directors, 120–7
Filmmakers, 6–7
Films, 2–4
  censorship in, 191–3, 196, 210; history of,
    117–33
  of émigrés, 131
  foreign, 143n.33
  permits for, 128–30
Finkelstein, L., 53–5, 58–60, 62–5, 76–8,
  113n.8, 194–8, 210
First Circle, 107, 111
Forbidden (censored) items, 18
Foreign Censorship Committee, 31
Foreign drama, censorship of, 183
Foreign publications:
  books, 159
  history of censorship of, 29–30
  translations, 194
Form:
  of Soviet works, 55
  Western influences on, 55
Foster, L., 101, 112
Friedberg, M., 21–8, 33, 54–5, 57, 61–2, 66,
  75, 78, 81–3, 101, 103, 105, 108, 111,
  147, 150, 163, 183, 199–206, 209, 212
Frumin, B., 131
Fulbright, W., 33–6, 40–1, 43–8
  and *The Arrogance of Power*, 33, 35–7,
    40–2, 43–8

Gabai, G., 131
Gaider, A., 193
Galich, A., 131, 179–82
Gershkovich, A., 1–12, 163–89, 211
Glad, J., 53, 60, 64, 108–9, 199, 202–3, 205
Glasnost, 5–6
Glavlit, 18–20, 57–8, 77, 89, 151, 193,
  197–8, 204

and films, 120–2, 126–7, 139, 142n.29, 192
and journalism, 155–9
Gogol, N., 25, 88, 111, 172–3
Golomshtok, I., 66–7
Golovsky, V. S., 117–43, 149, 193–6, 199, 209–10
Gorbachev, M., 1–6
Gorkii, M., 164, 181
Goskino, USSR (Film Committee), 126, 130–2, 137, 139
Grossman, V., 105, 177

Hemingway, E., 26, 82
Historical optimism, as literary style, 85
Hochhuth, R., 183
Humor, 108, 148, 156, 167
  in Soviet literature, 81–2

Iakobson, A., 98
Iarmatov, K., 120–1
Il'f, I., 108, 164
Imperial Russia, censorship in, 29–33
  compared to Soviet, 31–3
"Indian summer," of Soviet culture, 2–3, 11
India's Foreign Policy, 34–8, 40–2, 46, 50n.39
Individuality, 107–8
Ioseliani, O., 132
I Speak of Freedom, 34–7, 41, 44, 46

Jewish identity, 78
Jewish names, censorship of, 27, 151, 180–1, 183, 192–3
Jews. *See also* Anti-Semitism
  censorship of, 25, 157
  Soviet, 66
  treatment of in literature, 200–1
Journalism:
  censorship in, 147–53
  and Glavlit, 155–9
Journals, 2, 10. *See also Novyi mir*
  censorship of, 194
  émigré, 203
  foreign, in USSR, 22
Joyce, J., 56

Kalik, M., 131
Kapler, A., 145–6
KGB, 6, 18, 89, 93, 130, 193–4, 196
Khanzhonkov, A., 117
Khodasevich, V. F., 2
Khrushchev, N., 1–2, 19–20, 34, 40, 49n.12, 54, 95, 104, 158, 160, 183, 212

Klimov, E., 132
Klonskii, M., 64
Koestler, A., 15
Kohout, P., 183
Kolakowski, L., 57
Kopelev, L., 111
Korshavin, N., 151–2
Kosinski, J., 24–5
Kosygin, A., 56
Koval'chuk, E. I., 94–5
Kozhevnikov, V., 58
Kramarov, S., 131
Kriukov, F. D., 201
Kroshkin, M. G., 63, 197
Kundera, M., 183
Kuznetsov, F., 108, 112
Kuznetsov, I., 6

Language, Soviet, 95–9. *See also* Allusions.
  Aesopian, 101, 149
  metaphorical, 99
Lashkin, V., 20
Lavrov, P., 59
Lebedev, N., 118
Lenin, V. I., 4, 15–16, 20–1, 99, 101
  on films, 117–18, 133
  and theater, 4
Lermontov, M., 172–3, 193
Levin, I., 110
Libedinskii, Iu. N., 200
Libraries, Soviet, 23, 60
Literature:
  censorship in, 81–100
  erotic, 103–4
  foreign, censorship of, 60–1
  future of, 206, 208
  Russian, 188; history of, 169–74; strength of, 174
  screenplays, 127, 131
  subject matter of, 105–6, 111
  subtexts of, 106
Liubimov, Iu. V., 8, 77, 166–7, 169, 181–2, 184–8, 211
Lubrano, L., 76, 209
Lunacharskii, A., 118–21, 197–8

Magazines, 19–20
  censorship of, 197–8, 200
  U.S. in USSR, 61–2
Makaenko, 103
Malamud, B., 58
Malenkov, G., 82
Markish, D., 203
Marx, K., 15

Mass media:
  and censorship, 191–212
  military, 196, 198
Mednikov, A. M., 94
Medvedev, R., 3
Metaphor. *See* Allusions
Metropol', 112n.5
Mayerhold, V., 170, 177, 180, 185, 211
Mickiewicz, D., 77, 106
Mickiewicz, E., 75
Mikaelin, S., 131
Mikhalkov-Konchalovskii, A., 132
Miller, A., 26–7, 59, 183
Milosz, C., 24
Misharin, A., 9–10
Mistakes, 58
  arising from censorship, 98–9
  in translations, 38–9
Mowcow Helsinki Watch group, 71, 73
Movies. *See* Films
Mozhaev, B., 181, 184

Nabokov, A., 2, 78, 111–12, 206
Nabokov, V., 78
Nationalities, in literature, 200–1
Nehru, J., 34–8, 40–2, 46, 50n.39
Nekrasov, N., 176
Nekrasov, V., 11, 131
Newspapers, Soviet, 2. *See also Pravda*
Nicholas I (tsar), 77, 169–73, 175–6
Nicolson, H., 34–9, 41, 45–6
Nkrumah, K., 34–7, 41, 44, 46
NKVD, 125
Notes, in translations, 37–8
Novyi mir (journal), 2, 20, 61, 93, 104,
  107–8, 111, 148, 155–7, 160, 161n.5,
  194–5

OGPU, as censors, 193, 198
One Day in the Life of Ivan Denisovich, 20,
  102, 172, 204, 260
Openness, 6. *See also Glasnost*
Orlov, Y., 3
Orlova, R., 26
Ostrovskii, A. N., 4

Panfilov, G., 132
Paradzhanov, S., 131
Pasternak, B., 2, 5–6, 53, 99, 211
Peter the Great (tsar), 29
Petrov, Y., 108, 164
Picasso, P., 66–7
Playwrights, 4–5, 59, 102–3
Poets, 2, 5, 9

Pokrovskii, D., 185
Polevoi, N., 171–2
PolitControl, 198
Political writing, Western, censorship of,
  34–40
Politics, and censorship, 88–9
Pornography:
  of films, 123
  and Soviet literature, 103–4
Possev, 91
Pravda, 103–4
Printing plants, censors at, 17
Prokhanov, A., 11
Prokofiev, S., 185
Propaganda, Soviet, 5, 9, 98
  department of, 194
  translated, 54
Publication:
  abroad, 72
  in USSR, 66–7, 71
Publications, foreign:
  in imperial Russia, 30–1
  in USSR, 31, 61–2
Publishers, 194–5
Purishkevich, V. M., 117
Pushkin, A., 9, 21, 77, 95, 169–77, 184–9
  Boris Godunov, 77, 95, 174–5, 177,
    184–8
  Eugene Onegin, 170

Radio/television, U.S. vs. Soviet, 145–6
Raskol'nikov, F. F., 119
Rasputin, V., 3, 10–11, 20, 105, 108
Readership, 110–11
Repertory Control Committee, 118–19, 121
Research, scientific, censorship of, 71–2
Rewriting, as censorship, 32
Rostotskii, B., 178–9
Rozanova, M., 201–3
Rozov, V., 2, 102–3, 181, 183
Rudiak, I., 191–3, 210–11
Russophobia, 96, 109

Salinger, J. D., 82
Samizdat, 3, 20, 106, 161n.5
  émigré, 202
Satire, 102–3, 148, 164, 183
  censorship of, 156, 161n.6
Science:
  censorship and, 208–9
  censorship in, 71–7
  effect of censorship on, 56–7
  and foreign publishers, 72

Screenplays, censorship of, 127, 135, 142n.29
Secrecy:
  compared to U.S., 76–7
  in science censorship, 57, 72–4, 76–7
Self-censorship, 32, 54–5, 59, 92, 106, 152–3, 176
  and allusions, 150
  effects of, 153
  in theater, 163–4
  and translations, 32
Self-consciousness, 163
Self-expression, 163–4, 169, 171
Serban, A., 165–6
Sex, censorship of portrayals of, 27
Shalamov, V. T., 53, 109
Sharkov, O., 131
Shatrov, M., 2, 5
Sheremet'ov, B. B., 117
Shestakov, V., 185
Shishkov, V., 53
Shoenberg, H., 59
Sholokhov, 200
Shvedchikov, K. M., 119
Simmons, E., 163
Simon, N., 27
Sinclair, U., 25
Singer, I. B., 24
Siniavsky, A., 23, 61, 66–7, 81–3, 94–101, 104, 106, 109–10, 112, 153, 202, 206–7, 211
"Slipping through," 102–3, 148
Socialist realism, as literary style, 83–7
Solov'ev, S. M., 169
Sosin, G., 64
Solzhenitsyn, A., 96, 102, 104, 107, 110–11, 158, 160, 172, 182, 194, 198
  First Circle, 107, 111
  One Day in the Life of Ivan Denisovich, 20, 102, 104, 160, 172
Soviet culture. *See* Culture, Soviet
Soviet Jews, 66
Soviet Realism, 55
Stalin, J., 5, 95, 145, 157, 182, 191, 211–12
  as censor, 191
Stamp, of censor, 17, 157, 159
Stanislavskii, K., 164, 167, 170
State secrets, 17–18
Steinbeck, J., 26
Stepova, T., 197
Strada, V., 1
"Subtext," 99, 106
  uncontrollable, 77–8
  unverifiable, 88

Suchkov, B., 159–60
Surov, A., 83
Suslov, I., 19, 145–53, 158, 195
Suslov, M. A., 197–8
Svirskii, G., 160

Taganka (Comedy) Theater, 8, 77, 165, 167–9, 181–7
Talankin, I., 132
"Talmud," 18, 58, 62, 151
Tamizdat, 20, 106
Tarkovskii, Andrei, 210
Technology, 29
  effects of censorship on, 56–7
  effects on of censorship, 208–9
Television, censorship in, 145–6, 197
Tel'pugov, V., 93
Tertz, A. *See* Siniavsky, A.
Textbooks, Soviet, 62
Theater, 4–5, 8–10
  censorship in, 191, 163–89, 211
    of Jewish names, 180–1, 183
  contemporary trends in, 183–4
  criticism of, 169
  history of, 4–5, 164–5, 169–74, 179–80
  and Lenin, 4–5
  Russian vs. Soviet, 177–8
  strength of, 178
  vs. U.S., 165–8
Three Sisters, 165–8
Tiutchev, F. I., 111
Todd, A., 59–60, 62, 78
Translations:
  censorship of, 29–48, 199
  and censorship, 26
  changes in, 42–5
  compared to originals, 34–40
  of foreign books, 159
  image of Communism in, 40–2
  image of U.S. in, 40, 42–8
  image of USSR in, 40–2
  image of Western powers in, 40, 42–3, 45–7
  mistakes in, 38–9
  notes in, 37–8
  rewriting in, 45
  and self-censorship, 32
  of Soviet works, 53–4
  themes in, 40, 45–8
  of U.S. Supreme Court decisions, 54
  of Western political writing, 29–48
Trifonov, I., 7–9, 106–7, 165, 183
Turgenev, I., 111, 173, 193

Tvardovskii, A., 20, 104, 156, 158, 160, 172, 194
Tynianov, I., 170

Unbegaun, B., 64
Uncle Vanya, 4–5
Uncontrollable subtext, 77–8
United States:
  criticism of, in translations, 43–8
  image of, in translations, 40, 42–3, 45–7
  publications in, vs. USSR, 204
Universal Copyright Convention, and USSR, 32, 53
Unpersons:
  concept of, 25
  émigrés as, 60
Unverifiable subtext, 88
Updike, J., 27
U.S. books, censored, 24–7
U.S. Supreme Court decisions, translations of, 54
USSR:
  censorship of references to, 26
  image of, in translations, 40–2
  and Universal Copyright Convention, 32, 53

Vampilov, A., 182
Vidal, G., 26
Village writers, 104–5, 108
Vladimirov, L., 15–20
Vladimov, G., 131, 212
Voevodin, P. I., 118
Voice of America, influence of, 54
Voinovich, V. N., 61, 81–3, 87–94, 101, 104–5, 109, 152–3, 205–6

Volgin, I., 8
Vonnegut, K., 26–7
Voznesenskii, A., 2, 9, 108
Vronskaia, Z., 132
Vysotskii, V., 177

Weiss, P., 183
Western powers, image of, in translations, 42–3, 45–7
Western works, in USSR, 55
Willenz, E., 54–5
Wilson, H. (Sir), 56
Wouk, H., 25, 58
Wright, R., 25
Writers, Soviet, 93–4
  émigré, 108–9
  importance of in USSR, 91
  as Party's helpers, 102–3
  village, 104–5, 108
Writer's Union, 2, 93

Yarim-Agaev, Y., 60–2, 71–4, 78, 207–9
Yevtushenko, E., 2, 9, 19, 65
  Babi Yar, 19, 65
Yezhov's terror, 165, 211

Zaitsev, M., 163
Zakharov, M., 2
Zaks, B. G., 63–5, 76, 155–60, 193–6, 198–9, 208
Zalygin, S. P., 105
Zhukovskii, V. A., 171, 175
Zionism, 58